UNDERSTANDING EYEWITNESS MEMORY

PSYCHOLOGY AND CRIME

General Editors: Brian Bornstein, University of Nebraska, and Monica Miller, University of Nevada, Reno

The Perversion of Youth: Controversies in the Assessment and Treatment of Juvenile Sex Offenders
Frank C. DiCataldo

Jury Decision Making: The State of the Science
Dennis J. Devine

Deviant and Criminal Behavior in the Workplace
Edited by Steven M. Elias

Psychopathy: An Introduction to Biological Findings and Their Implications
Andrea L. Glenn and Adrian Raine

Gender, Psychology, and Justice: The Mental Health of Women and Girls in the Legal System
Edited by Corinne C. Datchi and Julie R. Ancis

Criminal Trials and Mental Disorders
Thomas L. Hafemeister

Criminal Trajectories: A Developmental Perspective
David M. Day and Margit Wiesner

Understanding Police Interrogation: Confessions and Consequences
William Douglas Woody and Krista D. Forrest

Understanding Eyewitness Memory: Theory and Applications
Sean M. Lane and Kate A. Houston

Understanding Eyewitness Memory

Theory and Applications

Sean M. Lane and Kate A. Houston

NEW YORK UNIVERSITY PRESS
New York

NEW YORK UNIVERSITY PRESS
New York
www.nyupress.org

© 2021 by New York University
All rights reserved

References to Internet websites (URLs) were accurate at the time of writing. Neither the author nor New York University Press is responsible for URLs that may have expired or changed since the manuscript was prepared.

Library of Congress Cataloging-in-Publication Data
Names: Lane, Sean M., author. | Houston, Kate A., author.
Title: Understanding eyewitness events : theory and applications / Sean M. Lane and Kate A. Houston.
Description: New York : New York University Press, [2020] | Series: Psychology and crime | Includes bibliographical references and index.
Identifiers: LCCN 2020039528 (print) | LCCN 2020039529 (ebook) | ISBN 9781479842513 (hardback) | ISBN 9781479877119 (paperback) | ISBN 9781479851157 (ebook) | ISBN 9781479886333 (ebook other)
Subjects: LCSH: Eyewitness identification—Psychological aspects. | Recollection (Psychology) | Memory. | Witnesses.
Classification: LCC HV8073 .L29 2020 (print) | LCC HV8073 (ebook) | DDC 363.25/8—dc23
LC record available at https://lccn.loc.gov/2020039528
LC ebook record available at https://lccn.loc.gov/2020039529

New York University Press books are printed on acid-free paper, and their binding materials are chosen for strength and durability. We strive to use environmentally responsible suppliers and materials to the greatest extent possible in publishing our books.

Manufactured in the United States of America

10 9 8 7 6 5 4 3 2 1

Also available as an ebook

CONTENTS

Introduction   1

1. Memory for Persons   27
2. Recognizing Familiar and Unfamiliar Faces   44
3. Genuine and False Memories   58
4. Distinguishing Between Genuine and False Memories   75
5. Emotion and Stress   100
6. Remembering Changes Memory   126
7. Helping Eyewitness Memory   143

   Acknowledgments   165
   Notes   167
   References   169
   Index   203
   About the Authors   213

Introduction

On an early morning in February 1981, a young woman in the northern Louisiana town of Chatham woke to find an intruder beating her with a wooden board. As she fought and pleaded with the man to stop, he raped her multiple times. After the brutal attack was over and the man had left, she called a cousin, who arrived to find blood spattered throughout the room and the victim severely injured. Soon after, her father arrived, and she told them that she knew her attacker—Michael Anthony Williams.[1] She said that she had seen his face and recognized his voice, as the intruder kept talking to himself throughout the attack. Michael, 16 years old at the time, was well known to the woman because she had previously tutored him. However, this arrangement had ended when he became infatuated with her, and he had recently been jailed after an altercation with her. After his release, he threatened to beat the victim. Given the victim's confidence and familiarity with her attacker, Michael was soon arrested for the crime, despite the lack of any physical evidence linking him to the attack. The police never located clothes matching the description provided by the victim, there was no blood found on his clothes, his shoes did not match the footprints outside the victim's home, and Michael had no cuts or abrasions on him. His grandmother and his cousin claimed that he had come home the previous evening from church around 11:00 and that he had not left the house during the night, nor had he taken a shower. Despite these issues, it is not surprising that the jury found the victim's testimony convincing at trial. After all, she had interacted with him on multiple occasions, had seen and heard him during the attack, and was extremely confident it had been him. At the trial's end, the jury quickly voted to convict Michael for the crime of aggravated rape. He received a life sentence and was sent to the Louisiana State Penitentiary in Angola, a prison well known for its harsh conditions.

To greater and lesser degrees, we rely on our memories to give us an accurate portrayal of our past experience. The potential consequences of failing to live up to this ideal are minimal in much of our daily life, such as when we misremember the name of a recent acquaintance during a conversation. Although such missteps can be embarrassing, there are situations in which the consequences can be much more profound, and we place a much higher premium on being accurate. An obvious example of such situations involves the memory of eyewitnesses. Indeed, legal decision-making by judges and jurors frequently involves an evaluation of whether a witness's memory accurately reflects what happened to him or her. Evaluating the quality of another person's memory might seem straightforward, particularly in circumstances like the Michael Anthony Williams case, where the victim allegedly knew the perpetrator before the attack. But, for a variety of reasons that we explore in this book, we are not always accurate in our assessment of other people's memories or even our own. The victim in the aforementioned case appears to have been mistaken—three separate DNA analyses of sperm taken from the victim's clothing and bedding excluded Williams as the source. At the age of 40, and after nearly 24 years in prison, he was released from Angola on March 11, 2005. In interviews, he described sexual and physical abuse that he had endured, particularly early in his incarceration. For her part, the victim remains convinced of the accuracy of her memory of Williams and has speculated that a second attacker may have been present. At this time, no one else has been arrested for the crime.

The press conference announcing Michael Williams's release was held at Louisiana State University's Hebert Law Center and coincided with a meeting the first author was attending there on the topic of eyewitness identification reform. Our discussions during the meeting that day primarily focused on what research studies have documented about the nature of eyewitness memory. However, Michael's story demonstrated in a much more personal and powerful way the importance we place on memory as *evidence* and how difficult it can be to ascertain the truth on its basis.

As heartbreaking a case as this was for all concerned, it is by no means the only documented example of eyewitness error. As of this writing, the Innocence Project (https://www.innocenceproject.org/) has documented a total of 375 DNA exonerations in the United States. These men served an average of 14 years in prison before exoneration, and 21 were on death row. Approximately 69% of these cases involved eyewitness misidentification—the leading cause of wrongful convictions. Criminal cases are not the only situations in which eyewitness memory is consequential. For example, witness accounts may provide key information when investigators attempt to reconstruct accidents that occur in industrial or other settings. If we are to use eyewitness evidence effectively, it is important to understand what factors can affect its accuracy and completeness.

Researchers have made progress in understanding this issue. There have been thousands of studies documenting factors that influence eyewitness memory (e.g., Wells & Olson, 2003; see Lampinen et al., 2012, and Cutler, 2013, for recent reviews). Many of these studies have been conducted in the laboratory using materials meant to simulate important characteristics of eyewitness situations (e.g., viewing mock crimes), and others have been conducted in the field (e.g., Platz & Hosch, 1988). For example, there is good evidence that people have a more difficult time discriminating between faces of other races than they do between faces from their own race (e.g., Malpass & Kravitz, 1969; Meissner et al., 2005), that they can incorporate information they acquire after an event into their memory of the event (post-event information; e.g., Loftus et al., 1978; Zaragoza & Lane, 1994), and that receiving positive feedback following a lineup identification increases a person's confidence that they picked the perpetrator (e.g., Wells & Bradfield, 1998). Furthermore, this work has matured to the point where researchers have clear recommendations for improving the way that eyewitness evidence is collected (e.g., Fisher & Geisleman, 1989; National Institute of Justice Technical Group for Eyewitness Evidence, 1999).

Despite these impressive achievements, there are good reasons to think that our understanding of eyewitness memory could progress more rapidly (Lane & Meissner, 2008; Turtle et al., 2008). One reason is that the field has often focused on documenting phenomena rather than building a richer theoretical understanding (e.g., N. Brewer & Weber, 2008; Turtle et al., 2008; although there are exceptions, e.g., Clark, 2003; Loftus et al., 1978). This is not just a trivial "academic" issue that only professors care about. The more thoroughly we understand the underlying mechanisms, the better we will be able to successfully support and evaluate eyewitness memory (Lane & Meissner, 2008). Another reason is that eyewitness memory researchers have tended to focus on work being conducted within their area and have paid less attention to research conducted by more "basic" researchers who study memory using simpler materials (e.g., pictures, words, simple objects) and tasks that less directly mirror the complexity seen in real-world eyewitness events. Yet, memory for eyewitness events depends on the very same psychological and neurological processes that are used to perceive and remember other everyday events we experience in our lives. Meanwhile, basic researchers[2] in perception and memory have made considerable empirical and theoretical progress on understanding these processes. Furthermore, many of the topics being studied have implications for eyewitness memory, even though basic researchers may not consider or highlight this relevance in their work. Eyewitness researchers are often unaware of a number of these developments. Keep in mind, however, that this neglect is not one-way. Basic researchers often study narrow, fairly circumscribed domains and may not have systematically considered how the processes they study could be influenced in more complex, real-world situations like those encountered by eyewitnesses. Similarly, they often do not know about related work being conducted by eyewitness memory researchers. Thus, it is clear that both types of scientists could benefit from an increased understanding of the scientific issues being explored by the other.

The Goals and Organization of This Book

In the chapters that follow, we review a number of important topics from basic research on perception and memory with respect to key findings and theories and relate this knowledge to what is known from eyewitness memory research. We also discuss the implications of these findings for our theoretical understanding of eyewitness memory and for potential applications that could help improve the quality and usefulness of eyewitness evidence. This focus on the implications of basic research for eyewitness memory is different from most books on the topic, which primarily review more applied research on eyewitness memory.

There are two, intertwined goals for this book. The first is to develop a deeper understanding of how people remember eyewitness events. The second is to bridge the divide that has often existed between basic and applied researchers (Lane & Meissner, 2008) and encourage a greater appreciation of each other's work, as well as foster collaboration between them. As we discuss in more detail later in the chapter, there are good reasons to conduct science in ways that increase such interaction.

The book is organized around six key questions: (1) How do we remember and describe people we've encountered? (2) How do we remember familiar and unfamiliar faces? (3) What is the nature of false and genuine memories? (4) How do we distinguish between false and genuine memories in ourselves and others (personal and interpersonal source monitoring)? (5) How does emotional arousal and stress affect what we remember about an event? and (6) How does the act of remembering change our memories? Each of these chapters discusses how basic research in a given area highlights factors influencing the accuracy of eyewitness memory and how it fits with findings of applied research. We also discuss what these findings and theories suggest regarding new research paths, hypotheses to be tested, or potential applications for supporting eyewitness memory. In the concluding chapter, we discuss how this understanding may be used to improve the quality of evidence given by real-world eyewitnesses.

Before we begin, it is important to cover some basic issues that are relevant to understanding the chapters that follow. In the remainder of this chapter, we cover three important topics. First, we briefly discuss some reasons for the divide between basic and applied research and articulate a general approach that could help bridge this gap and create a more robust science of eyewitness memory (Lane & Meissner, 2008). Second, we describe a number of characteristics of real-world eyewitness situations. A primary reason for doing this is that we cannot simply assume that the results of basic research studies, which are often conducted using tasks that are simpler and sometimes very different from real-world eyewitness events, will generalize to those situations. Instead, this is an important question *we* will need to ask ourselves when assessing the relevance of these results. To do this, it is important to appreciate some of the range and complexity of factors that influence memory for real-world eyewitness events. Finally, we cover some basic terminology and topics from the perception and memory literature that will be useful in understanding the research described in the chapters to follow.

The Basic–Applied Divide

Ulrich Neisser is considered one of the founders of the discipline of cognitive psychology—the study of processes that underlie thinking, perceiving, remembering, and problem-solving—and he wrote the first textbook on the subject in 1967. In this text, he discussed what had already been learned from basic research on these topics and laid out an exciting future for the field. It is perhaps a little surprising that just over 10 years later, Neisser (1978; see also 1982) wrote an influential paper that argued that basic laboratory-based memory research had contributed little to our understanding of how memory works in complex, real-world situations. In this paper, he distinguished between two types of research—"high road" and "low road." In this conception, high road refers to basic research conducted under controlled laboratory conditions, usually with relatively simple materials such as words or pictures. In contrast, low road refers to applied studies conducted under more ecologically realistic conditions (i.e., using tasks and materials that more closely mirror real-world environments). He proposed that researchers should focus more on low road research if progress was to be made. Ultimately, his call for change helped give rise to the Practical Aspects of Memory movement (e.g., R. Cohen, 1989), as many researchers began to study more ecological aspects of human memory, which included a renewed interest in eyewitness memory.[3]

As we discussed earlier, much has been learned about eyewitness memory in the intervening years. However, there were also some unintended side effects of this focus (e.g., Banaji & Crowder, 1989; Lane & Meissner, 2008; Turtle et al., 2008). For instance, eyewitness memory researchers have sometimes neglected to incorporate relevant insights from basic research on psychological and neurological processes (although not always; see, e.g., Clark, 2003; Loftus et al., 1978). This neglect has come about, in part, because researchers have sometimes adopted an overly strict ecological criterion for judging whether research studies are relevant to understanding eyewitness memory (Lane & Meissner, 2008). According to this criterion, if the tasks and materials used in a study differ substantially from actual eyewitness situations, the results are unlikely to be useful. More broadly, this viewpoint leads to the tacit assumption that eyewitness memory is special or unique, and thus, researchers should primarily focus on research on the topic. A second side effect of this approach is that researchers have tended to catalog factors that influence eyewitnesses rather than focus on building a more general theoretical understanding of eyewitness memory (e.g., Turtle et al., 2008).

If the low-road approach has impaired progress in the field of eyewitness memory, what might be the alternative? Lane and Meissner (2008) proposed a "middle road" approach to research as one possibility.

Whereas high- and low-road approaches see the relationship between basic and applied research as one-way (e.g., results from basic research are applied in the field or results from research in the field informs basic research), the middle-road view promotes greater interaction between the fields and diversity of research methods as a means to achieve stronger theoretical progress and improved application. They describe three major interrelated elements to this approach: (1) a focus on theory development, (2) greater interaction between basic and applied research, and (3) the use of convergent theoretical and methodological approaches.

The middle-road approach first argues that the focus of the field should be on building a more comprehensive theory of eyewitness memory. There are a number of advantages of focusing on theory building and testing instead of empirical cataloging. One is that this strategy brings greater coherence to the research process than the less systematic approach of looking at individual phenomenon in isolation. Another is that the better we understand the cognitive, neurological, and social processes underlying eyewitness memory, the better we will be able to design applications that support its use as evidence. Still another is that well-validated theories provide a stronger basis for predicting what is likely to happen in circumstances that have not been directly studied empirically. This is important because the results of eyewitness memory research are commonly criticized in court as being irrelevant for evaluating real-world cases, because the exact conditions of a particular case have not been precisely replicated in a study (for a discussion, see, e.g., Clark, 2008).

The second element focuses on the need for greater interaction between basic research and applied research on eyewitness memory. To accomplish such interaction, there must be the underlying belief that there is value in research from across the spectrum from the laboratory to the field (see also Herrmann & Gruneberg, 1993). Although the value of applying insights from the lab to the field may be apparent (although we discuss how difficult this can be later), basic researchers can certainly benefit as well. For instance, basic theories of perception and memory are often conceived to explain the findings from relatively simple laboratory tasks. There is much value in seeing whether such theories "scale up" with respect to their ability to predict performance in more complex, real-world situations. Beyond valuing each other's work, there is also a need for basic and applied researchers to be exposed to each other's ideas on a regular basis, whether by attending the same conferences, publishing in each other's journals, and so on. For reasons we describe later, this is a difficult task, although a very valuable one.

The third element of the middle road approach emphasizes the importance of embracing a diverse set of methodological and theoretical approaches to understanding eyewitness memory. In one sense, this is another way of describing a good general tactic for scientific progress, called *converging operations* (e.g., Garner et al., 1956). This tactic is usually described as the use of multiple tasks or measures to study a psychological process. For example, someone studying emotional reactivity might use physiological (e.g., heart rate), neurological (e.g. electroencephalogram activity), and behavioral measures (e.g., self-report). Using multiple measures allows researchers to overcome the weaknesses of any one measure, and to the extent they observe similar findings across measures, they can be more confident in their conclusions (e.g., Campbell & Fiske, 1959). Furthermore, such findings provide a stronger basis for the construction and testing of theories. In contrast, when researchers focus exclusively on a single task, a set of stimuli or measure, this can impede progress in a field (*methodological fixation*; Lane & Meissner, 2008; see also Cook & Campbell, 1979). Thus, diversity brings strength. However, this diversity requires us to consider results from different types of studies with respect to their relevance for understanding eyewitness memory. As mentioned earlier, eyewitness memory researchers have often used an ecological criterion—whether the task appears to have the same characteristics as faced by real-world eyewitnesses (e.g., Ebbesen & Konecni, 1996)—to determine relevance. Lane and Meissner (2008) argued that a better criterion for determining relevance is *generalizability* (Banaji & Crowder, 1989, 1994). The assumption is often made that the results of a field study are more likely to generalize to other real-life settings than laboratory studies. However, this need not be the case, as field studies conducted in very unique settings may actually be less generalizable. Furthermore, unless a laboratory or field experiment has internal validity (i.e., the research design is free of confounding factors), we cannot make firm conclusions from the results, and thus, the findings are not generalizable. For this reason, we may sometimes find that studies that use tasks that do not resemble a real-world eyewitness situation (e.g., because they use words, pictures, or other simple materials) may nevertheless be *more* useful for guiding a theoretical understanding of eyewitness memory than studies that more closely approximate it. Despite arguments about the special nature of eyewitness memory, the very same psychological and neurological processes used to perceive and remember eyewitness events are the same ones we use in other life activities, although the constraints of eyewitness situations may influence how such processes are deployed. We discuss some of these constraints in a later section of this chapter.

Altogether, the middle-road approach argues that the scientific study of eyewitness memory will be stronger to the extent it utilizes knowledge coming from both basic and applied research. However, the description of the basic/applied divide might give the false impression that researchers in one area have deliberately ignored developments in the other. We don't believe this is the case. For those unfamiliar with academic research, there are many reasons why basic and applied researchers do not often collaborate or frequently cite each other's work. One is that doctoral training in psychology is typically narrow and focused on helping a student to establish expertise in a particular domain. Those who go onto to academic positions at research institutions similarly find that tenure and other rewards are likely to come to those who specialize in a given topic. Similarly, academic researchers often have to juggle multiple aspects of their job—typically research, teaching, and service—and thus, time becomes a precious commodity. In addition, researchers from basic and applied areas often have different backgrounds. For instance, there are differences in the type of doctoral training received by students attending programs in basic and applied aspects of cognition. Basic and applied researchers often attend different conferences and publish in different journals, reducing the likelihood of cross-discipline exposure. Furthermore, there is sometimes prejudice against each other's field, with basic researchers claiming that applied work is not rigorous and applied researchers claiming that basic work is trivial and unrepresentative of real-world performance. Thus, it is not surprising that scientists in either group might be unaware of developments in the other's research area.

Despite these difficulties, the divide is far from insurmountable, and there are encouraging developments. These include greater academic and grant support for interdisciplinary research (e.g., Cacioppo, 2007), organizations that include both basic and applied researchers among their members (e.g., the Society for Applied Research in Memory and Cognition), and journals that explicitly encourage research that is theoretically-guided, yet with clear application to real-world issues (e.g., the *Journal of Applied Research in Memory and Cognition*; the *Journal of Experimental Psychology: Applied*). These are important steps, although there is much more that can be done. As argued earlier, a middle-road approach to research can lead to clear benefits for both basic and applied scientists. In particular, understanding how people remember eyewitness events is a worthy scientific problem for both groups, and this book is intended to encourage collaboration in this endeavor.

Eyewitness Events

To be able to adequately understand the implications of research for understanding eyewitness events, it is important to understand their basic characteristics, as well as develop some appreciation for how they may vary. As we will see, the task of an eyewitness is a difficult one.

CRIMINAL CASES. Imagine that you and your friend are on your way home from a night out. It is late, about 2:00 a.m., and you're joking with each other about things you've done this evening. Suddenly, a man steps out from behind a building, into your path, and you can see that he has a gun. You're the closest to the man, and you freeze as he yells for both of you to hand over your wallets and cell phones. Your friend Jim, who is farther away from the man, sees the gun and immediately runs in the other direction. The man yells at him to stop, and you consider running too until he threatens you. You feel your heart race and deep, intense fear. He repeats his demand for your wallet and cell phone, and you give them to him immediately. He grabs them and runs off quickly in the other direction. You then run back toward the bar, where you see Jim, and he tells you he has called the police. As you wait, you talk with each other about what the man looked like, what he was wearing, what type of gun it might have been, and what he told you. Later, a police officer takes statements from both of you about these details and says that a detective will follow up with you. A few days later, you go to the police station and view some mugshots, and a detective asks you some additional questions. A month later, a detective says he thinks they might have the person that robbed you, and he shows you a photo lineup with six faces. You aren't completely sure, but #5 looks very familiar to you. The detective thanks you and says he'll be in touch. Your friend Jim tells you he picked someone else out of the lineup. Six months go by, and you are contacted by the district attorney's office. You meet with the staff, and after asking you some questions about the robbery, they ask you to testify against the man you identified earlier. They tell you the man has been responsible for a series of robberies and that you can help keep him from victimizing anyone else. About 9 months after the crime, you meet with the district attorney, who briefs you about questions you are likely to be asked at trial. Subsequently, you appear in court and confidently testify that the man you earlier identified from the lineup was the one who robbed you.

You probably know from episodes of *Law and Order* (or other popular television series or movies) that a witness is supposed to "tell the truth, the whole truth, and nothing but the truth" in court. This is obviously a difficult task. In other words, people are expected to completely and accurately convey what happened during a witnessed event. As the preceding example demonstrates, this is difficult enough without considering a number of additional factors that make this task even more complicated. For instance, a person may have only witnessed the event briefly, or he or she might have focused attention on certain aspects of the event but not others. For example, it would not be surprising if you mainly thought about how to survive the robbery rather than trying to get a good look at the robber, or if you looked more at the weapon that his face (the *weapon focus effect*; e.g., Pickel, 1999; Steblay, 1992). As depicted in the example, it is also not unusual that witnesses feel fear or other intense emotions. After the event, he or she may learn information about the event from other witnesses, the media, or from investigators that he or she never observed (*post-event [mis]information*, such as the "fact" that the robber wore a green jacket rather than its actual black color). Although it is not unusual for a witness to be interviewed soon after a crime, it may be months or years before they are called to testify in court. Furthermore, witnesses are often interviewed or briefed about the event on many different occasions by different people (e.g., Kassin et al., 2007). During these different interviews, people may receive feedback about the accuracy of different aspects of their memories (e.g., such as when the person is told they identified the right person; Wells & Bradfield, 1998). Furthermore, witnesses may talk about the event many more times with family and friends. Note that we've described only a small number of factors that potentially affect an eyewitness's memory; there are many others (e.g., cross-racial identification; Malpass & Kravitz, 1969). However, even this small set gives a good sense of how difficult it might be for eyewitness accounts to meet the expectations of the legal system.

EYEWITNESS EVIDENCE. We can think about eyewitness memory as a type of evidence that is evaluated both by the witness/source and by others. For example, in the process of trying to remember an eyewitness event, a person might evaluate whether a particular piece of information that came to mind was something he or she actually saw during the event, or something heard afterward (e.g., M. K. Johnson et al., 1993). Consequently, the individual may only report something to the investigator if he or she has a clear and detailed memory of seeing it. More commonly, we think of memory reports as evidence that is judged by others. In criminal cases, these evaluators include investigators, judges, and jurors. When listening to eyewitness testimony, these people are judging whether or not the account seems to accurately reflect what happened during the witnessed event. As we will see in chapter 4, the characteristics people use to judge other people's memories are often similar to the characteristics they use to judge their own memories.

Just as with physical evidence, it is important to consider how eyewitness evidence is collected and maintained. In the case of physical evidence, it is well known that poor collection or storage procedures can compromise the integrity of a sample of DNA or blood, making it unusable. There is agreement among researchers, and among many in the law enforcement community (e.g., National Institute of Justice Technical Group for Eyewitness Evidence, 1999), that we should have a similar concern with the ways we collect and document eyewitness memories. In the chapters that follow, we discuss the implications of research for improving these methods. Furthermore, one can consider two general approaches for improving the utility of eyewitness accounts. The first is by supporting the eyewitness to provide a more complete or accurate account of what happened during the event. For instance, one technique from the Cognitive Interview (Fisher & Geiselman, 1989) involves having witnesses remember the context of the witnessed event prior to recall as a means of helping them remember details they might not otherwise remember. The second, less common approach is to help support people's (investigators, judges, jurors) ability to accurately evaluate the eyewitness accounts of other people. For example, researchers have had raters use the Memory Characteristics Questionnaire (M. K. Johnson et al., 1988) to help them distinguish between accurate and false memories provided by other people (e.g., Barnier et al., 2005). In this book, we consider both of these approaches to enhancing the utility of eyewitness accounts.

Experiencing and Remembering

Memory connects our past to our present[4] and involves translating our experiences into a representation that can later influence our behavior or contribute to a recollection. Furthermore, although we may spend a lot of time in school deliberately trying to learn information well enough to remember it later, this is not how we go about remembering most things in our lives. Instead, our brains appear tuned to help us make sense of what is happening around us and provide predictions about what is going to happen next (e.g., Bar, 2007). It is important to understand that the perceptual and reflective processes that help us comprehend an event not only contribute to the formation of a memory but are also influenced by memories of previous experiences (e.g., through the generation of expectations that affect where we look or how we interpret a stimulus). In other words, our experience of previous events influences how we perceive and comprehend later ones. As we'll see, this is only one of the ways that the process of creating and using memories is dynamic in nature. However, we'll first cover a few important terms that are commonly used in research on memory.

BASIC TERMS. Memory researchers typically think about the process of creating and remembering memories as following three general stages—*encoding*, *storage*, and *retrieval*. As discussed earlier, as events unfold, we try to make sense of them using both perceptual and reflective (elaborative) processes. Encoding describes the creation of a memory, as the information produced by these processes is translated into a format in which it can be stored in the brain. This representation is often referred to as a memory *trace*. Storage describes the period during which the representation is retained. During this period, memory traces are initially relatively fragile (this stage usually lasts for a few hours) but gradually are physiologically stabilized through a process of protein synthesis (e.g., see McGaugh, 2000). This stabilization process is called *consolidation*, and memories in this state are more resistant to disruption. Recently, researchers have discovered that even memories that are consolidated can be made unstable again by reactivating the memory (e.g., Nader et al., 2000). This process is called *reconsolidation*, and this appears to be one way that memories can be altered after being stored. The final phase, retrieval, describes the process of bringing back information stored in memory. Retrieval is often discussed using a spatial metaphor; people are described as searching for a particular memory. Most theories of memory assume that this search is cue-dependent. Cues can be conceived as internally or externally derived information that can be used to constrain the search process. For example, if you are trying to remember what you had for lunch yesterday, you might start by trying to remember where you had lunch. Remembering the location could help prompt your memory for what you ate and reduce the extent to which memories of other lunches come to mind. More broadly, the more closely the cues approximate the original experience, the more likely the memory will be retrieved (*the encoding specificity principle*; e.g., Tulving & Thomson, 1971). This has implications for interpreting performance on a given memory test as an index of memory. If someone fails to remember an item on a test, it does not necessarily mean that this information is not stored in memory. Rather, someone may simply not have sufficiently effective cues to retrieve it at that point in time. Researchers distinguish between *availability* (information is stored in memory) and *accessibility* (information can be retrieved at this particular moment) to make just this point (e.g., Tulving, 1983).

MEMORY AS A CONSTRUCTIVE ACTIVITY. If you stopped a person on the street and asked them how memory works, more than likely he or she would respond that memory is like a video recorder or a computer (e.g., Simons & Chabris, 2011). Researchers often refer to this notion of memory as *reproduction*. In this view, events are experienced, stored, and later brought back as they had occurred. Indeed, sometimes memory feels as if we are simply reexperiencing what happened previously (e.g., Tulving, 1983). Like many metaphors, it has some elements of truth (see basic terms discussed earlier) but is also incorrect in a number of important ways. To begin, let's compare just a few features of a video camera recording with human memory (see table I.1). First, as long as the camera is pointed toward an object and it is in view, that object is going to be recorded. This is not the case with human beings. A person can have their eyes directed toward an object, yet their attention can be directed somewhere else (e.g., on their thoughts). For instance, research has found that people can miss dramatic changes to the environment (e.g., the person they're talking with changes or objects change) if their attention is directed elsewhere (*change blindness*; for a review, see Simons & Rensink, 2005). Because attention influences whether or to what degree information is represented in memory, human memory is selective in ways that mechanical recorders are not. Second, the cognitive processes involved in memory are influenced by a person's physiological state (e.g., stress; Wolf, 2009) and the affective (emotional) properties of objects in the environment (e.g., Kensinger, 2009a), but no similar factors influence the quality of video recordings. Third, video recordings play back "word for word" the event that was initially recorded. Human memory is not verbatim; people often remember selectively what they experienced and may only remember the gist of what happened. As we discuss in much more detail later, human memory can also be in error, for example, by including details that were not initially experienced (e.g., Zaragoza & Lane, 1994). Fourth, when a video is recorded, your ability to play back that recording is not affected by other recordings elsewhere on the tape or hard drive. Yet, the ability to remember information in human memory *is* affected by the similarity of other memories. Researchers use the term *interference* to describe this situation. For example, when information you've learned recently (e.g., the Spanish word for *dog*) impairs your ability to remember previous related information you learned (e.g., the French word for *dog*), this is called *retroactive interference* (e.g., Melton & Irwin, 1940). When information you have learned previously impairs your ability to remember information learned subsequently, this is called *proactive interference*. Finally, let's say that we play back a video in an environment that is very different from the environment in which it was recorded. This should have absolutely no effect on whether we can watch the recording. But, differences in environment or context *do* make a difference for human memory (e.g., Smith, 1979). For example, people can sometimes remember information in one context but not another (e.g., Tulving & Thomson, 1971).

If human memory is not reproductive, how can we characterize it? The consensus view of researchers is that memory is *constructive* in nature (e.g., F. Bartlett, 1932; Neisser, 1967; Tulving, 1983). This is true from our very first perceptions of an event, which are inferences based on ambiguous sensory information from the environment (e.g., Helmholtz, 1867; Kersten et al., 2004). Furthermore, as discussed previously, an encoded memory trace is not a literal reproduction of reality but is selective, and includes elaborative activity such as what an individual was thinking and feeling at the time. Retrieval is no less (re)constructive. Our recollections are pieced together based on information provided in the memory cue (including the retrieval environment), what we selectively access from the memory trace, as well as inferences we make about this information based on other knowledge we possess (M. K. Johnson et al., 1993; Neisser, 1967; Tulving, 1983). Neisser (1967) likened this process to that of a paleontologist trying to reconstruct a dinosaur skeleton from fossil remains—"out of a few stored chips, we remember a dinosaur" (p. 285). Thus, remembering is better seen as a process of pattern completion than one that simply involves activating a stored memory trace. This view highlights, for instance, how differently we may remember an event depending on the available retrieval cues (e.g., E. Loftus & Palmer, 1974; Ochsner et al., 1997). We discuss the implications of this view of memory later in the book, but for now, it should be apparent that it conflicts with the view of memory commonly held by the public and the legal system.

MEASURING MEMORY. How can we evaluate whether someone remembers what they have experienced? There are several common types of memory tests that we'll encounter in the following chapters. One way of distinguishing between these tests is that they vary in terms of the specificity of external cues that are provided to participants. On *recognition tests*, participants are generally provided with stimuli (e.g., words, pictures, faces, scenes) that they have previously studied, called *targets*, and other stimuli they did not study, called *lures* or *distractors*. On the test, participants have to discriminate between these two types of items, for instance, by making an old/new judgment for each item or by picking which one of a set of items is old (a forced-choice test). Recognition tests thus provide fairly detailed external cues for remembering (in some cases, targets are the same stimuli they've viewed before), and thus, the need to search memory using your own internally generated cues is reduced. On *recall tests*, the external cues provided to participants are less specific and require that he or she produce some information in response. In *cued recall*, participants are given some information they studied (e.g., a person's face or several letters of a word) and asked to produce associated studied information (e.g., the person's name or the complete word). In *free recall*, participants are given a very general external cue, such as "Tell me all the words the words you just studied," and participants have to search memory using internally generated cues (e.g., "I know there were a number of animal names").

Another assessment tool in memory research is a *source memory test*. These tests involve decisions about the circumstances under which an item was encoded (e.g., its format or associated context) and usually take the form of source recognition. For example, a participant might indicate whether an item was previously shown as a picture or simply imagined, whether a word was previously presented in green or blue, or whether an item was viewed during a video or read in a questionnaire they had completed afterward. In some cases, participants see only items they previously encoded (i.e., all items are "old") and must indicate the source of the item. In other cases, the test includes both old and never-seen items, and participants have a response option that allows them to indicate if the item is new.

Each of these tests has its complement in real-world investigations. For instance, eyewitness lineups are a type of recognition test in which the witness must discriminate the perpetrator (if he or she is present) from other, similar individuals. During an interview, if the investigator asks the witness to "tell me everything you can remember about that night," he or she is asking the witness to engage in free recall. Furthermore, if an investigator showed a picture to a witness and asked him or her to remember the person's name, then that is a type of cued recall. Finally, if a detective asked a witness to try to remember which one of two people told her something, this would be a type of source memory test.

In the next two sections, we briefly introduce some distinctions that have been important for contemporary memory researchers (although they have also been subject to debate). Our intent is to provide a starting point for these topics, as many are covered in more detail in subsequent chapters.

TYPES OF MEMORY. Memory is multifaceted (e.g., James, 1890), and there are different ways of describing its various aspects. One key distinction is between a shorter term memory that is highly accessible and available to conscious awareness and memory that is a less accessible but a longer term store of our experiences (e.g., James, 1890). This general distinction has been reflected in the concepts of *primary* and *secondary memory* (James, 1890), *short-* and *long-term memory* (e.g., Atkinson & Shiffrin, 1968), and *working memory* and long-term memory (e.g., Baddeley & Hitch, 1974). Most contemporary researchers focus on the latter distinction (e.g., Cowan, 1999), and in this book, this is the focus as well. Although different theorists ascribe different mechanisms to working memory (e.g., Baddeley, 2000; Cowan, 1999; Engle, 2001), they broadly share the assumption that it describes mental processes that are used to manipulate and maintain information in an activated state so that it can be used to perform cognitive tasks such as understanding spoken and written language, mathematical calculation, and problem-solving (e.g., Cowan et al., 2005; Engle, 2001). The number of items that can be maintained in working memory is thought to be limited (e.g., 3–5 items), and information can be lost relatively quickly if not kept active (e.g., through rehearsal). One important finding is that people vary in their ability to effectively use working memory—*working memory capacity* (WMC; Kane et al., 2001), and this ability is highly correlated with intelligence and other important cognitive abilities. Among other things, people with high WMC appear to be more resistant to interference and better able to inhibit irrelevant or distracting information (e.g., Kane et al., 2007).

Researchers also distinguish between various types of long-term memory (e.g., N. Cohen & Squire, 1980; Tulving 1985) that differ with respect to the type of content, the potential for conscious remembering, and the associated brain systems. One broad classification contrasts *declarative* and *nondeclarative* memory (see Squire, 2004, for discussion). Declarative memory refers to memories that are represented in the brain in such a way that they can be consciously remembered, and it corresponds to what most people think of as "memory" (Squire, 2004). There are two types of declarative memory: *episodic* and *semantic* memory (Tulving, 1972). Episodic memory refers to memories of a person's own experiences that contain specific contextual features (information about "where, what, and when"; e.g., Nyberg et al., 1996) that allow the person to have a sense of reexperiencing the event. If, in thinking back to what you did for lunch yesterday, you remember that you ate a turkey sandwich while sitting on a park bench at the noon hour, you have an episodic memory for that event. In addition, the conscious recollection of episodic memories requires that one intentionally try to remember the past, what Tulving (1983) termed *retrieval mode*. This type of memory is the one most often studied by eyewitness memory researchers. Semantic memory involves facts or other knowledge about the world (e.g., "Martin Luther King was a pioneer of the civil rights movements in the 1960s"). One key feature that discriminates semantic from episodic memory is that although a person is consciously aware of the fact itself, this memory is not accompanied by a sense of remembering the context in which this information was initially learned. Nondeclarative memory describes the fact that memory for past experiences can also be conveyed in our behavior without our awareness (Squire, 2004). For example, people can ride a bicycle without needing to deliberately remember how to do so. This memory for how to do a task has been called *procedural memory* (Tulving, 1983; see also habit memory; Mishkin et al., 1984). Other types of nondeclarative memory include *priming* or *implicit memory*, in which information comes to mind without the sense of remembering (Graf & Schacter, 1985).

SIGNAL DETECTION THEORY AND SINGLE PROCESS VERSUS DUAL PROCESS THEORIES OF RECOGNITION. A substantial amount of theoretical and empirical work has examined how people make recognition decisions, particularly in the simple situation when they must choose whether a particular item (e.g., word, face, scene) was studied previously or not (*Yes/No or Old/New recognition*). In this situation, there are four different outcomes on each test trial (see table I.2) based on the participant's response and the actual status of the item. If the item was previously studied and the person correctly calls it "old," this is called a *hit*. If the item was previously studied and the person incorrectly calls it "new," this is called a *miss*. Conversely, if the item was not previously studied and the person incorrectly calls it "old," this is called a *false alarm*. Finally, if the item was not previously studied and the person correctly calls it "new," this is called a *correct rejection*. Memory researchers typically use a measurement model called *Signal Detection Theory* (SDT; Wickens, 2002) to evaluate the judgments made by participants on this type of test (for a more detailed discussion, see, e.g., Macmillan & Creelman, 2005). The model assumes that decisions are based on the amount of evidence retrieved from memory and the criterion set by a person for the amount of evidence required for an item to be called "old." The amount of evidence is assumed to be a continuous variable, and each test item will cue different amounts of evidence. Although new items may retrieve some evidence of prior presentation (familiarity), on average, old items will retrieve more evidence due to having been encountered during the study phase. This is usually represented as two normal distributions (old and new items), with the old-item distribution shifted to the right (indicating greater average amounts of evidence). These distributions often overlap, and the degree of this overlap indicates how well participants can discriminate between old and new items, independent of response bias. This overlap is characterized using the distance between the means of the two distributions and is called d' (d-prime). Where a participant places his or her response criterion along the continuum of evidence is represented as beta (although the measure C is reported most often in research studies; see Snodgrass & Corwin, 1988). Items that retrieve evidence that exceeds this criterion would be called "old," and those that fall below would be called "new." A criterion set to the right of the intersection of the distributions (an optimal criterion) is relatively <u>conservative</u>, in that more evidence is required to say "old." In terms of the response options discussed earlier, a conservative response criterion leads to fewer false alarms but also fewer hits. On the other hand, a criterion set to the left of the intersection is relatively <u>liberal</u>, in that less evidence is required to say "old." In this case, relative to an optimal criterion, hits will rise, but so will false alarms. SDT can also model situations in which people make confidence rather than old/new judgments, which is represented by the use of multiple response criteria corresponding to different levels of confidence. This also allows researchers to compute receiving operating characteristics (ROC) curves, a technique that can be very useful in distinguishing between different interpretations of data (for a description and an example of ROC curves in eyewitness identification research, see Gronlund et al., 2014; Wixted & Mickes, 2014). Altogether, SDT provides a very useful way of measuring performance on recognition tests. For more detail about the underlying assumptions, calculations, and other issues, see Macmillan and Creelman (2005), Wickens (2002), or Wixted (2007).

SDT is not only useful as a measurement model, but it can also be used as a conceptual model of recognition memory to generate theoretical predictions (e.g., Wixted & Stretch, 2004). There are two major types of theories that have been proposed to explain how people make recognition decisions. SDT can be considered a *single process* model because it assumes that a single continuous source of evidence can be used to make recognition decisions (e.g., for a discussion, see Donaldson, 1996; Wixted & Mickes, 2010). Beyond this shared assumption, single process models can differ with respect to assumptions that include how memories are represented, the way familiarity is computed from these representations, and the retrieval process (e.g., Gillund & Shiffrin, 1984; Hintzman, 1988; for a review of global matching models, see Clark & Gronlund, 1996; for more general models, see, e.g., Dougal & Rotello, 2007). In contrast, *dual process* models assume that more than one process is necessary to account for research findings on recognition performance (see Diana et al., 2006; Yonelinas, 2002). These models differ somewhat with respect to their specific hypothesized processes and assumptions (e.g., Jacoby, Kelley & Dywan, 1989; Mandler, 1980; Reder et al., 2000; Yonelinas, 1997). For example, Mandler (1980) proposed that recognition decisions are made on the basis of familiarity or a separate recall-like search process. In this paper, he provides a famous *butcher-on-the-bus* example to illustrate the distinction. In the example, he sees someone on the bus whose face is strongly familiar, yet he does not initially know the source of this familiarity. Consequently, after a search of memory, he realizes the man is the butcher at the local supermarket. Most dual process theories refer to the processes of *familiarity* and *recollection*, with the former referring to undifferentiated strength of evidence and the latter referring to the retrieval of item-specific and contextual information from the encoding event, although they differ in terms of other assumptions (e.g., whether recollection is based on continuous evidence or is a threshold process, compare Reder et al., 2000, and Yonelinas, 1997). Whether single or dual process models best account for recognition judgments continue to be debated (for reviews, see

Diana et al., 2006; Wixted, 2004; Yonelinas, 2002), although there are models that combine elements of single and dual process assumptions (e.g., Wixted & Mickes, 2010).

The Remaining Chapters

Now that we have covered some of the basic concepts about memory and eyewitnesses, the following chapters are organized around important issues regarding memory and eyewitnesses. Chapter 1 discusses how we remember people and describe them to others, particularly in the context of eyewitness situations. Chapter 2 covers our current understanding of how faces are remembered and the role of our past familiarity with them in influencing the accuracy of our memories. Chapter 3 describes the nature of true and false memories, while chapter 4 focuses on people's ability to distinguish between genuine and false memories, and discusses promising ways of effectively accomplishing this goal. Chapter 5 examines the influence of stress and emotional arousal on memory, both of which are commonly a part of the experience of eyewitness events. As we'll see, both clearly affect memory but not always in simple, straightforward ways. Chapter 6 looks at how the act of remembering can change our memories and affect what we are later able to remember about events. In the final chapter, we build on the previous chapters by taking a broader perspective on what we've covered. Specifically, we discuss the implications for applications to real-world witnessing, particularly how we might improve the ways we collect and evaluate eyewitness evidence.

TABLE 1.1. Selected Features of Video Cameras Versus Human Memory

Video Camera	Human Memory
Nonselective recording	Selective processing (e.g., attention)
No effect of stress or emotional arousal	Affected by stress and arousal
Verbatim playback	Nonverbatim remembering
Not influenced by previous recordings	Influenced by previous memories
Environment does not influence playback	Environment influences remembering

TABLE I.2. Possible Outcomes of a Trial on a Yes/No Recognition Test

Item Status	Response Type Old	New
Old	Hit	Miss
New	False alarm	Correct rejection

1

Memory for Persons

On February 1, 1989, Troy Webb received a sentence of 47 years for rape, kidnapping, and robbery in the state of Virginia. Troy had been identified by the victim from a photograph. The victim claimed she was 99% confident that the man in the photograph was her attacker and even claimed to recognize Troy from additional photos of him that had been taken when he was much younger. Troy Webb served almost 8 years in prison before DNA testing exonerated him from any connection to the crime (The Innocence Project, 2019a). The criminal justice system places immense weight on the ability of a witness or victim to accurately describe and then identify/recognize their attacker, who, in most cases, is a previously unfamiliar person to the victim/witness. In this chapter, the focus is on our ability to provide person descriptions. Unfortunately, research on the accuracy of person descriptions is sparse; therefore, we should be cautious of the weight that such descriptions currently hold in criminal investigations. One of the primary messages from this chapter is that further research is required if we are to fully understand the limitations of this kind of eyewitness testimony. First, this chapter considers the current literature on person descriptions and the inherent difficulties involved in describing people. Then, we consider issues of age and race in person descriptions. Finally, we consider whether there is a link between the ability to describe a perpetrator and the ability to recognize/identify one.

Person Descriptions

Being asked to provide a description of the perpetrator is one of the first things a witness or victim may be required to do when giving a statement to the police (perhaps second only to a description of the crime itself). This description is then used to locate a suspect, who is then subject to interrogation, lineup procedures, and possibly a trial. A wealth of research has focused on the conditions under which eyewitness identifications of suspects as perpetrators of crime can and do go wrong, but what about the description that leads to the arrest of a suspect in the first place?

In 2008, a famous Scottish actor, Robbie Coltrane (known for his roles in the Harry Potter movies and television series such as *Cracker*), was depicted in a wanted poster in New Zealand. While the New Zealand police made it very clear that Robbie Coltrane was not the person they were looking for and was innocent of any connection to the alleged crimes, they did claim that their suspect looked like a 16-year-old version of Coltrane. Importantly, the picture of Coltrane that the New Zealand police used was one in which he was 58 years old. The description from the poster reads: "Robbie Coltrane is not the burglar but imagine him aged 16 with lank greasy hair and you have the picture" (BBC News, 2008). Due to the Children and Young Persons Act 1989, the New Zealand police were not allowed to show an image of their 16-year-old suspect, so they used Robbie Coltrane as a look-a-like. On the whole, the police were lauded for their ingeniousness; however, this does raise the issue of how reliable an identification on the basis of this description can be? Furthermore, how do potential witnesses make sense of such descriptions?

In general, person descriptions tend to be vague, tend to follow population norms (average height, average weight), and tend to be applicable to the majority of the people local to the area of the crime (Meissner et al., 2007). In one of the first and most frequently cited archival studies on person descriptions from police reports, Kuehn (1974) found that most witnesses/victims of crime reported an average of seven person descriptors, with gender, age, height, and build among those most frequently reported. Kuehn found that features such as perpetrator race, weight, complexion, and hair color were described less frequently. By comparison, Ellis and colleagues (1980) conducted a laboratory-based study in which participants viewed an event and then, after a 1-hour delay, described the target individual. Ellis et al. found that participants (collapsed across genders) reported an average of 9.38 descriptors, which is a higher number than found in Kuehn. Because Ellis et al. is a laboratory study and Kuehn used field data, these findings raise the question of whether laboratory-based experiments may overestimate a person's ability to fully describe an unfamiliar person. Following up on this idea, Roderick Lindsay and colleagues (1994) compared person descriptions from staged crimes and real crimes. The staged crime was an undergraduate stealing a purse, whereas the real crimes were taken from reporting in a local newspaper and included fraud, sexual assault, kidnapping, assault, and armed robbery. Lindsay et al. found that witnesses to staged crimes reported an average of 7.35 person descriptors while witnesses to real crimes reported an average of 3.94 person descriptors. Therefore, laboratory-based experiments may produce person descriptions that contain more information than could be expected in the field.

In addition to comparing staged and real crimes, Lindsay et al. (1994) also looked at the categories of person descriptors that were being provided by participants who witnessed staged crimes, and witnesses/victims who experienced actual crimes. For the staged crimes, Lindsay et al. reported that 99% of participants who reported person descriptors reported clothing, 90% reported hair color, and 86% reported height, whereas less than 50% reported gender, age, and race/ethnicity. When facial features were reported, 43% reported information about the eyes, with all other facial features reported less than 25% of the time. By comparison, witnesses/victims of real crimes gave person descriptors that differed somewhat from the staged crime witnesses: 95% reported gender, 38% reported hair color, 60% reported clothing, 25% reported race/ethnicity, and less than 10% reported any facial features of the perpetrator(s). More recently, Van Koppen and Lochun (1997), using archival field data, found that less than 5% of person descriptors were inner facial features (eye, nose, lips) compared to external facial features (such as face shape).

Therefore, it appears that not only are person descriptors often incomplete but also rarely focus on identifiable features of the inner face. Furthermore, a good proportion of person descriptors tend to focus on information that needs to be estimated by the perceiver, such as height, weight, and ethnicity/race of the perpetrator. Meissner et al. (2007) argue that such estimates are often inaccurate and tend to be based on the perceiver's own height and weight and/or their knowledge of the population norm(s). As person descriptions are typically the first "lead" in an investigation, this research suggests that suspects may be first identified/contacted based on incomplete and estimated descriptions of their external body, such as their gender, race, height, weight, hair, and clothing. Despite person descriptions as a rule seeming to be vague and incomplete, there are factors that may undermine the accuracy and reliability of person descriptions even further. According to Meissner et al., the factors that influence the ability of a witness to form a memory of the perpetrator's appearance can be broken down into three categories: opportunity to view, stress and anxiety, and alcohol and drugs.

Opportunity to View

The two main factors that influence the opportunity of the witness to view are visibility (how clear a view of the suspect the witness is able to have) and exposure duration (how long the witness is exposed to the suspect for). While most mock crimes are staged during the day for research purposes, according to statistics from the Department of Justice (Office of Juvenile Justice and Delinquency Prevention, 2016), 24% of all violent crimes committed by adults occur between 8 p.m. and midnight, with activity reaching a peak in frequency at 9 p.m. Therefore, we must ask what effect the time of day might have on our ability to remember and recognize a perpetrator. Yarmey (1986) looked at participants' ability to describe and recognize a perpetrator at four levels of daily illumination: daylight, the start of twilight, the end of twilight, and night. Yarmey found that person descriptions were most complete for those who had witnessed the target individual during the day and at the beginning of twilight, compared to all other conditions. However, it is worth noting that identification of the target person was rather poor overall—in the daylight and start of twilight conditions accurate identification hovered around 50%. In the nighttime condition, accurate recognition from a lineup containing the target individual dropped to only 13% (Yarmey, 1986). While unfortunately little to no follow-up of this research has been conducted, it does suggest that for crimes that occur outside of normal daylight hours, the witness's ability to describe and recognize the perpetrator could be substantially diminished.

With regard to exposure duration, the intuitive answer appears to be the one supported by the data—the longer one views a perpetrator for, the more they will remember about him or her. Laugherty and colleagues (1971) found that the longer a participant was exposed to a target face, the better his or her subsequent recognition. Laugherty et al.'s finding has been replicated time and again (e.g., but not limited to, MacLin et al., 2001; Read, 1995; Shapiro & Penrod, 1986). However, rather unsatisfactorily, the research does not provide us with a consensus regarding the parameters of what should be considered adequate versus inadequate exposure duration. For instance, Laughtery et al. compared 10 seconds to 32 seconds, Read (1995) compared exposures of 30 to 60 seconds compared to 4 to 12 minutes, and for Maclin et al. (2001), the exposure durations were 0.5 seconds and 5 seconds. Therefore, the difficulty with this research is that no one can objectively say whether an exposure of 5 seconds is sufficient to produce a complete person description—5 seconds is better than 0.5 seconds, but is it enough? Or does a witness need to engage with a perpetrator for several minutes before a complete person description can be provided? To further complicate matters, research also suggests that we are very poor judges of duration and will often underestimate the duration of an event (cf. Ebaid & Crewther, 2018). Therefore, although it is clear that longer exposure to the perpetrator improves the ability of witnesses to describe them, what remains unclear is how long is long enough, and even if we knew what long enough was, whether witnesses and victims would be able to accurately estimate their exposure duration to the perpetrator.

Stress and Anxiety

The impact of stress and anxiety on memory is covered in extensive detail in chapter 5 and as such is only summarized here. Crimes are typically considered to be high-stress and high-anxiety events for those who witness them. The extant literature argues that the experience of heightened stress and anxiety, or negative emotion more generally, have a detrimental effect on the accuracy and completeness of memory reports (e.g., Deffenbacher et al., 2004). It is highly likely, therefore, that the experience of heightened stress and/or anxiety at the time of the crime will further decrease the reliability of the witness's testimony and their ability to fully describe the details of the crime event. However, some studies have demonstrated that, under the right conditions, negative emotions may improve memory for central details of an event (typically defined as details in the visual center of the scene) and only impair memory for peripheral details (typically defined as details in the visual periphery of the scene; e.g., Resiberg & Huerer, 2007) and may even increase recall memory for the perpetrator (Houston et al., 2013).

Intoxication

The third factor identified by Meissner et al. (2007) as affecting the encoding of person descriptions is intoxication of the witness at the time of the crime. Evans et al. (2009) surveyed police officers to determine how often they interact with intoxicated witnesses to crime, and the results were surprising—73% of officers reported that intoxicated witnesses were either common or very common, with 90% claiming to have interviewed an intoxicated witness in the past month. F. Palmer et al. (2013) found that 13% of 1,307 cases referred to the U.S. Prosecutor's Office had at least one intoxicated witness. In a study that focused specifically on sexual assault, 72% of college women who self-reported as being the victim of sexual assault claimed they were intoxicated during the crime (Mohler-Kuo et al., 2004). In spite of this seemingly high number of interactions between law enforcement personnel and intoxicated persons, our knowledge regarding the effects of intoxication on memory is rather limited.

One of the main issues with conducting research on intoxication and memory (be that alcohol- or drug-based) appears to be the field-versus-laboratory debate. In laboratory experiments, everything can be controlled to the extent that the researchers can be confident that only the alcohol or drug being tested has been ingested by the participant—a necessary component to assigning cause and effect relationships. However, where alcohol is concerned, due to ethical constraints, researchers cannot conduct research on individuals with blood alcohol levels similar to those that may be present in real-world witnesses to crime. In the lab, research participants can only be intoxicated up to a blood alcohol level of 0.08% (the legal drink/drive limit in the majority of the United States). A blood alcohol level of 0.08% is below the level often reported in archival studies of real crimes, which report an average blood alcohol level of 0.11% (Evans et al., 2009). However, upon moving one's research out of the lab and into the bar, for example, all experimental control is lost: There is no ability to control for whether all participants have only consumed alcohol or whether they have also consumed other substances (illegal or legal) that may alter their memory performance. These issues are important to consider, as laboratory-based studies that are capped at a blood alcohol level of 0.08% produce different findings regarding the effects of alcohol on memory than do field studies in which the blood alcohol level may increase to 0.29% (e.g., Altman et al., 2018).

Take, for example, Schreiber Compo et al. (2011) who, in laboratory-based research studies, compared intoxicated and placebo participants' memories of their conversation with a research assistant in the lab. Interestingly, intoxicated and placebo participants reported the same amount of information about their interaction with the research assistant; however, the kinds of information they reported differed (Schreiber Compo et al., 2011). Intoxicated participants reported more subjective information (e.g., opinions about the research assistant that were not linked to identifiable features, such as "he was nice") and less peripheral information (e.g., information about the location of the drinking event) than placebo participants. Furthermore, there were no between-group differences in the reporting of person descriptors (Schreiber Compo et al., 2011). By comparison, in a field study conducted in an actual bar, where blood alcohol levels ranged from 0.00% to 0.29%, intoxication impaired both the accuracy and completeness of recall but had no effect on the ability of participants to correctly identify the perpetrator of a mock crime from a photographic lineup (Altman et al., 2018). Therefore, findings from laboratory and field studies appear to present different implications for person descriptions, and memory more generally, of intoxication at the time of a crime. It is interesting to note, however, that neither laboratory nor field studies suggest that alcohol impairs the ability of a witness or victim to recognize the perpetrator.

According to the observations of Evans et al. (2009), alcohol is not the only intoxicating substance that police encounter with dealing with crime. While an estimated 18% of witnesses are under the influence of cannabis (Evans et al., 2009), very little is known about the ways in which cannabis intoxication may affect the ability of the consumer to describe the perpetrator of a crime. Prior research suggests that cannabis can impair memory; however, these studies have all been based on recall memory for word lists (e.g., D'Souza et al., 2004) and not for complex events that tend to involve emotional arousal, such as a crime. In a field study setup much like that of Altman et al. (2018), who visited a bar and tested intoxicated patrons, Vredeveldt and colleagues (2018) visited coffee shops in Amsterdam, which are alcohol-free bars that sell drugs such as cannabis to patrons aged 18 years or older. Vredeveldt et al. showed patrons a mock crime video and a lineup task. As no objective measures for cannabis intoxication exist, Vredeveldt et al. had to rely on patrons' self-reports for information on the number of cannabis cigarettes consumed that day and a subjective rating of how intoxicated each participant felt. Vredevelt et al. found that intoxicated participants provided significantly less correct information about the mock crime event than sober participants did; specifically, intoxicated participants provided less correct person descriptions. Conversely, intoxicated and sober participants performed similarly during an identification/lineup task (Vredevelt et al., 2018). It is important to exercise extreme caution in interpreting the results of preliminary studies, such as those conducted by Vredevelt et al. However broadly construed, this research suggests that while alcohol and cannabis intoxication may impair the ability of the witness to describe the perpetrator, intoxication with either substance may not affect the witness's ability to identify the target individual. With the legalization of cannabis in over half of the states in the United States, encounters with witnesses intoxicated with cannabis may become as prevalent as encounters with witnesses intoxicated with alcohol. Thus, it is clear that more research is needed in this neglected, yet crucial, area of eyewitness memory research.

While the opportunity to view, stress and anxiety, and alcohol and drugs have been considered here separately, it is not beyond the bounds of logic to argue that a crime could occur late at night or when the perpetrator's face is obscured, which causes the victim to experience stress and anxiety and which also occurs while the victim or witness, is intoxicated. Therefore, as any of these factors may impair the encoding of the information necessary to provide reliable person descriptions on their own, the potential combined effects are also worthy of consideration. Of course, this list is not exhaustive, and there are other important factors that can affect the accuracy of person descriptions. Two such factors are considered in more detail next, namely, what happens when the victim or witness providing the description is a child and what happens when the race of the perpetrator is different from that of the victim.

Person Descriptions by Child Witnesses

When it comes to person descriptions, children tend to provide far fewer person descriptors than adults (Pozzulo, 2007). Not only do children tend to provide fewer person descriptors, but the categories of descriptions that they provide also differ from adults. Early studies initially suggested that children may fail to provide any person descriptors at all (Dent & Stephenson, 1979); however, as research methods became more nuanced it was discovered that as children aged, their likelihood of providing person descriptors increased (G. Davis et al., 1989). G. Davis et al. found that when asked to describe an interaction with an unfamiliar person, young children (aged 6–7), on average, only provided one person descriptor about the target individual. However, older children, (those aged 10–11), provided on average 2.3 person descriptors (G. Davis et al., 1989). Unfortunately, a limitation of these early studies is that they investigated the likelihood of children providing person descriptions in isolation. Thus, the ability of children could not be compared to the ability of adults when it came to describing the same person. Therefore, we cannot say for sure if, under the same instructions and for the same target persons, adults would have performed differently (see Pozzulo, 2007, for an in-depth critique).

However, Pozzulo and Warren (2003) did directly compare the ability of children and adult witnesses to provide complete person descriptions. Pozzulo and Warren tested children aged 10 to 14 years old (referred to as "youths"), against adults aged 17 to 25 years old, by showing both groups a video of a previously unfamiliar man describing how to dress and act to stay safe when outside. Following exposure to the video, youths and adults were asked to write down everything they could remember about the appearance of the man in the video and what he was discussing. After completing a free-recall task, participants were further asked questions about the event and tasks that the man in the video had engaged in. Pozzulo and Warren found that youths provided significantly fewer person descriptors than adults did. In Study 2, Pozzulo and Warren largely replicated the design of Study 1; however, this time, instead of showing a video to youths and adults, the participants were asked to describe the appearance of a previously unfamiliar confederate to the study who had been brought into the room and had given a short talk. As in Study 1, youths again provided significantly fewer person descriptions than adults did.

These findings naturally lead us to two questions: Why is it that children are providing fewer person descriptors? and If children do provide person descriptors, what categories of information do they contain? Previous research has demonstrated that adult person descriptors tend to revolve around gender, age, height, weight/build, race, and hair color (Kuehn, 1974), with descriptors about hair typically being the most common (e.g., Ellis et al., 1980; Sporer, 1996). Interestingly, hair has also been found to be frequently reported by children (Ellis et al., 1980; Pozzulo & Warren, 2003; Sporer, 1996). However, in repeated studies, children and youths have been found to make errors when reporting height, weight, and age (Pozzulo, 2007; Pozzulo & Warren, 2003; Sporer, 1996).

There are several potential reasons for why children and youths provide fewer and less accurate person descriptors than adults. For example, it may be that external features of the face, such as face shape, hair length, hair color, and hairstyle, may be more salient and easier for young children to describe, so those are the features they focus on. It is also possible that given we see a developmental trend for increased person descriptors with age, it may be the case that younger children simply lack the experience and vocabulary necessary to provide accurate descriptors (see Pozzulo, 2007). Finally, it has also been argued that children and youths may suffer from an own-age bias, using their own ages as an estimate for those around them, resulting in their age estimates of adults being highly inaccurate (Pozzulo, 2007).

The extant literature appears to have focused exclusively on children's ability to describe previous unfamiliar faces. While such findings are important, research to date has neglected the fact that 90% of victims of childhood sexual abuse know their abuser (American Society for the

Positive Care of Children, 2019). While a child may be able to name their abuser if they are known to them, this may not always be the case. Depending on the age of the child, and whether their abuser is known to them by a familial name such as Aunt or Uncle, young and adolescent victims may have a harder time identifying their abusers by name simply because they don't know it. Therefore, investigating whether the ability of children to describe familiar persons is as poor as their ability to describe unfamiliar persons may be a worthy line of future inquiry.

Race and Person Descriptors

It has been consistently found in controlled laboratory studies that when the race of the victim/witness and perpetrator are different, the accuracy of the identification decision is impaired (see Brigham et al., 2007, for a review). This impairment in recognition ability is termed the cross-race effect, or own-race bias, and has been the subject of extensive research in the field of face recognition and eyewitness memory for the past 30 years. While there are many theories regarding what motivates a cross-race effect, the two main ones are the contact hypothesis (e.g., Brigham & Malpass, 1985; Finegold, 1914; Meissner & Brigham, 2001) and evolution (e.g., Goldstein & Chance, 1980; MacLin & Malpass, 2001; Rodin, 1987). The contact hypothesis argues that coming into contact with other races frequently will weaken the cross-race effect. The argument is that with increasing contact with other race faces, individuals learn to discriminate between faces of other racial groups, much in the same way as individuals learn to discriminate between faces from their own race (e.g., Brigham & Malpass, 1985). Evidence in support of the contact hypothesis is sporadic, however, with a meta-analysis demonstrating that contact accounted for only 2% of the variance in the cross-race effect; in other words, contact with other races had a very small influence on the ability to recognize other-race faces (Meissner & Brigham, 2001). One issue with empirically investigating the contact hypothesis, however, is that the primary measure relies on research subjects' ability to accurately estimate their contact with other races (Brigham et al., 2007). This has led to calls to instead investigate the contact hypothesis in cultures that typically have less or more contact with other races to get a more accurate estimation of contact (Brigham et al., 2007). On the other hand, the argument from evolution posits that we have simply not evolved with the capacity to process other-race faces with the same nuance with which we can process same-race faces. According to the evolutionary explanation, this inability to attend to the details of other-race faces stems from our genetic ancestors having to differentiate individual members of their tribe but only having to be able to categorize members of another tribe/race as an "other" (Brigham et al. 2007).

Unfortunately, although there is 30 years of research on the cross-race effect for face recognition, there are very few research papers on the effects of cross-race person descriptions. Two early studies found that regardless of whether one is describing an own-race or other-face face, the terminology used is the same (Ellis et al., 1975; Shepherd & Deregowski, 1981). In other words, when describing other-race faces, participants tended to report universal features (Ellis et al., 1975; Shepherd & Deregowski, 1981). For example, witnesses were found to comment that a Black face had brown eyes (Ellis et al., 1975; Shepherd & Deregowski, 1981). It has been argued that individuals in these studies were paying attention to features that are important to the differentiation of own-race faces (such as eye color) but that are less informative in the individuation of faces when applied to races for whom that characteristic is universal, thus resulting in a cross-race effect for person descriptions (Meissner et al., 2007).

Interestingly, in a further study to assess cross-race person descriptions, Falshore and Schooler (1995) found no cross-race effect for person descriptions but did observe the cross-race effect for person recognition. Falshore and Schooler asked participants to both describe and recognize a cross-race or same-race target person. When engaging in a lineup task, participants in their study were less able to accurately recognize the cross-race individual from the lineup compared to their ability to recognize the same-race individual. However, when independent judges, who had not seen the target individual before, were asked to complete the same identification task using only the participants' descriptions of the target individuals to guide them, they were equally accurate for same- versus other-race faces and did not show the cross-race effect (Falshore & Schooler, 1995). The findings from Falshore and Schooler may suggest that the own-race bias does not occur for person descriptions. However, it should be noted that in this study, the descriptions themselves were not coded for accuracy but were only evaluated based on the ability of independent judges to recognize individuals using the descriptions. Therefore, it is highly likely that the person descriptions were simply so poor that accurate identification was unlikely from either cross-race or same-race descriptors. That said, the discussion of cross-race effects does raise an interesting question about the relationship between person descriptions and lineup identification performance, which is the focus of the next section.

Relationship Between Person Descriptors and Face Recognition

While it may make intuitive sense that a witness who provides a full description of a perpetrator will be better able to recognize him or her from a photographic lineup, the research tells a different story. In most cases, the completeness and/or accuracy of the person description provided by a given witness has no association with that witness's ability to accurately pick a target person out of a lineup (e.g., Pigott & Brigham, 198), that is, at least until the witness is given an opportunity to reread his or her statement before the identification parade. While the accuracy and completeness of the person description have not been found to affect the accuracy of the lineup decision, rereading the statement has been found in some contexts to impair recognition ability (the verbal-overshadowing effect) and in others to facilitate accurate recognition (verbal-facilitation effect). The relationship between person descriptions and identification ability is thought to be lacking because describing a face and recognizing a face are two separate cognitive processes. Descriptions focus on a verbal representation of features of the face, while recognition relies on a visual match between memory and the faces presented to the witness as part of the lineup process (Meissner et al., 2007). Indeed, it is exactly this mismatch in cognitive processing that is thought to be behind verbal-overshadowing and verbal-facilitation effects.

Schooler and Engstler-Schooler (1990) conducted the first study to ever show a verbal overshadowing effect, and because of this, their work later became the cornerstone of the literature in this area. Schooler and Engstler-Schooler showed participants a mock-crime video. After viewing the video, half of the participants were asked to extensively describe the face of the target from the video or to complete a filler task. The purpose of the filler task was to ensure an equal passage of time between initially viewing the video and viewing the lineup, regardless of whether the participant had described the target face or not. Once the filler task/face description was complete, participants were then given a lineup and asked to visually identify the target from the mock-crime video. Schooler and Engstler-Schooler (1990) found that those participants who had described the face prior to the recognition test were less able to accurately pick the target out of a lineup when compared to those who had not previously described the target. Schooler and Englstler-Schooler (1990) argued that this effect, which they also replicated with the description and identification of colors, was due to a mismatch between the act of verbally describing a face and visually recognizing a face. The effect was termed the verbal-overshadowing effect and has been replicated many times (e.g., but not limited to, Fallshore & Schooler 1995; Schooler et al., 1996).

However, there are researchers who have failed to replicate the verbal-overshadowing effect, and yet others who have instead found a verbal-facilitation effect rather than a verbal-overshadowing effect (C. Brown & Lloyd-Jones, 2005; Itoh, 2005; Sporer, 2007; Sporer et al., 2016). Verbal facilitation refers to the finding that a participant's rereading of the person description prior to the recognition attempt can improve lineup task accuracy, compared to the performance by those who do not reread their descriptive statements (e.g., Sporer et al., 2016). Overall a meta-analysis of the verbal-overshadowing literature has found that there is a small but significant verbal-overshadowing effect (Meissner & Brigham, 2001). This meta-analysis suggests that while the verbal-overshadowing effect can be observed, it is a weak effect, and the literature cannot, at present, fully account for why it is sometimes observed and at other times it is absent (Meissner & Brigham, 2001; Meissner et al., 2007). As with most topics covered in this chapter, more research is clearly required to further untangle the effects of verbal-overshadowing, verbal facilitation, and the existence and nature of a possible relationship between a witness providing a description and an identification of a perpetrator, especially because both processes are integral to our criminal justice system.

Conclusion

Throughout this chapter, we have reviewed the extant research on person descriptions. Furthermore, we have considered issues ranging from their general vague and population-normative nature (average height, average build, and so on) to the influence of factors such as stress and anxiety, age, and race. Finally, we considered whether there is a link between the ability to describe a person and the ability to recognize the same individual, as well as how the link might be characterized if it does exist. Unfortunately, some of these topics have not been considered for decades, while others are more recent lines of inquiry and, as such, have been the subject of only a very few empirical investigations. Therefore, any definitive conclusions drawn from the extant literature may, at this stage, be premature. What does appear to be clear is that the current literature does not justify a recommendation for best practice in the gathering of reliable and complete person descriptions and that in itself is a concern, especially given that it is logical to assume that every witness or victim of crime is likely to be asked what the perpetrator looked like in their interviews with police. For now, all we can safely conclude is that, much like eyewitness performance during lineups, the accuracy and reliability of person descriptions can also be influenced by multiple factors related to the crime and to the witness themselves, often to the detriment in the accuracy and completeness of the information provided. Therefore, as with any other form of memory evidence, it is wise to treat person descriptions with caution.

2

Recognizing Familiar and Unfamiliar Faces

Winter in Philadelphia, 1985. A young woman is walking home alone, a little after midnight, when a car pulls up beside her. The male passenger gets out, points a gun at the victim, and forces her into the car, whereupon another male drives them away. After taking her to another location, the two men proceed to simultaneously and continuously sexually assault the victim. They steal her belongings and then push her, half naked and traumatized, out of the car. Five months after the crime occurred, the victim was walking down a street when she comes across a man walking with a woman and his young daughter. The victim believed she recognized this man as being one of her attackers, and she alerted the police. On the basis of this identification alone the man in the street, Vincent Moto, was arrested, taken to trial, and sentenced to 12 to 24 years in prison. DNA testing was not conducted on the victim's clothing until many years later. After serving 8 years of his sentence, DNA testing exonerated Vincent Moto of any connection to the crime—the victim had been wrong in her identification and had sent an innocent man to prison for a crime he did not commit (The Innocence Project, 2019b).

As Vincent Moto's case demonstrates, an eyewitness identification of a suspect can be the most compelling evidence in court. It can also be the single greatest contributor toward wrongful conviction (The Innocence Project, 2019c). The Innocence Project (2019c) estimates that mistaken eyewitness identification has been a main contributing factor in 70% of all cases of wrongful conviction they have worked with thus far. When an eyewitness identifies a suspect from a lineup, that evidence is interpreted by the criminal justice system as meaning that the eyewitness has recognized a member of the lineup as being the person who committed the crime. However, the ability to accurately recognize a face depends largely on whether that face is familiar or unfamiliar. In sexual assault cases, the likelihood of the perpetrator being previously known to the victim is high, with one National Institute of Justice (2008) study suggesting that 85% to 90% of sexual assaults reported by women were perpetrated by someone previously known to them. However, for other crimes the suspect may not be known to the witness, resulting in the witness having to identify an unfamiliar face. Research suggests that recognizing or identifying an unfamiliar face is a very difficult task: In general, recognition of unfamiliar faces often falls below chance level (Bruce et al., 2001; Burton et al., 1999). Unsurprisingly, recognition of unfamiliar faces is so poor that researchers suggest that unless the witness is personally familiar (i.e., a close friend) with the suspect, they will have little chance of being able to accurately recognize him or her in a lineup (Bruce et al., 2001; Burton et al., 1999).

Unfamiliar Faces, Source Monitoring, and Butchers on Buses

Unfamiliar faces are believed to be processed by different systems to familiar faces (e.g., Ellis et al., 1979). The difference in processing familiar and unfamiliar faces is further believed to lead to the high level of error that is encountered when one attempts to recognize an unfamiliar face. When that unfamiliar face is the perpetrator of a crime the consequences of an error could be to take the liberty, or even the life, away from an innocent person.

One argument for why the accurate recognition of an unfamiliar face is so unlikely (e.g., Bruce et al., 2001) is that recognition of an unfamiliar face may be based on external features of the face alone, such as hair color, hairstyle, and hair length. Ellis et al. (1979) found that familiar faces could be recognized from internal features alone whereas in unfamiliar face recognition, both the internal and external features were found to be of equal importance. This finding is supported, in part, by the more recent work of O'Donnell and Bruce (2001), which reported that as participants became more familiar with certain faces, they were able to detect subtle changes made specifically to the eyes of the stimuli. However, participants were unable to detect the same changes when the faces were unfamiliar to them. O'Donnell and Bruce, among others, have referred to findings such as these as a processing shift, whereby as a face becomes more familiar, successful recognition does not rely solely on external features but shifts toward a reliance on internal face features. Interestingly, Study 2 of O'Donnell and Bruce suggested that it was the eyes specifically that appeared to benefit from the shift toward the internal processing of a familiar face. Bonner and colleagues (2003) replicated the findings of O'Donnell and Bruce and reported that the internal features, specifically the eyes, nose, and mouth, were used as a basis in the recognition of familiar faces. Bonner et al. also found that the external features of a face (i.e., face outline, hairstyle, and color) were used more in the recognition of unfamiliar faces than of familiar faces. Such a reliance on external features for successful recognition of unfamiliar faces is problematic as external features are not only easy to change but do change frequently as well. Collectively, researchers use this pattern of evidence to argue that a processing shift occurs during the familiarization process whereby as a face becomes familiar the focus of perceptual processing moves toward the internal features of the face and their configuration rather than being reliant upon external features of the face (Bruce et al., 2001; Kramer et al., 2018).

To demonstrate the difficulty with which unfamiliar faces are recognized, even in seemingly perfect conditions, Bruce et al. (1999) conducted a face-matching study. Bruce et al. showed participants a high-quality still of a male target taken from a video. The video still was displayed next to a photo array of similar-looking male faces. Participants were asked to match the face seen in the video still with one of the faces in the array. Participants were given unlimited time to view the video still and the array and only made a judgment when they felt ready to do so (Bruce et al., 1999). Despite these conditions, participants were accurate only 70% of the time. Furthermore, participants were most accurate in conditions under which the facial expression and viewpoint of the target from the video still were identical to the target photo in the array, suggesting the participants were recognizing the image and not necessarily the face (Bruce et al., 1999).

One theory that attempts to explain why unfamiliar face recognition appears to be such a difficult task suggests that unfamiliar faces are processed by a generic object recognition system, rather than by a specific face identification system (e.g., Megreya & Burton, 2006). Megreya and Burton (2006) further argue that it is not until a face becomes familiar that it is processed by a face-specific processing system; until that point, the face is processed more akin to how the brain processes a pattern. Megreya and Burton showed participants pictures of familiar faces, unfamiliar faces, and everyday objects. Over a series of six experiments, participants had to match a target image to the stimuli image they were presented with—sometimes the stimuli image was a famous face, sometimes a previously unfamiliar face, and sometimes an object. In some trials, the stimuli image or the array containing the target was inverted; in others, they were not. Results revealed that participants were able to accurately match the inverted objects but that they struggled to match the inverted familiar faces, thus suggesting these two stimuli are processed by different cortical pathways. However, differences were also found within the recognition of inverted faces—inverted familiar and unfamiliar faces were seemingly processed differently by the participants. While participants found familiar inverted faces difficult to match, inverted unfamiliar faces were matched with a level of accuracy that was on par with inverted objects. In other words, participants' accuracy in recognizing inverted unfamiliar faces was more similar to inverted objects than to inverted familiar faces. Therefore, Megreya and Burton proposed that this similarity between unfamiliar inverted object and face recognition could suggest that different processes exist not only for the recognition of familiar faces compared to objects but also that unfamiliar faces may be processed more like patterns or objects rather than as faces. Megreya and Burton, however, also state that this theory does not fully explain their data and urge further research in this area.

In addition to the difficulty people have recognizing unfamiliar faces, a potential additional deficit concerns whether they can remember where the face/person has been encountered before. Have you ever had someone come up to you and say how nice it is to see you again, and although you recognize them, you cannot remember where you know them from? The experience of recognizing something (be it a face or an object) but being unable to remember where you recognize it from is known as an error of source monitoring. The ability to discern how memories from multiple sources are differentiated between has been the source of intrigue for researchers since Frederic Bartlett's work in 1932. In the 1970s, researchers began modeling the ways in which knowledge of memories could influence our ability to tell them apart from fantasy—the so-called Reality Monitoring Framework (see M. K. Johnson & Raye, 1981). Marcia K. Johnson and Raye (1981) demonstrated that we frequently misattribute details that we may have imagined about an event to being details we have experienced—thus committing an error in reality monitoring. One limitation of this model, however, was that it creates a dichotomy in memory whereupon memories are either "real" or "imagined" (D. Lindsay, 2014). The Source Monitoring Framework or SMF (M. K. Johnson, Hashtroudi & Lindsay, 1993), as we know it today, was first proposed as an elaboration of Johnson and Raye's reality-monitoring model. A central facet of the SMF is that the perceiver attributes a source to thoughts, feelings, and images. In other words, memories do not contain abstract labels that attribute a source: Rather, the source of a particular memory is inferred from the semantic and perceptual content of the to-be-remembered event (D. Lindsay & Johnson, 2000). For example, Notre Dame Cathedral recently suffered extensive damage due to a fire. Throughout the day, we encountered many sources of information about Notre Dame being on fire; it was an event covered extensively in the television news, on the radio, in conversation with friends, and, of course, across social media. We may remember where we were when we learned the news of the Notre Dame fire, but we may struggle to remember how exactly we first learned of the event: Did a colleague come by our office to tell us that Notre Dame Cathedral was on fire? Did we get a news alert on our smartphone? Were we watching or listening to the news? Or were we scrolling through social media? We may decide that given there is not a lot of importance placed on where we learned this information from, that we will construct the most likely scenario—we learned about the fire through social media, which we spend hours engaging with every day. However, what actually happened was that a friend alerted us to the fire at Notre Dame Cathedral and then we took to social media to find out more information. We have made a mistake in our source memory. Therefore, source monitoring errors arise when memories from one source are incorrectly attributed to a different source.

A source monitoring error can be innocuous, such as in the preceding example where we incorrectly attribute learning information about the Notre Dame fire to social media instead of our colleague who works two offices down from us, but such errors can have far-reaching consequences when they occur in the criminal justice system. An incorrect identification could occur because of source monitoring errors. Witnesses to crimes have been known to incorrectly claim that an individual who is innocent of the crime but who was encountered in a close temporal or spatial context to the crime is the perpetrator. After describing the innocent party to police, who apprehend them and place them in a lineup, further errors can occur. Upon encountering the individual in a lineup, the witness may incorrectly infer that the source of familiarity with the individual is due to their having seen that individual commit the crime. Rather, the witness has made a source memory mistake, and their familiarity with the individual is because they encountered them in close temporal and spatial proximity to the crime event. This is called the innocent bystander effect and has been replicated multiple times in the extant research literature (see Ross et al., 1994).

The unreliability of source memory attribution is further demonstrated by the "butcher-on-the-bus" phenomenon (Yovell & Paller, 2004). The butcher-on-the-bus phenomenon occurs because certain individuals (e.g., a butcher) tend to be associated with a specific context. Therefore, when such an individual is encountered out with that context, episodic memory errors occur. In other words, the perceiver is unable to recall where the butcher is known from, simply that the butcher is familiar (Yovell & Paller, 2004). Could this influence an identification judgment?

In the butcher-on-the-bus phenomenon, there is a source memory failure when the butcher is encountered out of context. A consequence of such an error could be that the witness will recognize an individual in the lineup but be unable to establish where the individual is recognized from. In such a situation, a witness is likely to conclude that the individual must be recognized because he or she committed the crime, and thus, a formal identification will be made, much like the innocent bystander effect. This could cause an incorrect identification. However, if the witness were familiar with the suspect, would they be better able to determine whether their familiarity with him or her is because he or she is the perpetrator or because he or she is their butcher?

Familiarity and Recollection

Familiarity and recollection are memory processes that historically have been thought to interact to generate recognition. The dual-process model of memory (see Diana et al., 2006; Gardiner & Java, 1993; Jacoby, 1991; Tulving, 1985; Yonelinas, 1994; see also Yonelinas, 2001, for a review) argues that recollection and familiarity work together to enable recognition. Familiarity is thought to be a fast process, responsible for alerting the perceiver that an object has been encountered before. In contrast, recollection is a relatively slow process and informs the perceiver where the object was previously encountered (Wixted, 2007). Evidence suggests that these two processes can be manipulated independently of each other: One can be affected while the other can remain intact. For example, Yonelinas and Jacoby (1994) found that increasing the length of a study list interferes with conscious recollection but not with the feeling of familiarity for the list items. In other words, by extending the length of the study list participants would feel familiar with test items but be unable to recollect why they felt familiar with them (Yonelinas, 1994). Consequently, recollection and familiarity enable recognition, but they may not always occur together (such as the butcher-on-the-bus phenomenon). Recent research by Rotello and colleagues argues that familiarity and recollection are two levels of recognition strength that differ quantitatively and not qualitatively (e.g., see Rotello & Macmillian, 2006). In other words, recollection and familiarity are two processes that combine to produce a single strength variable when deciding if an item is old/remembered (recollection and familiarity), old/known (familiarity), or new (Rotello & Macmillan, 2006).

In this view, accurate source monitoring is argued to occur when recollection is involved in recognition. Consequently, source monitoring errors occur when recollection is either absent or recollection is sufficiently weak to prevent an accurate inference of source (e.g., Yonelinas, 1994). In an eyewitness setting, determining where a face or person has been seen before can be of the utmost import, especially when faced with an identification decision. Familiarity for a face alone is an insufficient basis for an identification decision as such a decision will have been made in the absence of recollection, thus resulting in an identification made without an ability to infer a source to the familiarity experienced with the face.

How Does a Face Become Familiar?

Bruce and Young (1986) theorized that a familiar face is represented in the cognitive system by a set of structural, identify-specific semantic, and name codes. A *structural code* is a code that contains information about the structure of a familiar person's face. Ellis et al. (1979) began a line of research that suggests that the structural codes for familiar and unfamiliar faces differ significantly, such that structural codes for unfamiliar faces contain mostly external features and structural codes for familiar faces contain more information about internal features (see also Bonner et al., 2003; O'Donnell & Bruce, 2001). It therefore follows from this research that, as familiarity with a face increases, processing shifts from being dominated by the external features of a face to the internal features.

The Bruce and Young (1986) model proposes that as a face becomes familiar *identity-specific semantic codes* are also formed. These codes hold information about who a familiar person's friends are, what the familiar person's occupation is, and even information on where he or she might be encountered. However, the identity-specific semantic codes hold a largely arbitrary relationship to the actual structure of the familiar person's face. The relationship between the identity-specific semantic code and the face can be likened to the relationship between the structure of a word and its meaning (Bruce & Young, 1986). Finally, a *name code* is formed for the familiar face: This code contains the information about a person's name (i.e., what it is).

Everyday recognition of familiar faces can be described in terms of a sequential access to the codes posited by the Bruce and Young (1986) model. Information from the structural, identity-specific semantic, and name codes feed into a *face recognition unit*. Each familiar face has its own face recognition unit that contains the stored structural codes for that face. Therefore, when a face is encountered the face recognition unit sends a signal to the cognitive system. The strength of this signal is dependent on the level of resemblance between the stored code and the external input (Bruce & Young, 1986). Moreover, the stronger the resemblance, the better the individual will be at recognizing the seen face. Due to the signal strength being stronger for familiar faces, they will be recognized more accurately than unfamiliar faces. However, it is not yet clear whether, in such cases, source monitoring ability will also increase.

The Bruce and Young (1986) model suggests that familiar faces therefore, should benefit from the additional depth of processing and thus should be recognizable even in poor-quality viewing scenarios. Burton and colleagues (1999) investigated this supposition by questioning whether participants would recognize familiar individuals (targets) recorded on poor-quality closed-circuit TV footage. Burton et al. compared recognition performance of students, who were familiar or unfamiliar with the targets, to that of police officers, who were all unfamiliar with the targets but who had an average service of 13.5 years and so were ostensibly experienced with recognizing faces they were unfamiliar with. Burton et al. were interested in whether police officers were better at recognizing unfamiliar faces due to their professional experiences, compared to untrained students. Burton et al. found that participants familiar with the targets performed almost perfectly on the recognition task, whereas participants unfamiliar with the targets performed only slightly higher than chance level. Interestingly, there were no significant differences between the performance of police officers and students unfamiliar with the targets. It follows from this that if a face is unfamiliar witnesses may then find it very difficult to recognize that face, as predicted by Bruce and Young (1986). Bruce et al. (2001) replicated Burton et al. and again found that participants familiar with the targets performed significantly better on the recognition task than participants unfamiliar with the targets. These results collectively suggest that familiarity facilitates face recognition; even when the to-be-recognized image is of a low quality.

In studies of face recognition reviewed earlier, the familiar participants personally knew the targets: They were either students identifying their lecturers (Bonner et al., 1999) or colleagues identifying each other (Bruce et al., 2001). For this reason, both Bonner et al. (1999) and Bruce et al. (2001) conclude that only when a face is personally familiar does an individual have a good chance of accurately identifying that face. A problem encountered with this research is that only personal familiarity and unfamiliarity are investigated. But such a research focus leaves an unanswered question of how well could observers recognize faces that are only slightly familiar (i.e., only exposed on a couple of occasions)?

It has been shown that recognition judgments based on personal familiarity can produce high levels of accuracy (Bonner et al., 1999; Bruce et al., 2001). Similarly, it has been shown that recognition judgments of unfamiliar faces are highly error-prone (Bruce et al., 2001). However, what of faces that are slightly familiar? Likewise, will a witness's ability to accurately monitor where a face has been seen before be augmented by increasing levels of familiarity? How would a witness perform if their butcher were placed in a lineup: Would they incorrectly identify the butcher due to a high-level of familiarity coupled with no recollection, thus preventing accurate source monitoring? Or are there contexts in which low-level familiarity can occur with recollection and be sufficient for accurate source monitoring? In other words, how many times do we need to see a face before we can accurately determine why the face is familiar? Currently, there is no research that advises how well witnesses may perform under these conditions.

What of the Moderately Familiar Face?

A potential problem with identification from a few encounters is that a witness may become confused as to the suspect's identity. This can cause problems because it can result in an incorrect identification. An example of such an error is the mugshot exposure effect (Davies et al., 1979), which occurs when the police show a witness a mugshot of their lead suspect prior to the witness viewing the lineup. In the research literature, there is overwhelming support for the argument that witnesses shown a mugshot become likely to then identify that face (for a review, see Deffenbacher et al., 2006). The mugshot exposure effect is so robust that participants in laboratory studies have been known to identify the mugshot face over the suspect, even when the suspect is present in the lineup (Deffenbacher et al., 2006; Haw et al., 2007; Memon et al., 2002). It is thought that this situation arises because the witness confuses the feeling of familiarity toward the mugshot face in the lineup with having seen that face at the crime scene (Memon et al., 2002).

It could be argued from the SMF, that butcher-on-the-bus situations occur because the perceiver is unable to recall any form of semantic detail about the memory for the butcher or suspect. In such cases, the source of the memory cannot be inferred, resulting in the perceiver being unable to determine where they know the butcher or suspect from. If this information is tied to episodic memory, then recall is dependent on the successful recall of the episodic event; however, information in semantic memory (such as someone's name) can be recalled independently of the episodic event (e.g., S. Brown & Craik, 2000). This begs the question as to how many times an individual may need to encounter a suspect to be able to accurately recognize the suspect's face.

The method of familiarizing previously unseen faces through repeated exposure has been used with success throughout the literature (e.g., see Dubois et al., 1999). Clutterbuck and Johnson (2005) utilized this method and familiarized previously unfamiliar faces to the same level of familiarity as participants reported having with famous faces. Similarly, Dubois et al. (1999) found differential activation and blood flow in the brain when participants were asked to recognize faces familiarized via repeated exposure and unfamiliar faces, suggesting that the faces had been successfully familiarized. More recently, Robin Kramer and colleagues (2018) found that a computer/statistical model inputted with thousands of images of faces, all with slight variations, appeared to "learn" the faces in the same manner as humans do. In other words, the computer model began to show a bias toward processing internal features of faces as they were familiarized in the system (R. Kramer et al., 2018). Kramer et al. use these findings to argue that the process of familiarization with a face may rely on a statistical computation of idiosyncrasies of a given face, across multiple exposures to the face. While researchers are beginning to explore processes of becoming familiar with a face in more nuanced ways than were available to Bruce and Young (1986), and thus, the processes that occur between the binary stages of "familiar" or "unfamiliar" (e.g., Dubois et al., 1999; R. Kramer et al., 2018), this work is still in its infancy in terms of being applicable to the eyewitness domain.

Implications for Eyewitnesses

While statistics from the National Institute of Justice (2008) demonstrate that for sex crimes the majority (85%–90%) of female victims knew their attacker(s), little other data exist to suggest the role that familiarity with the perpetrator plays in the criminal justice system. It is therefore a reasonable assumption to make that for some types of crime perpetrators may be more likely to be known to their victims, while for other types of crime, the perpetrators may be previously unknown. Thus, understanding the effects of familiarity on accurate recognition of the perpetrator from a lineup is a matter of great importance. Another area, not yet explored, is whether law enforcement officers may experience a similar process: If they view images of a crime enough times, might they be able to later identify a suspect while on patrol? Such decisions would be predicated on a level of familiarity that is stronger than unfamiliar but weaker than true familiarity, and as such, the research to date would be unable to estimate the likelihood of accuracy in those decisions. This may be an important area of future research.

Conclusion

Throughout this chapter, we have reviewed research on familiar and unfamiliar face recognition. We began with the case of Vincent Moto, which highlighted the vulnerabilities of face recognition in criminal justice contexts. Researchers have typically argued that the reason why eyewitness misidentification is a contributor in the majority of wrongful conviction cases is because an eyewitness's identification may be of an unfamiliar face. As we discovered, unfamiliar face recognition is highly error-prone and tends to be based on external features of the face such as hairstyle and color, which can easily be changed and which change naturally over time. We discussed the research on how faces become familiar and the changes that such a switch from processing external features of face to processing internal features of a face as the face becomes more familiar entail. We then covered face learning whereupon participants have been found to be able to become familiar with faces in the laboratory through repeated exposure alone. This work was extended to a hypothetical scenario whereupon a law enforcement officer may learn a face through multiple exposures to images of the face/a crime and later feel sufficiently able to recognize the perpetrator when on patrol: a scenario that we would be unable to estimate the likelihood of accuracy or reliability for based on the current scientific understanding of how familiarity is established with faces.

The research literature and field data reviewed in this chapter suggest that eyewitness identifications of unfamiliar perpetrators are largely error-prone. While there are crimes in which the perpetrator is likely to be known to the victim, it is not a giant leap of logic to argue that crimes of opportunity will occur in which the perpetrator and victim are previously unknown. In those scenarios, the victim is faced with an extremely difficult task—to recognize a once-seen, or unfamiliar, face. Consequently, the research literature writ large suggests the resulting identification decision will be relatively unreliable. Altogether, the familiarity of the witness with the perpetrator can have a substantial effect on the likelihood that the witness will be able to accurately recognize him or her in a lineup (Bruce et al., 2001; Burton et al., 1999).

3

Genuine and False Memories

One hot summer afternoon during graduate school, I, the first author, was visiting my parents. Like many families, when we get together, we often reminisce about (usually embarrassing) events that happened to my brothers and me when we were kids. When it was my turn, I began to tell a story about my youngest brother when he was about 4 years old. My brother was an active young kid and at this time of his life loved pedaling a bright orange "John Deere" toy tractor around the neighborhood. He particularly liked to ride down from the top of our steeply sloping driveway because it allowed him to pick up quite a bit of speed. One day, he took off on his tractor and rode furiously down the driveway and out into the street. At the same time, a neighbor woman and her daughter were driving an old 1970s' era Ford station wagon—the kind with faux wood panels—down the street. At the last minute, the woman saw my brother and slammed on her brakes, hitting the tractor and breaking the "engine" off the frame. The woman frantically jumped out of her car to see what had happened. My brother, frightened but unhurt, jumped off the tractor and ran to our house.

After I had finished, I noticed my parents looking at me strangely. "You weren't there!" my mother told me. I began to argue with her because the memory was so rich and detailed that I felt it had to be true. How could I remember something so vividly that I had never witnessed? It turns out that my friend who lived next door had watched my brother's accident, and he had described it to me soon afterward. Furthermore, I knew the individual details exceedingly well and could easily imagine the rest. I was very familiar with my brother's bright orange tractor, had seen him ride it often, and observed its broken condition after the accident. I had also seen the neighborhood woman's car countless times and knew what she and her daughter looked like. The neighbor's story helped create in my mind a vivid reenactment of what had happened. The problem was that, over time, I no longer remembered that the event was something I was told about rather than witnessed (for a similar story, see Sacks, 2013).

This story is just one example of why it can be so difficult for us to distinguish between memories that genuinely reflect our past experiences and those that do not. Obviously, this issue is critical for the legal system. The rationale for using eyewitness testimony as evidence at trial rests on the assumption that witnesses are able to accurately convey what happened during an event. Furthermore, the issue has clearly been of interest to eyewitness memory researchers, such as work examining the effects of post-event misinformation on memory for the original event (e.g., E. Loftus et al., 1978; McCloskey & Zaragoza, 1985). But false memories also provide insight into how the memory system works, and for that reason, there is an even longer history of basic empirical research on the topic (e.g., F. Bartlett, 1932; Carmichael et al., 1932; Deese, 1959).

In this and the next chapter, we explore the issue of genuine and false memory: First, we discuss what it means for a memory to be false. Following that, we describe the *source monitoring framework* (M. K. Johnson et al., 1993) and other related theoretical ideas about how we discriminate between true and false memories. In the next chapter, we review research on genuine and false memories, focusing on studies that explore psychological and neurological features that might differentiate between them. We also discuss research on the types of features people use when evaluating the accuracy of other people's memories. Finally, we conclude by describing some directions for future research, as well as possible applications for investigators.

What Is a False Memory?

Memory researchers often use the terms *veridical (true)* and *false memory* to contrast situations in which a memory report is consistent with, versus different from, the original experienced event. False memories involve the distortion of old details or the addition of new ones (commission errors) rather than forgetting (omission errors). In the research literature, the term *false memory* applies to both minor and major errors. False memories can be said to occur both when a small detail is distorted (e.g., a red sweater is remembered as purple) and when an entire event that did not happen is recalled as having been experienced (e.g., as a child you spilled punch on the bride during a wedding reception; Hyman & Pentland, 1996). It is important to keep in mind that, in everyday memory, there is no "bright line" between true and false memories because, unlike in research studies, there is often no way of verifying the objective truth. Furthermore, as we've discussed, our experience of events is constructed (e.g., Neisser, 1967), and thus, one person's experience of an event can differ from another person's even if they were exposed to the same set of stimuli. However, even with these limitations, the term *false memory* can still be a useful one. In addition, the term is theory-neutral because it can be used regardless of the specific mechanism assumed to have produced the memory error.

Although we'll talk much more about how false memories occur, it is also important to ask *why* they occur (Newman & Lindsay, 2009). In short, false memories are a by-product of a cognitive system that allows us to integrate many different types of information, including memories and knowledge, to solve important real-world problems. For example, most people could easily imagine how an event might have turned out differently—what would be different today if John McCain rather than Barack Obama was elected president of the United States in 2008? This is called *counterfactual reasoning* (e.g., M. K. Johnson & Sherman, 1990), and it involves a fairly sophisticated rewriting of memory in combination with real-world knowledge. Similarly, our cognitive system allows us to make predictions about the future based on what we remember from the past and our general knowledge (e.g., see Szpunar, 2010, for a review). As noted by Newman and Lindsay (2009), this flexibility also allows people to maintain their sense of self over time (e.g., through dissonance reduction; e.g., Festinger, 1962) and facilitates their interactions with others (e.g., telling stories to each other in ways that differ from our original memory, e.g., E. Marsh, 2007). Although there are clear reasons why memories can be in error, this is not the same thing as saying that memory is hopelessly flawed. However, it does suggest why it can sometimes be so difficult to distinguish between true and false memories.

How Do We Distinguish Between True and False Memories?

Source monitoring refers to the process of inferring the origin of information retrieved from memory (e.g., M. K. Johnson et al., 1993). In the example that began this chapter, the first author made a source monitoring error because he initially believed that the memory of his brother's accident came about because he had witnessed it rather than identifying the actual source of that memory—the neighbor's story. We need to make source judgments frequently. Examples of everyday situations that involve source monitoring include the following:

Did I take my pill, or just think about taking it?
Did I read about this research breakthrough in the journal *Science* or in *People* magazine?
Did I come up with this idea or did you?
Is this a memory of something that happened to me or something I just know?

Although all these types of judgments could certainly have important consequences (e.g., mistakenly taking another pill could lead to poisoning), source monitoring judgments can be particularly consequential for eyewitnesses. For example, witnesses might need to judge whether a piece of information they remember is something they actually saw or heard at the time of the event, or whether it is something they saw or heard afterward from other witnesses, the media, or from a detective (*post-event misinformation*; e.g., D. Lindsay & Johnson, 1989; Zaragoza

& Lane, 1994). Source monitoring judgments even play a role in lineup identifications, as eyewitnesses who choose a lineup member are essentially attributing their memory for that person to the specific context of the crime (e.g., see discussion of face recognition in Rapcsak et al., 1999). This can be difficult as a lineup member may be familiar because he or she was the perpetrator of a crime or because the witness had seen them before in another context (e.g., Deffenbacher, Bornstein, & Penrod, 2006; Perfect & Harris, 2003).[1] Thus, understanding the process by which people make source judgments may provide insight into how these decisions can be supported to reduce the likelihood of false memories.

Source Monitoring Framework

The most widely used theoretical approach to understanding how people determine the origin of their memories comes from the source monitoring framework (SMF) of Marcia K. Johnson and colleagues (e.g., M. K. Johnson et al., 1993; M. K. Johnson & Raye, 1981, 2000; D. Lindsay, 2008; Mitchell & Johnson, 2000; see related developments for the MEM [multiple entry, modular] model, e.g., M. K. Johnson, 1992,1994; see also mathematical modeling of source monitoring, e.g., Batchelder & Riefer, 1990; Bayen et al., 1996; DeCarlo, 2003).[2] The SMF builds on a number of assumptions about encoding and retrieval processes that are consistent with the view that memory is constructive in nature. Perceptual and reflective processes deployed while experiencing an event become part of the memory trace (e.g., Kolers & Roediger, 1984). In other words, memory traces contain features that represent what was seen, heard, felt, and thought during the event, as well the products of more automatic processes that do not lead to awareness (e.g., lower level perceptual processes). These elements of perception and thought are often bound together in the memory representation (e.g., Johnson & Chalfonte, 1994; Johnson et al., 2005). Thus, different people seeing the "same" event can come away with dramatically different representations depending on where they focused their attention or the type of schema or prior knowledge that was activated. The SMF also assumes cue-dependent remembering (e.g., Morris et al., 1977; Tulving & Thomson, 1973). The likelihood that a memory trace will be retrieved depends on the overlap between the retrieval environment and the encoding environment (encoding specificity; e.g., Tulving & Thomson, 1973). Because of this, retrieval can be selective, such that some aspects of the memory trace are revived while others are not. For example, someone recounting a robbery to a friend might primarily remember how he or she felt, while the same person recalling the event for a police officer might primarily remember what the perpetrator looked like and what he did. Similarly, people sometimes remember a specific detail at one point in time but not at another time (e.g., during separate interviews with a police officer). Finally, remembering involves more than simply reinstating the memory trace. We also use information from the retrieval cue and the broader retrieval environment, as well as other memory traces or knowledge that are revived by the retrieval cue to construct our "memory" (e.g., M. K. Johnson et al., 1993; Neisser, 1967; Tulving, 1983).

Within the assumptions just outlined, it should be clear that memories are not associated with a tag or other code that uniquely identifies its source (e.g., "Bob told me this"). Rather, source monitoring processes evaluate the features that are activated at the time of retrieval. A memory of a conversation could contain perceptual detail (e.g., the color of a shirt or the sound of a voice), spatial detail (e.g., a table was in the corner), temporal context (e.g., this took place after coming home from the store), affective detail (e.g., I felt anger), and many others. These kinds of features can be used to determine with whom you had the conversation or the day it took place. Furthermore, source monitoring processes can take advantage of the fact that sources, on average, differ from each other on a number of dimensions. For instance, people often need to identify whether they are remembering a perceived event (e.g., taking a pill) or an imagined one (e.g., you thought about taking the pill). On average, memories of perceived events tend to contain more perceptual, contextual, and spatial detail than imagined events, and imagined events tend to contain more information about the cognitive operations involved in producing them (i.e., the process of imagining). People can also take advantage of less specific information in memory, such as the ease with which information is retrieved (retrieval fluency) or the sense that this information is highly familiar in the absence of specific details. Source decisions can be made based on both quantitative and qualitative differences in the characteristics of memory.

Source decisions can be made relatively quickly and nonanalytically (heuristic processes) or more slowly and deliberately (systematic processes; M. K. Johnson et al., 1993). In heuristic decisions, features that are activated at retrieval are compared to knowledge about the characteristics of different sources. For example, memories of recent events tend to be stronger and more vivid than memories of distant events, and as noted earlier, memories of imagined events tend to differ from perceived events. Besides these broader classes of events, one can also have knowledge about more specific sources (e.g., your friend Tyler is likely to make certain comments but not others). Because of this, certain features of a memory are likely to be weighted more heavily than others when this comparison process occurs. To the extent that the features of a memory overlap to a large degree with a particular source, the attribution is made that it came from that source rather than another. Furthermore, the person's agenda (goal) or the task context at the time of the decision can influence which sources are used for the comparison, as well as which characteristics of a source are emphasized. In contrast, systematic decisions involve greater cognitive control. For example, a person might deliberately search for associated information that can support or undermine a particular attribution. He or she might also evaluate the plausibility and consistency of a memory with other relevant knowledge or memories or use reasoning (e.g., "I thought I remembered hearing it at the meeting, but that was the week I was on vacation"). Despite being slower, systematic judgments are not necessarily more accurate than heuristic judgments. Instead, the outcome of systematic and heuristic processes can provide a check on each other (e.g., M. K. Johnson et al., 1993). For example, a person might initially believe that his friend Megan told a particular joke because she told a similar joke in the past (systematic) only to realize that his memory lacks perceptual detail of the conversation (heuristic). Both types of processes can evaluate quantitative and qualitative information from memory, and criteria can vary from strict to lax depending on a person's agenda in a situation. For instance, in a social setting, someone might use relatively lax criteria when telling a story about an event that happened earlier in the day to a family member. On the other hand, a witness should use relatively more strict criteria when providing an account of what happened during a witnessed event to a detective.

Altogether, the SMF suggests that monitoring is most likely to be accurate when the features activated at retrieval reliably distinguish between alternative potential sources, and these diagnostic characteristics are used effectively to make an attribution. In this conception, source errors can come about in a number of ways. First, errors are more likely when there is a high degree of physical or semantic similarity between sources (e.g., Ferguson et al., 1992; M. K. Johnson et al., 1979; D. Lindsay et al., 1991; Roediger & McDermott, 1995). As an example, participants in one study (D. Lindsay et al., 1991) were better able to discriminate the source of story details when the speakers were of a different sex and age (i.e., a teenage girl and an older man) than when the speakers were similar on these dimensions (i.e., two teenage girls). Besides such "preexisting" similarity, the type of processing an item receives can also increase the similarity of different sources of information. As noted earlier, memories of events that you have experienced tend to contain perceptual and contextual detail. Research has documented that repeatedly imagining events in vivid detail increases these characteristics and the likelihood that participants will later erroneously claim to have perceived them (e.g., Garry et al., 1996; Goff & Roediger, 1998; Suengas & Johnson, 1988).

Second, because source monitoring depends so heavily on the quality of memory records, factors that impair perceptual and reflective processes during the experience of an event, such as distraction, are likely to lead to an impoverished memory representation. For example, dividing the attention of participants while viewing an event increases the likelihood they will falsely claim to have seen things they only read about in the context of post-event questions (Lane, 2006). Furthermore, people may be more likely to rely on schemas or other knowledge to make source decisions in circumstances where memory for the original event is poor (e.g., Spaniol & Bayen, 2002). Third, even if diagnostic features are well encoded in the memory representation, they must be accessed and used during the source decision. If people have insufficient time or resources to access and evaluate these key features, this will harm source accuracy (e.g., R. Marsh et al., 2006; Zaragoza & Lane, 1998). People's expectations about which features distinguish between different classes of events must also be accurate. When this knowledge is incorrect or incomplete, errors are likely to occur (e.g., Gallo, 2013; Lane et al., 2007). Similarly, the way in which the source decision is framed can affect which characteristics of the memory trace are evaluated (e.g., R. Marsh & Hicks, 1998). When the highlighted characteristics are less diagnostic than others, this should harm source memory accuracy. Similarly, the retrieval situation can also influence the criteria adopted during the source decision. For example, source accuracy is generally higher when the testing format supports careful evaluation of memory characteristics (e.g., D. Lindsay & Johnson, 1989; Zaragoza & Lane, 1994). Fourth, source judgments can be affected by the extent to which related memory traces are activated at retrieval. Features of these memory traces can be "imported" such that they are incorporated into the original memory trace (Lyle & Johnson, 2006, 2007; see also *content borrowing*; Lampinen et al., 2005, 2008). For instance, participants who falsely remembered having seen a picture they only imagined often claimed to have seen the "picture" in the same color or location as a related picture they actually did see (Lyle & Johnson, 2006). This additional detail serves as particularly compelling (false) evidence that the person had seen the picture.

Other Related Theoretical Views and Mechanisms

Researchers have explored a number of theoretical mechanisms that are consistent with, and expand on, the processes described in the SMF.

DIFFERENT TYPES OF CONTROL AT RETRIEVAL. There are two main ways that people can control the accuracy of memory reporting at retrieval (Jacoby et al., 1999): *late correction* and *early selection*. Late correction roughly corresponds to the monitoring processes discussed earlier; people retrieve a memory record and evaluate its characteristics in the context of attributing its source (although this process may be iterative with additional memory search). In this case, errors can be "caught" only after retrieval processes have been initiated. In contrast, early selection refers to how people form their retrieval cues to constrain what is retrieved from memory (*source constrained retrieval*, e.g., Jacoby et al., 2005; see also research on *retrieval orientation*, e.g., Hornberger et al., 2004). Effective retrieval cues discriminate between sought-for and irrelevant memory traces. In such a situation, a person is more likely to retrieve target information and less likely to retrieve unrelated information. Put another way, whereas people relying solely on monitoring processes may have to evaluate both relevant and irrelevant information from memory, people effectively using source constrained retrieval are more likely to recover only sought-for information.

DIFFERENT TYPES OF MONITORING PROCESSES. Other researchers have distinguished between different ways of monitoring the accuracy of memory that are consistent with the SMF. One such comparison is between *diagnostic* and *disqualifying* monitoring (e.g., Gallo, 2004). Both types of monitoring can be used to reject an item as being from a particular source (and thus prevent a false memory). Diagnostic monitoring involves evaluating whether a retrieved memory record contains the characteristics expected of a given source and rejecting it when it fails this test (consistent with heuristic decision processes described in SMF). For example, when participants listen to lists of strongly associated words accompanied by pictures (vs. visually presented words), they are better able to reduce false recognition of associated nonpresented items. It has been argued that participants are able to use the lack of pictorial information in memory to correctly reject these items (*the distinctiveness heuristic*, e.g., Israel & Schacter, 1997; Schacter et al., 1999; for similar ideas, see Strack & Bless, 1994). There is also evidence that people can use idiosyncratically generated item-specific information (e.g., this item has some personal significance) to make diagnostic monitoring decisions (Lampinen et al., 2005). Disqualifying monitoring involves the use of reasoning to rule out that a memory originated from a particular source (consistent with the use of systematic decision processes in SMF). In most research on the topic, participants remember information during a test that allows them to conclude that they did not previously study an item (e.g., Gallo, 2004; Hintzman & Curran, 1994; Tulving, 1983; see also *recollection rejection*, e.g., Brainerd et al., 2003; Lampinen et al., 2004). For example, remembering that you studied the plural form of a word (e.g., *desks*) could help you to correctly decide that you did not study the word *desk* (e.g., Rotello et al., 2000). However, this particular strategy is only helpful when the situation is structured such that knowing certain information precludes other information from being correct. When it becomes difficult to recall information that is necessary to make such a judgment (e.g., when larger rather than smaller categories of information must be recalled) the utility of this strategy decreases (e.g., Gallo, 2004).

REMEMBERING AND KNOWING. The phenomenal experience that accompanies the retrieval of memories differs in a number of ways. One commonly used distinction (Gardiner & Java, 1990; Tulving, 1985) is between memories that are accompanied by a sense of reexperiencing the original event (remembering or recollection) and memories that feel highly familiar but do not contain specific detail (knowing). In most research on the topic, when participants indicate that they have recognized an item, they are asked to indicate which of these two bases were used for that decision (in some cases, a "not sure" or a "just guessing" response is also available; e.g., Eldridge et al., 2002). "Remember" and "know" responses are often affected differently by experimental variables (although not always; see, e.g., Bornstein & LeCompte, 1995). For instance, divided attention at encoding reduces remember responses (Gardiner & Parkin, 1990), and increasing item distinctiveness increases remember responses (e.g., Rajaram, 1998); know responses are unaffected. In contrast, increasing the fluency of items during recognition by briefly priming the item (e.g., Rajaram, 1993), or presenting them in a related semantic context (Rajaram & Geraci, 2000), increases know responses without changing the rate of remember responses. There has been much theoretical debate about whether these and other findings suggest that remember/know judgments are based on a single or dual process (e.g., see reviews by Dunn, 2004; Gardiner et al., 2002; Wixted & Mickes, 2010; Yonelinas, 2002). However, for the purposes of this chapter, the remember/know procedure can be seen as merely a way to characterize the phenomenal experience that accompanies true and false memories (e.g., Lane & Zaragoza, 1995; Mather et al., 1997). In this respect, it is important to note that the remember/know distinction divides the phenomenal experience accompanying memory retrieval into two broad categories, while the SMF views phenomenal experience as multifaceted. For example, SMF researchers often use the Memory Characteristics Questionnaire (MCQ; M. K. Johnson et al., 1988) as a means of evaluating phenomenal experience. In this instrument, participants rate different aspects of memory (perceptual detail, contextual detail, emotional reactions, thoughts) on a 1–7 scale and thus provide information about the degree to which their memory contains a particular feature. Regardless, both remember/know and the MCQ potentially provide important information about the phenomenal experience that accompanies true and false memories.

THE INFLUENCE OF NONMEMORIAL INFORMATION ON MEMORY DECISIONS. As discussed in the previous section, people often rely on the phenomenal experience that accompanies retrieval to decide whether a memory is veridical or not. In particular, the sense of reexperiencing or recollection appears to play a major role in such decisions (e.g., W. Brewer, 1996; Tulving, 1985). However, researchers have also noted that a person can believe an event happened in their past for other reasons. These *autobiographical beliefs* can be based on information provided by other people, the extent to which the event could have plausibly happened, and whether the "facts" of the event are consistent with other verifiable information, as well as other reasons (e.g., Mazzoni et al., 2010; Scoboria et al., 2015). Because of this, people can believe that an event did not occur to them despite having a recollection of that event (sometimes called a *nonbelieved memory*; Mazzoni et al., 2010). The story about the accident that began this chapter is an example of this type of memory. Despite having a vivid recollection of the event, the first author no longer believes he witnessed it because he trusts his parents' account of what happened and he now remembers talking with his neighbor about the accident. It is also possible for someone to believe an event happened to him or her without being able to recollect it. An example of this type of memory comes from research where participants come to believe they experienced an autobiographical event that did not happen (e.g., Garaerts et al., 2008; Hyman & Pentland, 1996), an outcome that has been argued to occur in some real-life cases of alleged abuse (Lindsay & Read, 1994). Both types of memory highlight the fact that a memory's status as being autobiographical is dynamic, and can change over time. Seen in the context of SMF, nonmemorial information (evidence) typically influences systematic processes that are involved in memory decisions (Johnson et al., 1993). As such, this information can provide a check on memorial evidence that becomes available via heuristic processes. For instance, when these two types of evidence conflict, additional processing can be triggered (e.g., a search for supporting information from memory) or the relative weight of evidence can be compared to arrive at a final decision.

Research in this area is growing and highlights the importance of considering information that people acquire from the environment and other people when making memory decisions (e.g., Jaeger et al., 2012; Scoboria et al., 2014). As described earlier, people sometimes decide that an event did not occur as remembered because someone else has told them the event did not happen or that it did not happen as remembered (e.g., Scoboria et al., 2014). Furthermore, research has demonstrated that people can integrate external cues to the probability of accuracy into their memory judgments (Jaeger et al., 2012). Such findings underscore the point that "memory," as we commonly talk about it, includes information that goes beyond what we are able to retrieve from prior experience (e.g., Tulving, 1985).

False Memory in the Lab and in Real-World Contexts

Of all the topics covered in this book, work on false memory perhaps best exemplifies how basic and applied research can fruitfully influence each other. For example, from very early on, research on eyewitness suggestibility focused on distinguishing between different basic theoretical explanations of the mechanisms underlying memory errors in this task (e.g., Christiansen & Ochalek, 1983; Lindsay & Johnson, 1989; Loftus et al., 1978; McCloskey & Zaragoza, 1985). In other words, researchers brought to bear what had been learned from laboratory studies of memory to help understand how real-life eyewitness suggestibility could occur. Conversely, basic researchers have also been influenced by false-memory issues that have been highlighted in more applied settings. One well-known example of this type of influence came from the *recovered (repressed) memory debate* that reached a peak in the early 1990s (for an insightful discussion, see Lindsay & Read, 1994). This debate concerned cases in which people claimed to remember a traumatic event (often abuse) after long periods when they ostensibly did not remember the event. In many instances, the "discovered" memory occurred in clinical settings after extensive use of *memory recovery* techniques (e.g., imagery, hypnosis; Loftus, 1993), and researchers questioned whether such accounts could actually be fabrications that resulted from the techniques rather than veridical memories. Although the debate ultimately led to general agreement that recovered memories can sometimes be accurate recollections of a past event and other times a fabrication (e.g., Geraerts et al., 2009; Lindsay & Briere, 1997), it also led basic researchers to think more deeply about the relevance of their laboratory studies to the issues underlying the debate (e.g., see the exchange between Freyd & Gleaves, 1996, and Roediger & McDermott, 1996) and produced new research that borrowed from both theoretical and applied domains (e.g., Arnold & Lindsay, 2005; Hyman & Pentland, 1996).

A broader question asked by researchers is whether the findings of experiments conducted in the laboratory apply to real-life situations. In the introductory chapter, we noted that this debate is long-standing (e.g., Banaji & Crowder, 1989; Neisser, 1978, 1982). A more specific question is whether false memories studied in the laboratory tell us anything important about how false memories occur outside of the laboratory. There are several lines of argument in favor of this proposition. First, variables that influence false memory in the laboratory with standard materials have also been shown to influence the creation of false autobiographical memories (Johnson et al., 2011). For example, false memories of pictures are increased when people repeatedly imagine the objects depicted by words (e.g., Johnson et al., 1979), and false memories of an autobiographical event that never occurred are increased when participants are asked to repeatedly imagine it (e.g., Hyman & Pentland, 1996). Second, individual differences in performance on false memory tasks are often correlated with autobiographical memory accuracy (see discussion by Gallo, 2010). For instance, research has documented instances where errors in the Deese–Roediger–McDermott paradigm (DRM; Deese, 1959; Roediger & McDermott, 1995) are more prevalent in people who have autobiographical memories of questionable authenticity. Participants who had remembered being abused while being exposed to suggestive therapy techniques were more likely to falsely recall or recognize DRM theme words than participants who had recovered their memories of abuse spontaneously (Geraerts et al., 2009). Similarly, participants who claimed to remember past lives were more likely to falsely remember DRM theme words than control group participants (Meyersberg et al., 2009).

Other findings suggest that there might be differences between performance on laboratory tasks and autobiographical memory. One recent line of research has focused on people with highly superior autobiographical memory (HSAM; e.g., LePort et al., 2012; Patihis et al., 2013). HSAM people have remarkably detailed memory about events in their lives, including the ability to remember what they were doing at a specific time on a random day years ago. Furthermore, when verifiable, almost all these details are determined to be accurate (LePort et al., 2012). Despite this incredible accuracy, HSAM participants are not superior to control participants on standard laboratory tasks of memory (LePort et al., 2012) and are just as likely (and, in some situations, more likely) to make errors in standard false memory tasks such as the DRM and Misinformation paradigms (Patihis et al., 2013). Such findings demonstrate that even people with highly accurate memories nevertheless rely on constructive processes to remember. More broadly, however, this suggests that there can be differences between memory in the lab and in the world. Patihis and colleagues (2013) argue that HSAM individuals have expertise in using the structure of their everyday lives to help remember autobiographical events accurately. In situations where this advantage is removed (i.e., laboratory memory tasks), they tend to show more normal performance (for an analogous finding with chess masters, see Chase & Simon, 1973). Of course, this argument suggests that only some people take advantage of the narrative structure of everyday life to avoid memory error. An alternative explanation is that retrieval processes differ between laboratory tasks and autobiographical memory tasks, and one could be better at one than the other (Roediger & McDermott, 2013). The primary evidence for this argument is a recent meta-analysis (McDermott et al., 2009) comparing brain activation in functional magnetic resonance imaging studies of laboratory memory tasks (primarily recognition) and autobiographical memory tasks (typically using the "Crovitz" technique of cueing memories using words or pictures). The results revealed little overlap in the brain areas involved in retrieving memories in these two types of tasks. Although further research will be needed to compare these tasks in more precise ways, the findings at least raise the possibility that different brain networks and cognitive processes contribute to remembering laboratory and autobiographical memories.

Although the findings of the literature are generally supportive of a link between the lab and memory "in the wild," a more nuanced question is perhaps appropriate given the evidence discussed earlier. Although it is clear that the same fundamental cognitive processes are available to operate in both situations, the nature of task constraints in each affects how and which processes might be deployed. Furthermore, there is much variability within various laboratory-derived and real-world memory tasks. Thus, a better, more generative question might be, Which characteristics are shared and which are unique across situations (Gallo, 2010)? Research guided by such a question is more likely to reveal satisfying theoretical explanations and more targeted applications aimed at reducing real-world false memories.

Conclusion

False memories are a by-product of a constructive memory system that allows us to perform a great number of useful tasks in our lives (e.g., Newman & Lindsay, 2009). Although many false memories are of a mundane variety (one example being the story that began this chapter), others are of greater consequence. In situations such as criminal or accident investigations, inaccurate memories can lead to major errors in decision-making including wrongly incarcerated individuals, inappropriate conclusions, or missed opportunities to increase worker safety. As we have discussed, research focusing on understanding how the memory system works and factors that influence false memory creation can be used to create new and better ways to support memory accuracy in these critical contexts. In the next chapter, we go more deeply into the ways we might be able to better distinguish between genuine and false memories.

4

Distinguishing Between Genuine and False Memories

Researchers have convincingly demonstrated that it is possible to create false memories in the laboratory. For example, people can come to falsely remember hearing nonpresented words that were associated with words they had heard (e.g., Deese, 1959; Roediger & McDermott, 1995), report information that was only inferred on the basis of general knowledge (e.g., F. Bartlett, 1932; Bower et al., 1979), say they saw items during an eyewitness event that were only suggested afterward (e.g., Lane & Zaragoza, 2007; E. Loftus et al., 1978; Zaragoza & Lane, 1994), recall autobiographical events that were suggested as having come from a family member (e.g., Hyman & Pentland, 1996; E. Loftus & Pickrell, 1996), remember seeing pictures they previously lied about seeing (e.g., Vieira & Lane, 2013), and claim to have perceived events they only previously imagined (e.g., Garry et al., 1996; Goff & Roediger, 1998). One interesting question that arises from this research is to what extent veridical and false memories can be distinguished. If there are cues or markers to reliability, this suggests the potential to identify and reduce false memories. For instance, it may be possible to help witnesses better discriminate between information they experienced during the witnessed event and information acquired from other sources. It may also be possible to help interviewers or other people (e.g., jurors) to consider aspects of witness testimony that are more diagnostic of accuracy.

In the research described in the following sections, two broad classes of cues to reliability are explored. The first is internal to the person remembering—the phenomenal experience generated at the time of retrieval (although this information is expressed overtly in the form of judgments or descriptions). The other type of cue comes from physiological measures, such as the brain activity associated with remembering, that may not be accessible to awareness. As we discuss research in both areas, keep in mind that the source monitoring framework (SMF; as well as similar theories, e.g., Schacter et al., 1998) predicts that the ease of discriminating true from false memories will depend on a number of factors previously discussed (e.g., similarity of sources, specific sources to be discriminated, access to features at retrieval). Thus, in some cases, false memories might be indistinguishable from true memories, and in others, they can be easily discerned. Furthermore, even the most diagnostic cues are unlikely to be useful in all situations.

Before we discuss research on this topic, it is important to briefly consider the different ways that false memories may arise in the context of a forensic setting (for an excellent review, see Davis & Loftus, 2007). Following an event, a witness can be exposed to information from a wide variety of sources. For instance, someone could hear the event described on a newscast or learn new details when interviewed by a police officer or from a conversation with another witness. He or she might also try to recall the event on their own and, wittingly or not, fill in missing details using his or her imagination or schematic knowledge. A witness might also tell a story about the event to family and friends. In such situations, it would be common to focus on some aspects of the event (e.g., how it felt) and neglect others (e.g., the perpetrator's appearance) and, consequently, influence the availability of features in memory (e.g., E. Marsh, 2007). False memories can also occur when people are asked to make identification decisions (e.g., "Do you remember seeing this man?"). A person in a lineup, for instance, may be familiar for reasons other than being the actual perpetrator or target individual. For instance, a person may feel familiar because they had been seen earlier in a mugshot (e.g., Deffenbacher et al., 2006) or previously encountered in an entirely different context (*unconscious transference*; e.g., Ross et al., 1994). Altogether, there are a variety of circumstances that can make it difficult for witnesses to accurately monitor the source of their memories. This task can be even more difficult in settings where an individual may be asked to remember unremarkable events that happened long ago (Evans et al., 2010).

Phenomenal Experience

One major question researchers have asked is whether the conscious subjective experience that accompanies retrieval is similar when a person is accurately remembering the past and when he or she is remembering in error (e.g., Lane & Zaragoza, 1995; Roediger & McDermott, 1995; for an excellent review of the literature, see Lampinen et al., 1998). The phenomenal experience of true and false memories has been measured in a number of ways, including confidence judgments (e.g., Payne et al., 1996), remember/know judgments (e.g., Roediger & McDermott, 1995), verbal descriptions (e.g., Schooler, Gerhard, & Loftus, 1986), think-aloud protocols (e.g., Lampinen et al., 2008), and ratings of specific features of memory (e.g., Suengas & Johnson, 1988). Despite the potential strengths and weaknesses of each type of measure, and general concerns about the use of introspection (see Lampinen et al., 1998, for discussion), research on the topic has converged on two major conclusions: (1) some false memories are remembered as vividly as accurate memories, and (2) on average, false memories are frequently distinguishable from accurate memories on one or more characteristics of memory. In our selective review of the literature on this topic, we distinguish between research that uses more specific measures of phenomenal experience (e.g., remember/know, Memory Characteristics Questionnaire [MCQ]) and those that use confidence judgments, which can potentially be made based on relatively specific or relatively general properties of experience (e.g., recollection and familiarity; Wixted & Mickes, 2010).

QUALITATIVE CHARACTERISTICS. False memories can be especially pernicious when they are accompanied by a rich sense of reexperiencing the event—what you saw, heard, and thought—and in more complex events, where you were, who you were with, and what you felt. There is ample evidence that false memories can have any or all of these qualities (e.g., Heaps & Nash, 2001; Lampinen et al., 2008; Lane & Zaragoza, 1995; Mather et al., 1997; Neuschatz et al., 2002; Norman & Schacter, 1997; Odergard & Lampinen, 2004; Roediger & Mc-

Dermott, 1995; Schooler et al., 1986). For example, Lane and Zaragoza had participants view simple line drawings of objects and words (object names), and make ratings that encouraged them to form mental images. Forty-eight hours later, participants took a source memory test that included items they had studied (as pictures and as words) as well as new items. For each item, they indicated whether the item had been seen as a picture and, if so, whether their memory of it had been accompanied by a sense of recollection or familiarity (a remember/know judgment; Tulving, 1985). Across two experiments, participants were most likely to claim to recollect items they had actually seen as pictures, next most likely to recollect seeing imagined items as pictures, and least likely to recollect seeing never-presented lure items as pictures. More broadly, false memories that resulted from imagination were more often than not accompanied by recollection, while false memories resulting from other processes (e.g., plausibility, semantic similarity to items that were seen as pictures) were more often accompanied by only a feeling of familiarity. Similar findings have been documented with the remember/know procedure using other false memory paradigms. For example, "remembering" is higher for objects seen in a naturalistic event than for objects that were falsely recognized based on schema consistency (Neuschatz et al., 2002), for items that were viewed in a witnessed event than for items suggested in the context of post-event questions that were falsely attributed to the event (Zaragoza & Mitchell, 1996), and for correct identifications of perpetrators in a lineup than for false identifications of foils (M. Palmer et al., 2010).

The vividness of false memories has also been strongly documented in the DRM paradigm (Deese, 1959; Roediger & McDermott, 1995; see Gallo, 2013, for a review). In this task, participants study lists of words that are highly associated with a critical nonpresented theme word (e.g., for the theme word *thief*, list words include *steal, robber, crook, burglar,* and *cop*). Participants often falsely recall these theme words, or endorse them on recognition tests (in some cases, at rates that exceed recognition of list words; e.g., Roediger & McDermott, 1995). Research using remember/

know judgments finds high rates of "remembering" in the false recognition of theme words (see, e.g., review of remembering/knowing studies in Gallo, 2013, p. 76), sometimes at rates indistinguishable from accurate recognition of list words (e.g., Roediger & McDermott, 1995, Exp. 2). Similar rates of remembering of true and false DRM memories are more likely when the list presentation is auditory rather than visual (see Gallo, 2013), and when lists are grouped by theme rather than mixed (e.g., Payne et al., 1996). Finally, the false recollection of recognized theme words also routinely exceeds recollection of unrelated lures, suggesting the important role of activation in creating false memories during the presentation of related word lists (Gallo, 2010).

Although the remember/know procedure has proved useful in investigating the phenomenal experience associated with false memories, the technique has limitations too. For example, phenomenal experience is broken into two broad categories (three, if researchers provide a "guessing" or "not sure" option). Because of this, information can be lost about which particular aspects of phenomenal experience are present. For instance, researchers have distinguished between *criterial recollection* (recollected features that are relevant to the test judgment, such as the font in which a word appeared when the test requires this discrimination) and *noncriterial recollection* (recollected features that are irrelevant to the test judgment, such as what you thought about when saw the word presented; e.g., Yonelinas & Jacoby, 1996). Furthermore, standard remember/know judgments do not assess the degree to which something is recollected or familiar.

Some researchers have attempted to address these issues using tests that require criterial recollection (e.g., Gallo et al., 2004) or by adding ratings to remember/know judgments, such as a rating of the number of unique recollected details (e.g., Scimeca et al., 2011; see also the graded recollection measure of M. Palmer et al., 2010). Others have sought more information by eliciting verbal descriptions and categorizing their features (e.g., Lampinen et al., 2008; Schooler et al., 1986), or having participants rate their memories on a range of different specific features (e.g., Karpel et al., 2001; Lane et al., 2007; Mather et al., 1997; Norman & Schacter, 1997). This work has also documented the richness of false memories and provided clues to potential differences from true memories.

As a first example, Schooler et al. (1986) had participants in an eyewitness suggestibility study provide descriptions of an object (e.g., a yield sign) they claimed to have seen in an event when it either had actually appeared in the event or had only been suggested in post-event questions. Qualitative analyses revealed that the descriptions of true memories were more likely to include sensory details (e.g., color, size), less likely to include information about cognitive operations (e.g., their thoughts or reactions when viewing the part of the scene where the sign "appeared"), and were shorter and more likely to include verbal hedges (e.g., "I think") than false memories. Similarly, Lane et al. (2007, Exp. 1; see also Karpel et al., 2001) had participants in an eyewitness suggestibility experiment rate the clarity of their memories for several features of items they claimed to have seen in the original event (on an immediate test or after a 24-hour delay). The key comparison was between objects they had actually seen in a slide sequence and objects they had only read about in the context of post-event questions. They found that participants rated their memories for *object appearance* and *object location in the scene* as significantly clearer for true than false memories on an immediate test, and on the delayed test, true memories were also rated significantly clearer than false memories for the *time during the event when the object was viewed* and *thoughts, emotions or reactions they had when they saw it during the event* (in addition to object appearance and location). In this particular study, the differences between true and false memories actually grew over time (for a similar effect, see Suengas & Johnson, 1988). Similar findings have also been obtained in other false memory tasks. Mather et al. (1997) and Norman and Schacter (1997) examined false memories in the context of the DRM paradigm. Both studies included conditions where participants rated their memories on a number of features for each word they claimed to recognize at test.

Across the two studies, participants rated their accurate memories of studied items significantly higher than false memories of theme words for *the sound of the word's presentation, reactions or feelings they had when hearing the word*, and *the position of the word in the list* (Norman and Schacter only). Interestingly, the strength of memory for *associations* that had come to mind did not differ between studied items and falsely recognized theme words.

The pattern of findings across different studies and different measures of phenomenal experience is fairly consistent. The sense of reexperiencing that accompanies a nonperceived item or event can, under some circumstances, be as rich and vivid as the strongest true memories (e.g., Roediger & McDermott, 1995). Thus, there is no feature or set of features in phenomenal experience that uniquely distinguishes between true and false memories. That said, the majority of research also finds that false memories are, on average, less vivid and detailed than true memories (at least for some features, such as perceptual or contextual detail; e.g., Lane et al., 2008; Mather et al., 1997). This finding is consistent with neuroscience studies that find that accurate recognition is more likely to be accompanied by activation of brain areas involved in perception than is false recognition (the *sensory reactivation hypothesis*; e.g., Schacter & Slotnick, 2004). Altogether, this suggests that the phenomenal experience that accompanies memory retrieval may contain cues that are diagnostic with respect to memory accuracy (e.g., Lane et al., 2008). It also suggests that people may commonly fail to utilize these cues. Keep in mind that in the studies discussed earlier, participants are rating or describing their phenomenal experience *after* they claimed to have remembered an item. Consequently, it is unclear whether participants are failing to notice these cues during test decisions or whether it is simply too difficult to use the cues (e.g., because differences are too subtle). This raises the question of whether it is possible for people to use mnemonic cues to improve accuracy if they are able to learn its utility.

USING FEATURES OF PHENOMENAL EXPERIENCE TO AVOID FALSE MEMORIES. One way of reframing this research question is to ask the broader question of whether it is possible to change people's expectations about the retrieval task (*metamnemonic knowledge*; e.g., Lane et al., 2007; Starns et al., 2007; see also Gallo, 2013) in ways that increase the accuracy of their memory decisions (e.g., Dodson & Schacter, 2002; Ghetti & Castelli, 2006). The goal of a typical memory test is to discriminate between different classes of items or events (e.g., studied and nonstudied items, items perceived during an event vs. items encountered afterward), and participants will generally have some idea of how to do this before they begin the test. These expectations can come from the instructions of the experimenters (e.g., Koriat & Goldsmith, 1996), from lay theories (beliefs) about memory (Koriat et al., 2004; Lane & Karam-Zanders, 2014), or even prior experience with the task. This knowledge thus influences retrieval and postretrieval decision processes. To the extent that this knowledge is well calibrated (i.e., it accurately reflects task constraints such as the type of mnemonic evidence that distinguishes between item classes), participants can use it to construct more discriminative retrieval cues (e.g., Jacoby et al., 2005; Marsh et al., 2009) or more diagnostic criteria for evaluating retrieved memory records (e.g., M. K. Johnson et al., 1993). Conversely, false memories may often occur because participants' metamnemonic knowledge is inadequate, in error, or not considered during a memory decision (e.g., Lane et al., 2007; Mather et al., 1997; McDuff et al., 2009).

In this view, there are a number of ways that metamnemonic knowledge can be updated in ways that improve accuracy. General warnings given after encoding but before the test often clarify the nature of the items to be discriminated (e.g., Chambers & Zaragoza, 2001; Neuschatz et al., 2001; Starns et al., 2007). For example, in DRM studies, warning instructions often highlight the fact that theme words are likely to have been thought about during the presentation of list words. Although not all studies find significant reductions in the false recognition of theme words (e.g., Gallo, et al., 1997), the overarching pattern is most consistent with the proposition that participants retrieve less memorial evidence for critical theme items when they have been warned about the nature

nature of the items than when they have not (Starns et al., 2007). For instance, Starns et al. (2007) used a signal detection model to fit the results of 12 prior DRM experiments that used test warnings to evaluate their effects on recognition performance. The results of model fitting and two additional experiments strongly suggested that warnings lead participants to retrieve less evidence of having studied critical theme lures. In signal detection terms, the d' between list items and critical theme lures *increased* (the distributions moved farther apart). Although a change in discrimination rather than response bias may seem unusual, it is possible if you assume that people can change the type of evidence they focus on at retrieval (e.g., M. K. Johnson et al., 1993). Starns et al. argued that the pattern of observed findings was consistent with a change in the type of evidence considered at test, with warned participants shifting from a reliance on relational information (e.g., how the items are conceptually linked) to more diagnostic item-specific information (e.g., the sound of the words—phonological features).

There is also evidence that people may benefit from receiving information about the types of features that normatively discriminate between true and false memories (e.g., Lane et al., 2007, 2008). For example, in a series of experiments using the DRM paradigm, Lane et al. (2008) found that participants who had been told to use features of phenomenal experience (*sound of the word, word location in the list, and reactions when they heard word presented*) that had been found to discriminate between list items and nonpresented critical themes in prior research (Mather et al., 1997; Norman & Schacter, 1997) significantly reduced false memories relative to a control condition that simply rated these characteristics without being instructed to use them in their decisions. Similar reductions of false memories were obtained in an eyewitness suggestibility experiment using different features (i.e., object appearance and location; Lane et al., 2007, Exp. 2). Thus, it may be possible to directly instruct people about diagnostic features as a means of improving accuracy (see Schooler et al., 1986, for an example involving ratings of other people's memories). However, not everyone appreciates the utility of provided metamnemonic knowledge. In Lane et al. (2007, Exp. 3), a post-experiment questionnaire revealed that about a quarter of warned participants chose not to use the features described in the warning, and the false recognition rate for this subset of participants was similar to that of the unwarned control group.

Another means of increasing accuracy involves manipulating test format to increase the likelihood that a person will consider diagnostic features in his or her decision. To use an earlier example, criterial recollection tests are expressly designed to have people make memory decisions based on a particular feature (e.g., Gallo et al., 2004, 2010; for a similar approach, see R. Marsh & Hicks, 1998). To the extent that the features on a test are diagnostic of source in a particular situation, this would be expected to improve performance relative to when less diagnostic features are relied on. In addition, tests that increase the extent to which people systematically evaluate the features of their memory generally improves accuracy (e.g., Mather et al., 1997; Zaragoza & Lane, 1994; although see Hicks & Marsh, 2001). For instance, relative to yes/no recognition tests, people are less likely to claim to have seen post-event suggestions in a witnessed event when the test requires them to consider different potential sources of test items (e.g., Lindsay & Johnson, 1989; Zaragoza & Koshmider, 1989; Zaragoza & Lane, 1994). Similarly, having participants rate features of their phenomenal experience (using the MCQ) at test reduces false recognition of critical theme words when these false memories are weak rather than strong (i.e., when study lists included words from randomly intermixed themes rather than blocked by a single theme; Mather et al., 1997).

Finally, there is evidence that people can sometimes learn from the process of making test judgments to focus on features that are more diagnostic of the source. For instance, studies using multiple study-test phases have found that participants can learn from repeated testing such that they consequently improve on later trials (e.g., McDermott, 1996; Tauber & Rhodes, 2010). McDermott (1996, Exp. 2) had participants complete multiple study-recall trials using word lists from the DRM paradigm. Over trials, list word recall increased and theme word recall decreased. Of course, in this and similar studies, what is learned during the test can be applied to the encoding strategies that are adopted on the following trial. However, at least under some conditions, participants can learn from test judgments such that the accuracy of subsequent test judgments is improved without additional encoding of items (Lane et al., 2007, Exp. 3). In Lane et al. (2007) participants watched a mock crime on video, answered a post-event questionnaire that included misleading information about the crime, and later completed a source memory test. The test was broken into two phases: a training phase and an assessment phase. Participants in a correct feedback condition received accurate feedback about their source judgments during the training phase (i.e., the actual source of the test item was displayed after their source decision; e.g., "This item as only in the VIDEO"), participants in an incorrect feedback condition received systematically inaccurate feedback about their responses (half of the feedback was incorrect), and control condition participants received no feedback. Subsequently, all participants received a source memory test with no feedback (assessment phase). Importantly, different items appeared on the two tests. Thus, any effects would suggest the transfer of what had been learned from the first test to a different set of items. Results revealed that correct feedback during the training test reduced subsequent false claims of having seen suggested items in the video relative to the other two other conditions, and incorrect feedback increased source misattribution errors. This latter finding suggests that participants were indeed using the information provided in the feedback rather than responding to the general provision of feedback (e.g., becoming more conservative or systematic). Finally, the time to make source judgments during the assessment test was similar in the correct-feedback and control-condition participants, suggesting that correct feedback did not simply lead participants to more carefully evaluate their memories. Lane et al. interpreted their findings as suggesting that participants were able to use the feedback to learn features that better distinguished between event and post-event sources (although answers to post-experiment questions suggest they were not necessarily aware that they had learned anything).

There is also evidence that feedback on the test might be more helpful under some testing conditions than others. Specifically, researchers examining the utility of feedback for recognition test performance have found it typically has no effect or affects only response criterion (e.g., see Kantner & Lindsay, 2010; Lindsay & Kantner, 2011). This suggests more research is necessary to understand the conditions under which feedback might improve memory decisions and when it could be ineffective or even impair performance. One possibility is that the effectiveness of feedback for improving accuracy depends on the type of evidence used in the recognition judgment. It has been argued that participants primarily rely on familiarity when making old/new recognition decisions (e.g., Malmberg, 2008). Under such circumstances, it may be difficult to adjust how this (unidimensional) evidence is evaluated other than by a simple criterion shift. In contrast, feedback may be more helpful when the test leads people to make more fine-grained evaluations of memory evidence such that adjustments can be made to the features used in the decision (e.g., a greater reliance on recollection; Malmberg, 2008; Wixted, 2007).

Altogether, the literature just reviewed suggests that it is possible for people to update their metamnemonic knowledge in ways that reduce false memories on memory tasks (e.g., Gallo et al., 2004; Lane et al., 2007; Mather et al. 1997; McDermott, 1996). However, it is important to note that it is rare for any of these manipulations to eliminate false memories entirely (for an exception, see the misinformation effect in the high discriminability condition of D. Lindsay, 1990). Because of this, it is unlikely these techniques will provide a panacea for the problem of false memories in forensic contexts, although they do provide a starting place to develop new, stronger techniques, and even a modest reduction in memory errors is likely to be welcomed in these situations (see also N. Brewer & Weber, 2008).

These studies also raise a number of other interesting research questions. For instance, are there important differences between techniques that provide metamnemonic knowledge explicitly and those where metamnemnonic knowledge is acquired more automatically with little or no awareness (i.e., implicitly)? This question relates to a larger debate within the literature as to whether metacognition necessarily involves conscious awareness (e.g., Nelson, 1996) or whether it can be implicit (e.g., Reder & Schunn, 1999). Our findings on the influence of feedback on source memory (Lane et al., 2007; see also Han & Dobbins, 2009) are more consistent with the notion that knowledge can be updated using relatively implicit (automatic) processes, but it is also clear that such knowledge can be updated in ways that involve more explicit, reflective processes (e.g., using warnings, see Lane et al., 2007, or through experience with repeated study-test trials, Dunlosky & Hertzog, 2000). It remains to be seen whether differences in the way this knowledge is acquired has implications for how it is subsequently used (e.g., the degree to which knowledge learned in one situation transfers to another).

CONFIDENCE. We next focus briefly on research that has looked at the utility of confidence for distinguishing between accurate and false memories (for a review, see Roediger et al., 2012). Confidence judgments are designed to reflect phenomenal experience in a graded quantitative manner and do not differentiate between different qualitative bases that might give rise to that feeling of confidence (cf. remember/know judgments or the MCQ). Thus, confidence integrates across different types of memorial evidence. In signal detection theory, confidence is expressed through the use of multiple criteria placed at different points along the evidence distributions of old and new items. Thus, confidence expresses the degree of "oldness" for an item on a recognition test.

Historically, researchers from basic research traditions and eyewitness identification researchers have come to very different conclusions about whether confidence is a good predictor of memory accuracy (for reviews, see N. Brewer & Weber, 2008; Roediger et al., 2012). Basic memory research has generally found that high confidence is associated with accurate performance (e.g., van Zandt, 2000; Wixted & Mickes, 2010), and at least in initial studies, eyewitness identification research generally found low confidence–accuracy correlations (e.g., see literature reviews by Sporer et al., 1995; Wells & Murray, 1984).

Many eyewitness researchers thus concluded that confidence is a poor predictor of accuracy (e.g., 78% of experts in Kassin et al., 2001, thought the statement "An eyewitness's confidence is not a good predictor of his or her identification accuracy" was scientifically reliable). However, other researchers in the field took issue with this blanket conclusion for reasons that include (1) the role of potential moderator variables, (2) the way confidence was measured, and (3) the design of prior studies. First, Sporer and colleagues (1995) called attention to the finding that the confidence–accuracy relationship was stronger for certain subgroups of participants. Specifically, they highlighted the finding that the correlation is stronger for participants who picked someone from a lineup ("choosers") than for participants who said the lineup did not contain the perpetrator ("non-choosers"). Given that district attorneys are only likely to call choosers to testify in a criminal case, this suggests a somewhat more optimistic view of the utility of confidence for real-world settings. Second, the use of correlation as the most appropriate measure of the confidence–accuracy relationship was called into question (e.g., Juslin et al., 1996; Weber & Brewer, 2003; see Roediger et al., 2012, for a discussion). Instead, it was argued that it is more appropriate to assess the calibration of witnesses (i.e., plot the probability of a correct response against the level of confidence expressed). Research using this approach found that participants could show a high degree of calibration even if confidence–accuracy correlations were low (Juslin et al., 1996). More important, across studies, the relationship between confidence and accuracy was positive and linear, although participants do often show overconfidence (e.g., N. Brewer & Wells, 2006; Weber & Brewer, 2003). Finally, there is also evidence that the design of typical eyewitness identification studies, because they hold encoding and test conditions constant, constrains the size of correlation that can be obtained between confidence and accuracy (e.g., Lindsay et al., 1998). When conditions allow more variability (as would be expected in real-world situations), correlations are substantially larger (Lindsay et al., 1998). Altogether, this body of work suggests that investigators would be ill advised to completely disregard the utility of witness confidence when evaluating the reliability of their memory.

Although confidence does appear to be a marker of accuracy, it is important to consider factors that influence its usefulness. First, even when participants are strongly confident (e.g., 100%), substantial error rates can still be observed (e.g., over 20%; see Sauer et al., 2010). These rates are large enough to merit concern about relying on the testimony of a highly confident witness to convict a defendant without additional corroborative evidence (Roediger et al., 2012), although such rates might be acceptable from an investigative perspective (e.g., whether to spend more time gathering and evaluating evidence about a potential perpetrator). Second, confidence is malleable. In the studies described earlier, confidence is obtained at test. However, jurors primarily base their decisions on the confidence expressed by witnesses in court, which may be months or years after the identification. A number of post-identification factors can also inflate witness confidence without affecting accuracy, including post-identification feedback ("Good you identified the suspect"; e.g., Wells & Bradfield, 1998, 1999), having an individual reflect on the reasons for his or her confidence in an identification before making a judgment (Wells & Bradfield, 1999), repeated questioning (Shaw & McClure, 1996; but see Knutsson et al., 2011), feedback from a co-witness (e.g., Semmler et al., 2004), and briefing as to the type of questions a witness can expect in cross-examination (Wells, Ferguson, & Lindsay, 1981). These factors are fairly likely to occur in real-world cases and thus provide a good rationale that confidence should be recorded at the time of identification (as well as additional safeguards; see recommendations of Technical Working Group for Eyewitness Evidence, 1999). Third, although research consistently finds choosers to be fairly well calibrated, the same is not true for non-choosers (e.g., Sauer et al., 2010; see bottom panel of figure 1 therein). In other words, the confidence someone expresses in *rejecting* a lineup does not tell you much about how accurate they are in that assessment.

In addition to research on the confidence–accuracy relationship, other work in this domain has sought ways to maximize the usefulness of confidence judgments in discriminating between accurate and false identifications (e.g., N. Brewer et al., 2012; Sauer et al., 2008). In many ways, this work is a good example of research that fruitfully combines basic theory and an understanding of the memory task confronting eyewitnesses. Based on assumptions underlying signal detection theory (e.g., Wickelgren & Norman, 1966) and accumulator theories of decision-making (e.g., van Zandt, 2000), Sauer et al. (2008) proposed that having participants judge the similarity of the match between each lineup member and the memory representation of the perpetrator (i.e., *ecphoric similarity*; Tulving, 1981) might be a way to reduce the influence of various factors on response criteria that are adopted during recognition decisions (e.g., see Wells, 1993, for descriptions of factors influencing real-world witnesses). In a series of four studies using face recognition and lineup identification tasks, they compared the performance of participants who made ecphoric confidence rating judgments for each face (i.e., confidence that a person's face had been studied or was the culprit in a mock crime on a 0–100 scale) with participants who made binary old/new judgments followed by a rating of their confidence in that decision (0–100). To ascertain the accuracy of the ecphoric rating participants, Sauer et al. used a classification algorithm to choose an optimal decision criterion. Across the four experiments, ecphoric confidence ratings led to more accurate identification decisions than old/new binary judgments. Subsequent research has replicated these effects (e.g., Sauer et al., 2012). These findings not only suggest the possibility of new ways of assessing eyewitness identification but also raise intriguing questions about the specific nature of the disruption that may occur when people have to make binary judgments. Research has also found that it may be possible to improve ecphoric confidence judgments even further by modifying the format of the lineup identification (N. Brewer et al., 2012). Specifically, Neil Brewer et al. (2012) had participants make their confidence judgments under deadline pressure (3 seconds) as a means of reducing any reflection participants might engage in that would increase the likelihood that they might false alarm to a foil lineup member. In a series of experiments, participants in this speeded ecphoric confidence condition were substantially more accurate than participants in a control condition (yes/no judgments and no deadline pressure). Furthermore, the discrepancy in confidence expressed by participants between the top and next-highest lineup member was highly predictive of accuracy—when it was large, participants were almost always accurate (for more recent work, see N. Brewer et al., 2020). As noted by the authors, this work may be extended in the future by utilizing theories that model response time and confidence (e.g., Ratcliff & Starns, 2009) to better understand the mechanisms underlying identification decisions.

Neural Activity

Consistent with the findings reviewed above and the assumptions of the SMF, studies examining brain activity that underlies true and false memories have found many similarities and a few differences (e.g., Johnson et al., 2012; Mitchell & Johnson, 2009). Much of this research has used functional magnetic resonance imaging (fMRI) to identify specific anatomical areas and networks involved in the encoding and retrieval of memories in the context of typical false memory tasks (e.g., DRM, misinformation, reality monitoring; Cabeza et al., 2001; Gonsalves et al., 2004; Okado & Stark, 2005). One hypothesis that has garnered support is that, at retrieval, true memories are more likely to involve the reactivation of sensory information from encoding than are false memories (*the sensory reactivation hypothesis*; see Slotnick & Schacter, 2004, for a discussion; for converging evidence from research using event-related potentials, see, e.g., Fabiani et al., 2000). For instance, Cabeza et al. (2001) had participants listen to related (DRM) lists of words and subsequently complete a recognition test. In this study, although hippocampal activation was similar for accurate recognition of list words and false recognition of critical theme words, activity in the parahippocampal gyrus was greater in the former than in the latter (consistent with greater reactivation of sensory information; see also Dobbins et al., 2003). Similarly, Schacter and Slotnick (2004) had participants view abstract shapes and later had them complete a recognition test that included the studied shapes, "related" shapes (prototype shapes that were perceptually similar to studied shapes), and never-seen shapes. Participants often false alarmed to the related shapes, and brain activity was stronger in early visual processing areas (Brodmann areas [BAs] 17 and 18) for accurate than false recognition, but activity was similar for these two types of recognition in late visual processing areas (BAs 19 and 37). Of key importance is that the former areas are typically activated during perceptual priming, a type of implicit (unaware) memory. This suggests that this difference in neural activity may not be reflected in the phenomenal experience that accompanies participants' remembering, and thus, they are unable to use it to influence their memory decisions.

Research in this area also suggests why it may be so difficult to discriminate between memories that originate from similar sources. Gonsalves et al. (2004) scanned participants while they viewed and imagined pictures (using the object name as a cue) and later had participants complete a source memory test. They found that imagined items that were subsequently claimed to have been seen as a picture showed greater activity in the precuneus and inferior temporal cortex than imagined items that were accurately attributed to imagination. These brain areas are known to be activated during visual imagery tasks (e.g., Kosslyn & Thompson, 2000), and this is consistent with the explanation that the features generated during vivid visual imagery were later interpreted as evidence of having perceived the picture. More broadly, research has found that perceiving and thinking about specific types of perceptual features (e.g., faces and scenes) activate similar areas of the brain (e.g., M. R. Johnson et al., 2007; O'Craven & Kanwisher, 2000).

Research on the neuroscience of false memory (and memory more broadly) continues to expand, and this brief section only reviews a small part of this literature (for more extensive reviews, see, e.g., Mitchell &

Johnson, 2009; Schacter & Slotnick, 2004b; Straube, 2012). Perhaps reassuringly, many findings to date are consistent with behavioral studies and cognitive theory in suggesting that, despite their similarities, true memories often differ on average from false memories. For the purposes of this chapter, however, we need to consider whether it is possible to use specific brain activity as a marker of accurate memory in ways that might be useful to an investigation (e.g., for a discussion, see Bernstein & Loftus, 2009; Schacter & Loftus, 2013). One promising aspect of using brain activity is that it is possible that some diagnostic markers to accuracy are not accessible to awareness (e.g., Johnson et al., 2012; Schacter & Slotnick, 2004), and therefore such measures could provide information above and beyond what could be gleaned from reports of phenomenal experience. Yet, there are other issues that suggest limitations of this research (e.g., Schacter & Loftus, 2013). In these studies, the signals that discriminate between true and false memories are averaged over trials and individuals. Yet, in a legal case, investigators are interested in what can be determined about the accuracy of a particular witness. The types of tasks and stimuli used in these studies also differ dramatically from the more complex situations faced by real-life witnesses. For instance, participants in these studies are typically tested only a short time after encoding, in contrast to the lengthy delays often faced by witnesses. The stimuli used in these tasks also tend to lack the perceptual richness, context, and personal significance that are present in real-world events. This may be a nontrivial issue, as there is evidence that retrieval processes can differ when people are remembering in typical laboratory tasks (such as those used in fMRI research) and autobiographical memory tasks (McDermott et al., 2009). In addition, false memories themselves may be richer and more vivid when they are constructed over time and rehearsed, and this is not reflected in the brief induction procedures typically used in laboratory tasks (e.g., DRM-related word lists). Altogether, these limitations to the current literature suggest that brain imaging or other neuroscience techniques are unlikely to be useful in the near term for a *definitive* determination of whether someone is having a false memory (see also Rissman et al., 2010), although these techniques may be useful in a more probabilistic sense (see discussion in the chapter 7). From a scientific perspective, however, these techniques can tell us valuable things about the nature of memory (e.g., Levy & Wagner, 2013).

Judging Other People's Memories

In forensic settings, people are often called on to evaluate the likelihood that an account of a past event is credible. These evaluators include investigators, attorneys, judges, jurors, and other personnel. This can be a difficult task, as the evaluation is often high-stakes, the person being interviewed may be motivated to be less than truthful (e.g., for a review see Vrij, 2008) and the evaluator is unlikely to know the interviewee well.[1] In situations in which an evaluator has reason to be skeptical of a person's memory, what types of cues might be used to make an assessment?

QUALITATIVE CHARACTERISTICS OF REPORTS. There is evidence that when people judge the likelihood that a person's memory is based on an event they personally experienced, they use features that are highly similar to those used to judge their own memories (M. K. Johnson et al., 1998; Schooler et al., 1986). Johnson et al. (1998) use the term *interpersonal reality monitoring* to refer to situations where people are evaluating whether another person's memory originated from perception or imagination. Consistent with the prediction that people should use features that they use when evaluating the reality of their own memories (e.g., M. K. Johnson & Raye, 1981), participants judge memory accounts as more likely to be accurate when they contain perceptual and contextual detail (e.g., M. K. Johnson et al., 1998; M. K. Johnson & Suengas, 1989; Keogh & Markham, 1998; Schooler et al., 1986). For instance, in Schooler et al. (1986, Exp. 3), participant-judges read a series of accounts describing a yield sign that had been generated by other participants who had either seen the road sign during a slide sequence or who had only read about the sign in a post-event narrative. For each account, they decided whether the person had seen the item or it had been suggested to them, and provided a rationale for their decision. Participants' ability to discriminate between true and false memories was modest (~60%) but significantly above chance (similar size effects are common in the literature; see, e.g., Exp. 1, Clark-Foos et al., 2014). In addition, participants' reasons for deciding that an item had been perceived commonly included sensory details (e.g., color) and spatial location. Along these lines, some researchers have found evidence that witnesses who provide more detailed testimony, even when the details are about peripheral objects, are more likely to be believed by jurors (e.g., Bell & Loftus, 1988, 1989; Wells & Leippe, 1981).

The foregoing findings suggest that although people can reliably distinguish between other people's veridical and false memories, when left to make judgments on their own, their accuracy is modest at best. Not surprisingly, this has led researchers to investigate ways that these monitoring judgments can be improved (e.g., Blandón-Gitlin et al., 2009; Clark-Foos et al., 2014; Schooler et al., 1986; Short & Bodner, 2011; Sporer & Sharman, 2006). One major focus has been to teach participants specific criteria to use in their judgments. For instance, in early work on the topic, Schooler et al. (1986, Exp. 4 & 5) provided instructions to a group of participant-judges that described the key features that had distinguished between true and false memories in their first experiment. Discrimination in the instructed condition was better than the no-instruction condition, but this improvement was modest, as was absolute accuracy (just above 60% at best). Subsequent studies have often provided participants with a more formal evaluation procedure and training to increase accuracy (e.g., Blandon-Gitlin et al., 2009; Short & Bodner, 2010; Sporer & Sharman, 1995).[2] For example, criteria-based content analysis (CBCA) is a technique that involves coding features of statements to distinguish between accurate and fabricated accounts of events (Undeutsch, 1989; see Vrij, 2005, for review). Recently, Blandón-Gitlin et al. (2009) examined its utility for distinguishing between true memories, false memories, and fabrications. In their second experiment, participants completed a series of actions (e.g., placing Play-Doh in a box) and came back a week later for an interview, where they were asked about an action they had performed, an action the interviewer said they had performed but had not (suggested), and an action for which they were told to fabricate a description. Transcripts of the interviews were given to trained CBCA raters, and overall scores differentiated true memories from false and fabricated memories. However, when the suggested accounts were divided into those where the participant simply described the action (partial false memory) and those where he or she gave indication they remembered performing the action (full false memory), the findings were different. CBCA was less effective in discriminating between true and false memories in the former than the latter type of false memory. Researchers have also used a version of the MCQ to help discriminate between true and false memories (judgment of memory characteristics questionnaire, JMCQ; e.g., Sporer & Sharman, 2006). The general finding across studies is that JMCQ ratings do distinguish between true and false memories, particularly with respect to clarity and vividness (e.g., see discrimination of about 70% in Short & Bodner, 2011). Furthermore, it has been suggested that further improvements might be made using statistical techniques (e.g., logistic regression) to optimize the use of features to discriminate between classes of memories. Finally, other researchers have provided evidence that, even without the aid of formal evaluation procedures, it is possible to increase the discrimination performance of participant-judges using training or feedback (Clark-Foos et al., 2014).

Take as a whole, research on people's assessments of the veracity of other people's memories suggests a reliance on the presence of details (e.g., Bell & Loftus, 1988), although people can change their weighting of such factors in their decisions depending on contextual factors (e.g., *suspicion*; M. K. Johnson et al., 1998). Different people may also apply different standards when evaluating another person's account of an event, depending on their abilities to describe their own experiences

(Nahari & Vrij, 2014). However, untrained people generally have only modest success distinguishing between true and false memories of others (e.g., Schooler et al., 1986). Performance can be improved somewhat with training and formal evaluation procedures (e.g., Blandón-Gitlin et al. 2009; Bodner & Short, 2011; Clark-Foos et al., 2014). However, it is clear that there is much room for improving the diagnosticity of these judgments and that future research on the topic is likely to be fruitful.

CONFIDENCE. People often rely on confidence when deciding whether they should trust other people's perceptions, opinions, and so on (e.g., Bahrami et al., 2010; for a discussion, see Frith, 2012). Furthermore, the content of people's descriptions of their memories often provides cues to their confidence in them (e.g., Selmeczy & Dobbins, 2014). In a previous section, we discussed the question of whether confidence is diagnostic of accuracy. However, a related question concerns the degree to which people rely on confidence when assessing other people's memories. Most of this research has been conducted in the context of work examining how jurors assess the veracity of witness testimony. One impetus for this focus was the U.S. Supreme Court's decision in *Neil v. Biggers* (1972) that expressly stated that confidence should be considered by triers-of-fact when evaluating witness accuracy. Research on the topic has reached several general conclusions. First, survey research suggests that laypeople generally believe confidence is associated with memory accuracy (e.g., Deffenbacher & Loftus, 1982; Kassin & Barndollar, 1992; Lane & Karam-Zanders, 2014; Simons & Chabris, 2010; see Desmarais & Read, 2011 for a meta-analysis), with similar findings for law enforcement personnel and judges (e.g., Benton et al., 2006). That said, prior research has been criticized with respect to question wording and the fact that it is ambiguous as to whether the survey question used in most studies refers to confidence at the time of identification or at trial (e.g., Read & Desmarais, 2009, see also Alonzo & Lane, 2010). Second, when judging the accuracy of eyewitnesses in trial simulation research, mock jurors clearly weight confidence highly, and their ability to discriminate between accurate and inaccurate witnesses is poor (e.g., Cutler et al.,

1988, 1990; D. Lindsay et al., 1989). As discussed earlier, confidence may be a better marker for accuracy when collected at the time of identification rather than at trial (e.g., Roediger et al., 2012). However, a key issue is whether this evidence of initial confidence, or, more precisely, any *increase* in confidence from identification to trial, can be used effectively by jurors to assess witness accuracy. Research suggests the answer is that this *mere inflation* (Bradfield & McQuiston, 2004) is only used by jurors to adjust their evaluations of witness accuracy when a defense attorney highlights the discrepancy between initial and subsequent confidence (although this heightened sensitivity can be reduced if mock jurors are provided an acceptable reason for the discrepancy, e.g., an "epiphany"; see Jones et al., 2008). These findings suggest the tendency to rely on confidence as a cue to accuracy is strong and that future research exploring whether there are more optimal ways of presenting confidence information to decision-makers (e.g., numeric ratings) is merited.

As noted earlier, taking a calibration perspective may be useful when considering the usefulness of confidence as a cue to accuracy (e.g., Juslin et al., 1996; Roediger et al., 2012). Consistent with this notion, work by Spellman and colleagues suggest that people can take a more nuanced view when assessing the confidence of others (e.g., Tenney et al., 2007, 2008). Specifically, these researchers have found that participants will use information about a mock witness's calibration with respect to confidence. In these studies, participants receive information about two witnesses who differ in terms of their confidence regarding a target event and two other details. One witness has high confidence about the target event and the other details; the second has high confidence for the target event and one other detail but low confidence about the other. Given this information alone, participants find the first witness more credible. Participants then learn that both witnesses were right about one of the other details and wrong about the other. In the key condition, the second witness was correct for the high-confidence judgment and incorrect for their low confidence judgment (and hence better calibrated than the first witness). In this scenario, participants find the second witness more credible than the first. Thus, people's reliance on confidence as a cue to accuracy can also depend on the information provided about whether the person being judged has a history of good metacognitive resolution. However, a question for further research is whether this type of metacognitive information actually does predict greater witness accuracy on a critical detail (for an argument that it might not, see Fisher et al., 2009). Furthermore, an applied question worthy of exploration is whether such kinds of information can be brought into court proceedings in a valid and useful way. For instance, prosecuting and defense attorneys might be tempted to highlight different aspects of an event, and a witness's associated confidence about these aspects, to gain an advantage in a case.

Next Chapter

We've discussed ways that it might be possible to distinguish between genuine and false memories of eyewitness and other events from our lives. But there is another important variable that can influence the characteristics of our memories. Most, although not all, of the research discussed in this chapter has explored memory in situations in which people are relatively relaxed and stress levels are low. However, witnesses to crimes are much more likely to be in a physiologically aroused state during and after the event. What is the impact of such arousal? In the next chapter, we explore what research tells us about how emotional arousal and stress influence memory. As we will see, the conclusions of such research suggest a complex picture.

5

Emotion and Stress

Jennifer Thompson was a 22-year-old college student in North Carolina. The year was 1984. One night, a man broke into Jennifer's apartment and raped her at knifepoint. Throughout the attack, Jennifer made sure to keep her eyes open and focused on her rapist—she wanted to make sure she remembered what he looked like so she could identify him. Jennifer later identified Ronald Cotton from a police lineup, and due to her testimony, Cotton was convicted at trial. A few years later in 1987, Cotton was granted an appeal because another inmate, Booby Poole, had confessed to being Jennifer's rapist. However, when Poole was presented to Jennifer in court for her identification, Jennifer claimed she had never seen him before and Cotton's appeal was denied. Years later, in 1995, and with the advent of DNA testing, Cotton was exonerated and Poole was found to be Jennifer's rapist. Ronald Cotton spent almost 11 years in prison for a crime he did not commit (The Innocence Project, 2019d).

Although it may be fairly easy to accept that our everyday memories are fallible, the idea that we may misremember crucial aspects of an emotional event seems unlikely to our commonsense beliefs. However, the experience of Jennifer Thompson and the consequences to Ronald Cotton suggest that our memories for emotional events may not be as reliable as we think they are. In other words, it would appear that the negative emotion associated with an event may further increase the potential for error in the already fragile, reconstructive process of memory retrieval. Eyewitness scenarios such as these raise important questions such as whether a witness would be able to provide accurate details of the negative emotional event that was witnessed? And would the witness be able to identify the perpetrator?

As the literature on the effects of stress and negative emotion on memory appear to be interlinked and are often cited together, we begin this chapter with an evaluation of the effects of stress on eyewitness memory. Then, we proceed to evaluate the effects of negative emotion on recall, recognition, and the encoding of new memories. We consider the argument that the terminology of "emotion" is too broad and that to further our understanding of the interactions between emotion and memories for emotional events (e.g., crimes) the investigation of specific, individual emotions may need to be considered. Finally, we review the literature on older adult eyewitnesses, a sometimes neglected topic of eyewitness research, with attention paid to how emotion and memory interact in later life.

The Effects of Stress on Eyewitness Memory

The studies conducted by Charles Morgan III and colleagues (Morgan et al., 2007, 2004) are considered by many to be a cornerstone of the literature on the effects of stress on memory. Morgan and colleagues investigated the memories of military personnel completing training exercises that involved a direct personal threat and heightened stress. The participants in Morgan et al.'s (2004, 2007) studies were active-duty military personnel enrolled in survival school training. Although there are multiple elements to survival school training (see Morgan, Wang, Mason, et al., 2000; Morgan, Wang, Southwick, et al., 2000; and Morgan et al., 2001, for a full description), for the purposes of the research Morgan and colleagues focused on the wilderness evasion phase, which culminated in the trainees' captivity in a simulated prisoner of war camp. As part of this phase of training, all personnel were subjected to food and sleep deprivation over a period of 48 hours. They were also isolated from their colleagues and interrogated in a well-lit room for 30 minutes at a time. The participants were subjected to multiple interrogations, separated by approximately 4 hours. Morgan et al. (2004) investigated two interrogation "conditions": a high-stress and a low-stress interrogation. High-stress interrogations involved verbal threats and physical confrontation aimed at the subject, and the low-stress interrogations involved verbal threats and deceit in an attempt to gain the subject's cooperation (Morgan et al., 2004). All the personnel assessed for the purposes of the study were subjected to both the high-stress and low-stress interrogations.

Morgan et al. (2004) found the military personnel were significantly worse at identifying any of their high-stress interrogators than they were at identifying any of their low-stress interrogators, even though they had been exposed to the interrogators for periods of up to 30 minutes at a time. Morgan et al. (2004) argued that these data provided strong evidence that eyewitnesses who encounter heightened stress and personal threat while attempting to encode details of the event and/or perpetrator are likely to be highly error-prone when asked to subsequently identify the perpetrator. In a subsequent study, Morgan et al. (2007) found more than a third of the personnel who had undergone highly stressful interrogations were unable to recognize their interrogator.

Taken together, the Morgan et al. (2004, 2007) studies raise interesting questions and issues surrounding the effects of negative emotion or stress or memory. Morgan and colleagues argue that these results are directly generalizable to the eyewitness scenario and are more ecologically valid than a laboratory simulation of a crime event. This may be true, as laboratory simulations of stress and/or crime events are often limited by ethical guidelines for research with human subjects, preventing participants from being subjected to experiences that may cause them long-term psychological distress. However, it can be argued that eyewitness identification decisions may be impaired to an even greater extent by heightened stress than is depicted by Morgan et al.'s (2004, 2007) results. All participants in Morgan et al.'s (2004, 2007) research were military personnel and as such they are more likely to have undergone specific training prior to interrogation. Such training may have involved how to cope with a situation akin to that encountered during the course of survival school training. General public eyewitnesses are unlikely to have had such training and therefore may react in an even more negative way to the same stressors.

However, the issue of biological duress experienced by Morgan et al.'s (2004, 2007) participants may be a limiting factor for these findings. As the military personnel suffered from both food and sleep deprivation, this would have resulted in biological distress that, in turn, may have increased susceptibility to the potential effects of stress on their memory performance (Reisberg & Heuer, 2007). Reisberg and Heuer (2007) argue that, because of the biological duress experienced by the military personnel, the findings may only be applicable to circumstances whereby a witness has also been deprived of food and sleep. Therefore, conclusions from Morgan et al.'s (2004, 2007) research should be treated with caution in their application to scenarios where eyewitnesses are not under substantial stress during encoding.

One way to address these limitations is to conduct research in a highly controlled laboratory environment. Then, researchers can compare laboratory findings to field studies, such as those conducted by Morgan et al. (2004, 2007), to investigate whether similar effects can be found using videotaped crime scenarios. For example, early studies by Clifford and colleagues (Clifford & Scott, 1978) reported that participants who viewed a violent crime event were significantly less accurate in their recall of details of the crime than participants who viewed a nonviolent but highly comparable event. Clifford and Scott's (1978) findings suggest that negative emotion or stress experienced during the witnessing of a violent event impairs the accuracy of recall memory, which is consistent with the more recent field studies conducted by Morgan et al. (2004, 2007).

In a subsequent study, Clifford and Hollin (1981) again reported that participants who viewed a violent event were significantly worse at recalling details of the event than participants who had viewed a nonviolent event. As the participants in Clifford and Hollin viewed either a violent or nonviolent video, an argument could be made that effects observed were due to the differences in the content of the videos. However, the content of the videos used by Clifford and Hollin was stringently controlled to enable equality between each video type regardless of the fact that they depicted different scenarios. On the basis of this, Clifford and Hollin argue that it is unlikely the observed differences could be attributed to an artifact other than stress or negative emotion elicited as a direct result of the violent video.

Additionally, Clifford and Hollin (1981) investigated the effects of stress or negative emotion on recognition memory by presenting participants with an identification task for the main perpetrator depicted in the videos. Interestingly, Clifford and Hollin found no statistically significant differences between the violent and nonviolent groups in identification performance. Clifford and Hollin argue that these findings further highlight the difficulty and unreliability of an identification task, even when an event is nonviolent. This research illustrates that the difficulty of an identification task may mask or override any differences found in the recall performance of participants. Numerous researchers since 1981 have also observed the problems posed by the inherent difficulty of an identification task (see Wells et al., 2006; Wells & Olson, 2003).

In 2004, Deffenbacher and colleagues reviewed all the available research on heightened stress and memory performance. Deffenbacher et al.'s meta-analysis analyzed 27 instances of the effects of high stress on face recognition tests in addition to 36 tests of heightened stress on eyewitness recall performance. Their work found that heightened stress experienced during encoding impaired both eyewitness recall and recognition memory. Consistent with this conclusion, recent research by Valentine and Mesout (2008) found that individuals who experienced heightened stress while touring an interactive horror maze (The London Dungeon) provided fewer correct descriptors of a target individual they interacted with during the experience. The high-stress subjects also provided more incorrect descriptors of the target individual and fewer correct identifications compared to those who experienced lower levels of stress (Valentine & Mesout, 2008).

Taken together, research on the topic suggests that heightened stress impairs both the accuracy of a statement that the eyewitness provides to the police and the accuracy of an identification decision. Although these conclusions are drawn from literature that has primarily focused on the effects of stress on eyewitness memory, their findings are often applied to the effects of negative emotion on memory. In fact, the majority of the studies already cited in this chapter use terms such as *stress* and *negative emotion* interchangeably. While the argument appears to be that the experience of heightened stress almost universally impairs recall and recognition memory, the argument for the effects of negative emotion on memory may be more complex: Negative emotion may enhance memory for certain aspects of an event but not others (e.g., Christianson, 1992; Reisberg & Heuer, 2004, 2007).

The next section addresses questions such as whether recall and recognition memory are impaired by negative emotion differently to the effects of heightened stress. We begin by reviewing the literature on memory retrieval: first recall and then recognition memory for negatively emotional stimuli. The section then concludes with a discussion of whether the way in which emotional information is encoded is likely to have an effect on memory retrieval.

The Effects of Negative Emotion on Memory
Recall Memory

The early literature on emotion and memory conflated stress with negative emotion and drew conclusions about negative emotion impairing recall and recognition memory holistically. However, more recent research has instead found that individuals who witness a negative emotional event may have enhanced memory for the gist or core idea of the event but impaired memory for details on the periphery (e.g., Reisberg & Heuer, 2007; Safer et al., 1998). This has been termed the "central and peripheral effect" in the literature (e.g., Reisberg & Heuer, 2004) and is routinely explained by reference to the work of Easterbrook (1959). Easterbrook argued that the detection of an emotional/anxiety-provoking stimulus would result in tunnel vision, the result being that an individual may only encode information that is central to attention and disregard peripheral information.

Easterbrook (1959) argued that a reduction in the encoding of environmental information may be advantageous as it may allow the perceiver to exclude irrelevant (peripheral) information from memory. Easterbrook terms this phenomenon "attentional narrowing" because negative emotion appears to cause attention to narrow to the extent that only central details of the scene/event are encoded. Easterbrook's theory suggests that an eyewitness who experienced negative emotions during the witnessing of a crime may have a better memory for details that are the focus of attention. However, the same eyewitness could also have an impaired or even incomplete memory for other important details of the crime that were excluded from encoding because they were peripheral details.

Although Easterbrook's argument was made just over 60 years ago, it has received little scrutiny and/or revision. Consequently, one important aspect of Easterbrook's (1959) theory remains underspecified: What constitutes a central detail? It appears implicit in Easterbrook's paper that central details refer to those details that are central to attention; however, this begs the question as to which details are central to attention.

This problem was identified by Reisberg and Heuer (2004), who argue that categories must be defined with care because if multiple researchers use multiple, different definitions then the generalizability of their findings is reduced dramatically. For example, Christianson and Loftus (1991) define central details as details that are spatially central or in the foreground of the scene that participants are shown. Thus, peripheral details are details that are in the background of the scene (Christianson & Loftus, 1991). On the other hand, Heuer and Reisberg (1990) define central and peripheral details in terms of centrality to the plot of the scenes shown to participants. Therefore, it is no surprise that the results of Heuer and Reisberg differed from those reported by Christianson and Loftus. Christianson and Loftus reported enhanced memory for central details and impaired memory for peripheral details whereas Heuer and Reisberg did not. One possibility for why these studies reported conflicting results could be that each group of experimenters used different definitions of central and peripheral details.

Furthermore, there is a second consideration in applying Easterbrook's (1959) theory of attentional narrowing to human memory. The majority of Easterbrook's research used animal participants, not human participants, and "anxiety," or increased emotional states that were induced by depriving the animals of food for long periods. Although animals are routinely used in neurological research it is questionable how generalizable an effect such as attentional narrowing may be to a human population. In an eyewitness context, the witness is likely to experience multiple stressors leading to the experience of various different emotions (see Reisberg & Heuer, 2004). However, in Easterbrook's scenario, the rodents experienced one stressor only. Furthermore, the kinds of emotions elicited by food deprivation may be different from those experienced by witnessing a violent conflict between two people (for example). On the other hand, given the similarity in stress induction methodology, Easterbrook's research may be more applicable to the Morgan et al. (2004, 2007) experiments than to the majority of research that does not induce emotion through food deprivation/biological distress. Despite these concerns, a participant's enhanced recall of the central details of a negatively emotional event is strongly supported by the majority of the current literature (e.g., Reisberg & Heuer, 2004, 2007; see also Burke et al., 1992; Edelstein et al., 2004).

Although more work is needed concerning the definitions of central and peripheral details that researchers employ, it follows from these findings that an emotional eyewitness may fail to pay attention to peripheral aspects of a crime event. Instead, the eyewitness may focus on details that are directly in their line of sight or that are plot-relevant, and this could result in an incomplete recall of the crime. Therefore, one conclusion to draw from this literature is that eyewitness recall may be impaired by negative emotion and stress but this likely affects only recall of peripheral details, which may or may not be important during a police interview. This is because it is logical to assume that one detail that is central to both attention and the plot during a crime is likely to be the perpetrator. However, as the next set of studies show, even the perpetrator may not always be "central to attention."

Recognition Memory

As the process of an eyewitness reporting a crime will typically involve a recall task (statement) and, in more serious cases, will also involve a recognition task (identification) it is important to determine whether the experience of negative emotion is likely to affect recall of the crime and recognition of the perpetrator. Research suggests that attentional narrowing can occur for recognition memory as well as recall. For example, Safer et al. (1998) presented participants with either a neutral or an emotional set of slides. In both sets a woman is depicted in a park: In the neutral set the woman is shown talking to a man, and at the end of the series of slides, a close-up is shown of the man's gloved hands giving the woman a set of keys. The man is then shown driving away. In the emotion condition, however, instead of having keys in his hand as in the neutral set, the man's hands are depicted holding a bloody knife. The next slide shows the woman on the ground with her throat cut open. While testing participants with a recognition task, Safer et al. presented participants with four versions of each critical slide: one that was the original slide and the other three were increasing close-ups of the critical information. Safer et al. were interested in whether participants who viewed the emotional set would recognize a modified critical slide depicting a close-up of only the central details of the critical incident (the woman with her throat cut) as the originally presented slide. Safer et al. argued that if this occurred, it would further support the literature on attention narrowing during encoding of negatively emotional events.

Safer et al. (1998) found that when participants were exposed to a negative event, their attention narrowed to the extent that only details that were critical to the negative emotion were recognized. Safer et al. found that 26% of participants identified close-ups of the negative slide that depicted the woman with her throat cut open as compared to 2% identifying a close-up of the neutral critical slide as the originally encountered photograph. This suggests that the participants distorted the boundaries of what they encountered by focusing on the plot-critical information, resulting in the recognition of an image that depicted only the central information of what was originally encountered (Safer et al., 1998). These findings suggest that attentional narrowing may influence recognition as well as recall memory. However, the implication that attentional narrowing during encoding may increase the chances of an eyewitness accurately identifying a perpetrator from a lineup is unclear from this experiment alone.

The literature on the so-called weapon focus effect may help to shed light on any potential implications of attentional narrowing for accurate recognition of a perpetrator. The weapon focus effect refers to the diminished ability of a witness to accurately identify a perpetrator when a weapon has been present during the crime (Carlson et al., 2016; Kramer et al., 1990; E. Loftus, 1987; Pickel, 1998, 1999; Pickel et al., 2006). In a classic study of the weapon focus effect, Elizabeth Loftus et al. (1987) showed participants slides depicting customers queuing at a fast-food restaurant in America. In the weapon series, the perpetrator presents a gun to the cashier, who, in turn, hands over money. The control slides depicted the same individual paying for food. Loftus et al. reported that only 11% of participants in the weapon condition correctly identified the perpetrator from a lineup compared to 38.9% correct identifications in the control condition. This suggests that the presence of a weapon impaired the witnesses' ability to recognize the perpetrator.

Elizabeth Loftus and her colleagues (1987) supported their claims with data from an eye-tracker that was able to provide details of where the participants were looking, providing the researchers feedback on where participants' attention was directed. Crucially, Loftus et al. found that participants fixated more often on the gun than on the perpetrator's face (3.72 fixations compared to 2.44) and for longer (242 ms vs. 200.3 ms, respectively). This finding adds further support to the hypothesis that the reason for the decrease in accurate identifications in the weapon scenario was because the participants' attention became focused on the weapon involved and was therefore diverted away from the perpetrator's face.

Following repeated replication of this finding, weapon focus is now thought to be a stable and reliable phenomenon (Fawcett et al., 2016; Steblay, 1992), with 77% of psychological experts surveyed reporting that they would testify in court to the existence of the weapon focus effect (Kassin et al., 2001). Furthermore, between 57% and 87% of psychological experts, judges, law enforcement personnel, and jurors in the United States agree about the existence of a weapon focus effect (Hosch et al., 2009). Traditionally, the weapon focus effect has been explained by the Easterbrook (1959) hypothesis of attentional narrowing. More specifically, the emotion caused by the event and the associated threat of the weapon result in the witness focusing their attention on the weapon involved rather than on the perpetrator (see Steblay, 1992).

Work by Pickel and colleagues (Pickel, 1998, 1999, 2007; Pickel et al., 2006) suggests that not only the emotion of encountering a gun but perhaps also the unusualness of such an encounter may motivate the weapon focus effect. For instance, Pickel (1998; Pickel et al., 2006) has found that making a gun more unusual by the addition of neon reflective stripes worsens the participants' memory for the perpetrator but improves their recall for details of the gun. Pickel (1998) also found that the production of an unusual and unexpected object, a raw chicken, resulted in a weapon focus effect whereby participants were less able to describe a man when he held a raw chicken compared to when he did not. In a similar vein, Carlson et al. (2016) examined whether the object itself motivated the weapon-focus or unusualness effect or whether it is the way in which the object is used. For example, if someone is hit in the head with a stapler (typical object, unusual action), would a weapon focus effect be observed in the same way as if someone is threatened with a gun? Carlson et al. observed a weapon focus effect only for the crime scenario involving a handgun; they did not find the weapon focus effect for an unusual object (a stuffed toy), nor did they replicate the weapon focus effect when an everyday object (the stapler) was used as a weapon. Regardless of whether it is the unusualness or emotionality of the encounter (or some combination of the two) that results in the weapon focus effect, it still remains a plausible argument that the experience of negative emotions during the witnessing of a crime may impair not only recall memory but also recognition memory for details that are peripheral to the attentional focus of the witness. As this research shows, even the perpetrator can be peripheral to attention under certain circumstances.

Does the Presentation Medium of Emotion and Memory Experiments Matter?

As encoding and retrieval are intrinsically linked (S. Brown & Craik, 2005), the way in which an emotional event is presented to a participant in the laboratory could itself have an effect on the retrieval of emotional information. Previous studies (with a few exceptions) have shown horrific still images to participants (e.g., Candel et al., 2003; Wessel & Merckelbach, 1996) to induce negative emotion(s) and investigate their effects on memory retrieval. A potential problem with such a paradigm is that an eyewitness is likely to experience a dynamic event and not a still image when witnessing a crime. Therefore, it is important to determine whether the presentation of pictures affects the encoding and retrieval of emotional information differently than when the emotion is engendered via staged events or videos of events.

In one of the first studies to directly address this question, Laney and colleagues (2003) argued that emotion is unlikely to be generated in a pictorial fashion outside of the laboratory; rather, emotion is likely to be thematically induced through unfolding events. Laney et al. differentiate between thematic arousal, which is the generation of emotion via involvement in and empathy with an unfolding event, and visually induced reactions, which Laney et al. do not define, instead claiming that visually induced reactions are what have been involved in previous studies. This leaves one to assume that what Laney et al. mean by visually induced reactions is that participants react to a still image with an emotional response.

Laney et al. (2003) asked participants to describe several flash-bulb memories that the participants would later be asked questions about. A flash-bulb memory is a memory that can be recalled with extreme clarity and is typically encoded only for highly emotional events (Schooler & Eich, 2005). Laney at al.'s participants rated how emotional the event was when it occurred and also how emotional it was to recall the memory during the experiment. Participants were also instructed to only list memories that they would be comfortable with a third party verifying accuracy. Transcripts of the verifiable memories were then sent to the elected third parties (usually close family members) for verification of their accuracy. Finally, Laney et al. coded the memories as either visually arousing (the participant described an individual event in some detail and focused on a particular item in their description) or thematic (if the memories did not meet the visually induced criteria).

Laney et al. (2003) reported that 80% of the participant's memories were instances of thematic arousal. This led Laney et al. to conclude that laboratory studies that investigate visually induced emotion may only be investigating a form of emotional processing that occurs 20% of the time in human life. Laney et al.'s results are intriguing and suggest that future research on the effects of emotion on memory may need to adopt a different methodology to the tried-and-tested approach of showing emotion-provoking slides or pictures. However, there are a number of limitations with Laney et al.'s methodology that limit the applicability of their findings. First, the large proportion of thematic memories reported could be attributed to the descriptive abilities of the participants rather than reflecting the true proportion of events or memories that are thematic or visually induced. Second, Laney et al. found no significant difference in the accuracy of thematic or visually induced memories. Therefore, even if previous conclusions concerning emotion and memory have been drawn from studies of visually induced reactions, their conclusions are still probative.

However, in a follow-up experiment, Laney et al. (2004) addressed these concerns. Laney et al. presented participants with either a neutral or emotional slide sequence through which negative emotion was conveyed by means of a narrative, and thus, any emotional arousal was categorized as thematic. The neutral and emotion slide sets were identical except for one critical slide and the accompanying narratives. In the neutral condition, participants heard a narrative of a successful first date between a couple at a woman's flat that ends in a friendly manner. The critical slide in this sequence is a slide of the man and woman in a friendly embrace as the man leaves. The emotional narrative, on the other hand, depicts the man as aggressive and the woman becoming nervous in his company and finally asking him to leave and ending the date. The emotional narrative was intended to convey that the man was likely to assault the woman, and the critical slide in the emotional condition was of the man restraining the woman and seemingly pushing her backward onto a sofa.

Laney et al. (2004) reported that memories for thematic emotional events show no evidence of a central and peripheral, or attentional narrowing, effect. In other words, tunnel memory or attentional narrowing does not appear to occur when emotions have been thematically induced. Laney et al. also reported that both central and peripheral aspects of the events were remembered more accurately in the emotional than in the neutral condition. These findings suggest that thematic arousal may affect memory differently to visually induced arousal and that thematic arousal of negative emotions may universally enhance memory and remove the so-called central/peripheral effect.

Nevertheless, it should be noted that Laney et al. (2004) did not directly compare the recall of central and peripheral details between thematic and visual stimuli; rather, they tested participants on thematic stimuli and drew conclusions from previous literature about the relevant comparisons. Furthermore, as we have already seen, much depends on the exact definition of central and peripheral details; thus, it is possible that definitions employed by Laney et al. may have been different from the literature to which they compared their effects. Therefore, a direct comparison of thematic and visual stimuli would be required to ensure that Laney and colleagues could succeed in measuring the central and peripheral effect in their stimuli that utilizes a visual-induction of emotions.

The debate between visually induced and thematically induced emotion is still ongoing and needs further research to determine whether different encoding and retrieval processes are associated with these different categories of emotional memories. Nonetheless, Laney and colleagues make an interesting point by suggesting that an eyewitness is more likely to encode a crime under thematic conditions than under visual conditions (unless they discover the aftermath of a crime that may then be classified as a visually induced reaction). Laney et al.'s (2003, 2004) research poses interesting questions for criminal justice practitioners and the courts of law: For instance, how is eyewitness memory affected by thematically induced negative emotions?

Most studies assessing the effects of negative emotion on cognition have used Deese–Roediger–McDermott word lists (see Kensinger, 2009a, for a review; see also Knott et al., 2018), or affective pictures (e.g., threatening pictures of snakes; Meyer et al., 2015) to assess the effects of negative emotion on memory, judgment, and decision-making. However, Houston et al. (2013) explored the effects of negative emotion elicited during the witnessing of a crime event, on later recall, and recognition memory. Houston et al. compared the completeness and accuracy of free and cued recall for the negatively emotional crime event to a matched neutral event. Houston et al. found across two experiments that, compared to participants who viewed the neutral event, those who witnessed the negatively emotional crime scenario produced more complete accounts of the perpetrator but were less able to provide a detailed account of his interaction with the victim. Furthermore, Houston et al. found that although they were able to provide more complete accounts of the perpetrator, emotional participants were less likely to accurately recognize him from a photographic lineup than neutral participants were. Given the extant literature points to the importance of attentional focus in determining central details, which, in turn, become more likely to be accurately recalled or recognized, a reasonable presumption is that the perpetrator of a witnessed crime would be central to attention. However, the results of Houston et al. do not fit into a traditional central–peripheral effect categorization because while negative emotion resulted in more complete descriptions of the perpetrator, it also resulted in less complete descriptions of his actions. Presumably, if attention were focused on the perpetrator such that he became central to attention, a memory benefit would be observed for his appearance *and* his actions. Furthermore, negative emotion reduced the likelihood of an accurate identification during a recognition task, which again appears to not align with the central–peripheral effect literature. These data, taken together with the work of Laney and colleagues, suggest that we may process a memory of witnessing a crime in real time differently from a memory of still images or word lists and that such thematic negative arousal may result in different patterns of memory enhancement and/or impairment than those found in the majority of the literature on this subject. Furthermore, Houston et al. measured discrete emotional responses and found that their participants experienced a mixture of sympathy, disgust, sadness, and anger. Therefore, may it be possible that the experience of discrete emotions differentially affects memory?

Are All Emotions Equal?

For some researchers, it is sufficient to equate emotion with arousal: Numerous researchers use the terms *arousal* and *emotion* interchangeably and rely on self-report measures of arousal to infer the experience of emotion by their participants (e.g., Bornstein et al., 1998; see also Reisberg & Heuer, 2007; Safer et al., 1998). However, other researchers argue we experience more than simply "arousal" and that as a psychological construct, a measurement of arousal may not be adequate to investigate the effects of emotion on memory (Levine & Pizarro, 2004). Levine and Pizarro (2004) further argue that an understanding of how emotion affects memory depends on the acceptance of the argument that while arousal may be involved in the experience of emotion, it cannot be used as a term in place of *emotion*. In other words, "arousal is to emotion as brightness is to colour; an essential component to be sure but one that fails to capture some of the most fundamental properties of the phenomenon" (Levine & Pizarro, 2004, p. 539).

Levine and Edelstein (2009) further argue that reports of the intensity of emotional arousal in the extant literature are "insufficient to explain when emotion enhances, and when it impairs, memory" (p. 844). For instance, it has been argued that positive and negative emotions are likely to have different effects on memory. When experiencing a positive emotion, people may be more likely to engage in the use of heuristics to process information: In other words, they engage in non-effortful processing (Levine & Pizarro, 2004). On the other hand, when experiencing a negative emotion, people may be more likely to engage in effortful processing, using fewer heuristics than "positive" people and are also far more cautious about the information they retrieve, perhaps monitoring the information for accuracy to a higher extent than when experiencing a positive emotion (Levine & Pizarro, 2004).

Although a distinction between positive and negative emotion is likely to be more insightful than investigating "arousal," the question must be raised as to whether such a distinction is sufficient to describe the various possible effects of emotion on memory. It is possible that by categorizing all negative emotions as the same (i.e., anger as a negative emotion, fear as a negative emotion, sadness as a negative emotion) previous and present research may have merely scratched the surface concerning the effects of discrete emotions on the encoding and retrieval of memories. To move the literature forward, Levine and Pizarro (2004) suggested that research attention should focus on individual emotions in an attempt to further pull apart the confusing and sometimes contradictory effects of "emotion" on memory. Furthermore, eyewitness testimony is one area where the effects of discrete/different emotions on the completeness (ability to report details) and accuracy of memory are important (Levine & Edelstein, 2009).

According to appraisal theories of emotion, discrete emotions are experienced when a goal is violated or achieved (Rolls, 2007; Scherer, 1999). Depending on which goal has been violated or achieved, a certain emotion will be experienced that, in turn, will direct attention toward information relevant to the achievement or nonachievement of that specific goal (Levine & Pizarro, 2004). In this way, goals are constantly being appraised and emotions act as a means of organizing the myriad information in the world into categories of information that is useful/relevant to the observer and information that is not (Scherer, 1999).

Levine and colleagues favor the goal-relevance approach of appraisal theories of emotion whereby the definitions of which details are central and which are peripheral depend on which emotion a subject is experiencing. For instance, Levine and Pizarro (2004) argue that while the source of a perceived threat is likely to be a central detail when someone experiences fear; when someone is happy, the general environment that person is acting in is likely to be a central detail. Therefore, details that are central to attention may be likely to shift and change as different emotions are experienced. Such a theory is consistent with the finding that anger, for example, motivates a retaliatory/defensive posture toward a causal agent whereas fear leads to a focus on methods of escape (Seitz et al., 2007). Recently, Angie and colleagues (2011) conducted a meta-analysis on the influence of discrete emotions on judgment and decision-making, focusing primarily on the literature assessing anger, fear, guilt, sadness, and happiness. Angie et al. found that discrete emotions have differential effects on judgment and decision-making, even emotions with a similar valence, such as anger, sadness, and fear. However, as the extant literature has not investigated the effects of discrete emotions on eyewitness memory, the question remains as to what effect discrete emotions may have on the completeness, accuracy, and reliability of eyewitness memory reports.

How Does Age Play a Role in the Effects of Emotion on Memory?
The Older Adult Eyewitness

The literature reviewed thus far has concerned only younger adult eyewitnesses, as this is the mainstay population tested in psychological research. However, with an increasingly aging global population (U.S. Census Bureau, 2016) the presence of older adults as eyewitnesses to, and victims of, crime is likely to increase. In comparison to younger adults, previous research suggests that older adults may be less accurate as eyewitnesses to crime, especially when attempting to identify the perpetrator of a crime (e.g., Bartlett & Memon, 2007; Searcy et al., 1999). Consequently, the next section of this chapter focuses on older adult eyewitnesses. First, we compare the performance of younger and older adult eyewitnesses on memory completeness and accuracy. Thereafter, we consider the changing nature of the effects of emotion on memory throughout the life span of an individual. Finally, we discuss the implications of this literature for practitioners why must rely on older adult eyewitnesses—can the research translate into recommendations for practice?

According to a recent review of the eyewitness literature, research on older adults as eyewitnesses is somewhat sparse (Bartlett & Memon, 2007). Eyewitness memory studies that have directly compared younger adults (in general aged between 18–30 years old) to older adults (generally of an age range of 60–80 years old) have found older adults to be less complete and accurate in their recall of a crime than younger adults (e.g., Moulin et al., 2007) and less accurate when attempting to identify a perpetrator from a lineup (Searcy et al., 1999).

Explanations for the observable age differences in the completeness and accuracy of eyewitness recall and recognition memory are largely based on neurological and cognitive research. Researchers have posited that, due to structural changes in the brain caused by normal aging, older adults may experience a reduction in the attentional resources that are available to them (Zacks et al., 2000). As a result of this reduction in attentional resources, successfully completing demanding cognitive processes such as the encoding of new memories and retrieval of old ones becomes more difficult for older adults (Anderson & Craik, 2005). Thus, reduced attentional resources are likely to result in an impairment in recall ability, in comparison to younger adults.

An alternative explanation for the differences in recall and recognition performance between older and younger adults is that the deficit in older adults' memory performance may be due to a reduction in the ability of older adults to process stimuli quickly. For instance, Raz (2000) and Salthouse (1996) argue that declines in the cerebral white matter of the brain could lead to a cognitive change resulting in a reduction in the speed with which stimuli are processed. Therefore, during encoding, older adults may be unlikely to encode as many details as younger adults within the same period of time. Slower encoding speed, therefore, could also serve as a possible explanation for why older adults may provide less complete recall responses than younger adults (e.g., Yarmey, 2000).

These theories are supported by early research conducted by Searcy et al. (1999), who found that older adult eyewitnesses were more likely to make a false identification of an innocent lineup member than a young adult was, regardless of whether the perpetrator depicted in their stimuli was present in the lineup. The finding of increased choosing rates from lineups among older adult eyewitnesses coupled with exaggerated levels of false identifications has been replicated in various other experiments and is now considered by researchers to be a fairly robust and reliable effect (e.g., Memon & Bartlett, 2002; Memon et al., 2002; Rose et al., 2005).

When we look at recall performance in elderly persons, in comparison to younger adults, we see a similar pattern to that which is presented in the recall literature. An early but still highly cited experiment by Brimacombe et al. (1997) found that older adult eyewitnesses, in comparison to younger adults, described fewer physical and clothing characteristics of a perpetrator depicted in their stimuli. The older adults in Brimacombe et al.'s experiment were also less accurate when their recall of these details was compared to younger adults. More recently, Yarmey (2000) summarized the results from three experiments (Yarmey, 1982; Yarmey et al., 1984; Yarmey & Kent, 1980) and reported that older adults were, on average, 15% less complete in their descriptions of the perpetrator than their younger counterparts. Findings such as these have led Wilcock et al. (2008) to conclude that, in general, older adult eyewitnesses may be less accurate than younger adult eyewitnesses when describing the crime and/or attempting to identify the perpetrator from a lineup.

However, there are factors that can reduce age differences in eyewitness memory performance. A review by Anderson and Craik (2005) suggests that if older adults were in an environment that supported effortful encoding or guided retrieval then the negative effects of aging could be offset (see also, Craik, 1983). This is called the environmental-support hypothesis (Anderson & Craik, 2005; Craik, 1983; see also Schonfield & Robertson, 1966). Free-recall tests involve instructing participants to describe everything they can remember about their experience, without any prompts being provided. Recall tasks such as these require the participant to devise their own retrieval strategy (and therefore contain no environmental support). Therefore, free-recall tasks are argued to demonstrate the largest age-related impairments in memory (Anderson & Craik, 2005; Prull et al., 2000). Cued-recall tests, on the other hand, which require participants to answer specific questions regarding the to-be-remembered stimulus (and thus provide environmental support by way of prompts), are less cognitively demanding than free-recall tests as the cues provide a ready-made retrieval strategy for the participant (Anderson & Craik, 2005). Therefore, one way to offset the potential for age differences may be for older adult eyewitnesses to be directly questioned about the crime event (e.g., Describe the perpetrator's hairstyle? Describe the perpetrator's clothing?) rather than be asked to simply "describe what happened."

Furthermore, recognition tests generally show less evidence of age-related differences in performance than recall tests. Recognition tests require little effortful strategy; the individual can make a response on the basis of familiarity with a previously encountered stimulus (e.g., Jacoby, Woloshyn, et al., 1989; Vokey & Read, 1992), whereas recall requires the production of information. Therefore, age differences may be reduced when attempting to identify a perpetrator of a crime in comparison with attempting to provide a statement of what/who was encountered to the police. It is important to remember, however, that although age differences may be reduced in recognition performance, differences still remain (e.g., Searcy et al., 1999; Memon et al., 2002).

Taken together, these findings suggest that structural changes in the brain that occur with increasing age may have an impact on the encoding and retrieval of memories of crimes. One consequence of this is that older adults may provide less complete and accurate descriptions/accounts of what happened than younger eyewitnesses. Furthermore, older adult eyewitnesses appear to also be more prone to incorrectly making an identification of an innocent lineup member. Therefore, it appears that on the basis of available evidence older adults may be less reliable eyewitnesses to crimes than younger adults.

Of all the possible explanations put forward for the observed differences in the performance of older and younger eyewitnesses, emotion is seldom, if ever, among them. This is slightly perplexing because crimes are highly emotional events, and there have been numerous studies charting the changes in the interaction between emotion and memory as an individual gets older. In the next section, we address this issue by exploring older adult memory for emotional events in particular, of which crimes are an obvious subset, and by discussing the changing interaction of emotion and memory as the age of an individual increases.

Aging and Memory for Emotional Events

Are emotional memories also affected by the potential lack of attentional resources as eyewitness memory appears to be? Recent work by Mather (2004) suggests that due to a faster deterioration of areas of the brain associated with nonemotional memories, emotional information may be assigned a higher importance or priority during encoding due to areas of the brain associated with emotional memory deteriorating at a slower rate. Earlier research by Fung and Carstensen (2003) appears to support Mather's theory. Fung and Carstensen showed older and younger adults both emotional and knowledge-based (nonemotional) advertisements and then tested their memories for them. Fung and Carstensen found that while younger adults showed equivalent memory performance for both the emotional and knowledge-based advertisements, older adults remembered the emotion-based adverts more accurately and more frequently than the nonemotional adverts. Fung and Carstensen's findings suggest that the processing of emotional information may be enhanced or prioritized in some way by older adults.

However, a subsequent study by Charles et al. (2003) suggests that the prioritized encoding of emotional information by older adults may not be as clear cut as Fung and Carstensen (2003) posit. Charles et al. found support for the hypothesis that older adults tend to shift toward a bias to process and recall positive information rather than negative information. They presented younger adults (18–29 years old), middle-aged adults (41–53 years old), and older adults (65–80 years old) with images taken from the International Affective Picture System (IAPS; Ito et al., 1998). After a 15-minute delay, participants wrote down descriptions of all the images they could remember being shown. Upon completing this task, participants were then given an old/new recognition task that required them to respond yes/no or old/new to indicate whether an image has been previously seen. Charles et al. found that older adult participants tended to recall and recognize more of the positive images compared to neutral and negative images. However, the younger adults tended to remember and describe a similar number of positive and negative images (Charles et al., 2003). These findings suggest that only memory for negative emotional events may deteriorate with age, and memory for positive emotional events remains relatively intact. One potential implication of these findings is that older adult eyewitnesses may be unlikely to give as accurate or complete a description of the negative aspects of a crime event as their younger counterparts.

More recent research sheds further light on the "emotional processing shift" that appears to occur as an individual ages. Murphy and Issacowtiz (2008) conducted a meta-analysis of the literature and found that younger adults tend to recall more negative information than neutral or positive information. Older adults, on the other hand, were found to recall more positive information than neutral or negative information. One possible explanation for these results is Carstensen's socioemotional selectivity theory (Carstensen et al., 1999), which argues that, as an individual ages, they become increasingly aware of the finite nature of their existence. This awareness results in older individuals becoming orientated toward the goal of making themselves feel good and of regulating their emotional state (Carstensen et al., 1999). Recent revisions to this theory have resulted in Carstensen and colleagues arguing that aging-related changes in orientation toward stimuli results in the exclusion of almost all negative information from memory because processing has become more focused on the positive aspects of events (see Carstensen & Mikels, 2005; Carstensen et al., 2006).

What implications may this shift from a negative preference in young age to a positive preference in old age have on eyewitness memory? Are older adults more likely to simply not encode (or retrieve) the negative aspects of the crime than younger adults? Are older eyewitnesses, therefore, likely to only be reliable for events leading up to and after the crime but have a limited memory for the most negative aspects of the crime event? Also, are younger adults less likely to be able to provide details of the events leading up to the crime but provide more complete accounts of the specific crime than an older adult?

Even though studies investigating aging and emotional memory are on the increase, there is much more work required to explain the various ways that emotion may affect eyewitness memory in an aging population. Furthermore, although research on older adult eyewitnesses is increasing, a connection appears to be lacking between the literature on the effects of emotion and age on memory performance and the application of such research into the eyewitness testimony domain. For instance, if an older adult experiences negative emotion during the witnessing of a crime what effect is that likely to have on the completeness and accuracy of their eyewitness testimony?

One drawback to the current literature on emotion and aging is that emotion is investigated through the use of stimuli such as the IAPS. If future research is to gain an understanding of the role of emotion in older adults' memory for crimes, then researchers will need to employ more ecologically valid techniques, such as thematic arousal.

Conclusion

From the extant literature, it appears that negative emotion may impair the reliability of eyewitness recall and recognition memory. However, this effect may be mediated by whether the information is central or peripheral, depicted pictorially or thematically, which discrete emotions are experienced, and whether young or older adults are tested. So what does the presence of these relationships between emotion and memory mean for the criminal justice system, which deals with emotional eyewitnesses, perpetrators, and victims on a daily basis? Unfortunately, this literature currently poses more questions for researchers than it provides answers for practitioners. The current literature certainly suggests that the experience of negative emotions further undermines the already-fragile process of memory encoding, storage, and retrieval. However, it also suggests that there are aspects of memory that may see increases in accuracy and completeness due to the experience of emotions (such as central details). However, it is currently unclear whether any impacts on central and peripheral detail may shift with the experience of discrete emotions or even during a thematically presented event.

As new and emerging areas of research interest arise, it can be useful to consider how our current understanding of emotions and eyewitness memory may be of application to other domains. The most common-sense application of emotion and eyewitness testimony research is in a policing/forensic context wherein the focus has been on the understanding of factors that threaten the accuracy and reliability of memory evidence from victims or innocent bystanders/witnesses to crime. However, further areas of relevance for this research may be to consider the perpetrator's memory for the crime committed. While a broad assumption exists in the eyewitness memory literature that negative emotions will be experienced and thus their influence on memory needs to be understood, this may not necessarily hold true for perpetrators. Therefore, to be relevant to these emerging areas of research interest, the focus may need to shift away from the study of negative emotions and toward a study of the effects of positive emotions on memory performance. We understand very little about the effects of positive emotions such as pride and happiness on memory creation, storage, and retrieval, which may be a useful avenue of future research to consider.

6

Remembering Changes Memory

Forty-three years old, and the war occurred half a lifetime ago, and yet the remembering makes it now. And sometimes remembering will lead to a story, which makes it forever. That's what stories are for. Stories are for joining the past to the future. Stories are for those late hours in the night when you can't remember how you got from where you were to where you are. Stories are for eternity, when memory is erased, when there is nothing to remember except the story. . . .

. . . The thing about a story is that you dream it as you tell it, hoping that others might then dream along with you, and in this way memory and imagination and language combine to make spirits in the head. There is the illusion of aliveness.
Tim O'Brien, *The Things They Carried*

The Things They Carried (O'Brien, 1990) is a collection of related short stories that explores, among other themes, how the characters' memories of the Vietnam War are changed through the process of imagination and storytelling in ways that help create meaning from their experiences. Put another way, O'Brien's (1990) book describes how memories can be transformed from (relatively) factual retellings to narratives that represent deeper truths about the characters even if they are not necessarily faithful to the original events on which they are based. Storytelling is but one way that we remember our personal and communal past. The act of remembering has the potential to shape the nature of our memory representations—modifying how easily we can access them in the future or what specifically we later remember about the original episode.

This characteristic of our memory system differs from the mechanical recording systems that we often utilize in our daily lives. For instance, replaying a digital video of a birthday party will not change the recording. If you play the video again 2 days or 2 years later, the representation of the party on the recording medium will be the same. In contrast, human memory representations are dynamic, and thus, your memory of the same birthday party may be changed dramatically by how you have remembered it in the past.

As noted in the introductory chapter, memory is a constructive process (e.g., F. Bartlett, 1932; Neisser, 1967; Tulving, 1983), and our recollections are based on memory cues, selectively accessed elements of the memory trace, imagination, and inferences based on general or personal knowledge (e.g., M. K. Johnson et al., 1993; Tulving, 1983). Furthermore, it is not uncommon for people to repeatedly recall personally experienced events, particularly ones they find consequential or salient. And, as illustrated by the earlier quotes, sometimes this remembering is used in service of goals such as connecting with others or trying to make sense of one's own life experiences (e.g., Hirst & Echterhoff, 2012; Marsh, 2007). Thus, memories are repeatedly constructed, sometimes in ways that may make it difficult to ascertain which components may be the result of imagination and inference and that are reflective of the circumstances under which a memory was originally encoded (e.g., see the discussion of source monitoring framework in chapter 3; M. K. Johnson et al., 1993). More broadly, the act of remembering can influence whether someone subsequently remembers or forgets an event, as well as what they remember (e.g., Anderson, 2003; Marsh, 2007; Roediger & Karpicke, 2006).

The issue of how memory representations are affected by prior retrievals is an important one for understanding eyewitness memory. For instance, we know from surveys of law enforcement personnel that witnesses are routinely interviewed multiple times during the course of an investigation (Kassin et al., 2007). Furthermore, if a case goes to trial, witnesses will undoubtedly meet with prosecutors or their staff prior to arriving at the courtroom. Crimes are also generally rare and salient events in people's lives, as well as emotional in nature, and therefore are likely to be discussed with others. Additional retrievals of the event will occur when witnesses describe their experience to other witnesses, family, friends, the media, or other individuals. Thus, it is likely that any witness appearing in a court case has previously remembered the crime on many different occasions.

In this chapter, we discuss how remembering changes memory and see that these effects can enhance (e.g., increasing ease of subsequent retrieval, remembering prior unremembered details) or make it more difficult (e.g., forgetting or adding new information) to access the details associated with the original event. We first review research that generally documents the benefits of retrieval on later memory, with a particular focus on the substantial literature on the testing effect (e.g., Roediger & Karpicke, 2006). Next, we review research examining situations in which retrieval can have at least some negative effects on subsequent memory. For instance, remembering can selectively enhance some aspects of an event while impairing access to others (*retrieval-induced forgetting* [RIF]; Anderson et al., 1994; see Anderson, 2003, for a review). There are also a number of studies that demonstrate that *how* you recall an event can influence what is later remembered about it (e.g., E. Marsh, 2007); this work highlights the social nature of remembering, such as the impact of telling stories about one's experience. In the final section of the chapter, we discuss areas in need of further research, as well as the implications of this research for better supporting eyewitness memory.

Remembering Enhances Memory

As discussed earlier, it is commonplace for law enforcement personnel to repeatedly interview witnesses to crimes (Kassin et al., 2007). One potential impact of such interviews is that they increase the total amount of information remembered about the witnessed event. Basic laboratory research on memory has long documented that repeated recall can lead to the recollection of new information. For example, when participants engage in repeated recall of studied information, they often remember items on later tests that they did not recall previously. This phenomenon is called *reminiscence* (see Payne, 1987, for a review). During repeated recall, it is also common for participants to fail to recall information on a test that was recalled on a previous test. When the amount of reminiscence exceeds recall failure, it is called *hypermnesia*. Assuming that interviewers would aggregate the total information recalled across interviews, one would think the additional detail that results from repeated recall of a witnessed event would be seen a highly positive benefit. Instead, recalling new information during a subsequent interview can be viewed with suspicion in the context of the legal system (for an extensive review, see Fisher et al., 2009). For example, imagine that an eyewitness did not initially recall that the perpetrator had a scar on his arm immediately after the crime but remembered this detail during a subsequent interview. Under these circumstances, the newly recalled detail could be used by a defense attorney to discredit the witness based on the assumption that memory should always be better soon after the crime than at a later point in time. In this situation, the defense attorney's (and presumably jurors') naïve beliefs about memory would be wrong. Research has shown that these reminiscences are often very accurate (e.g., see the summary of findings from 19 mock-crime studies in Fisher et al., 2009).

Research spanning more than a century has documented the beneficial impact of initial retrieval of information on subsequent memory (e.g., Gates, 1917; H. Spitzer, 1939). One research topic that has received much attention is the *testing effect* (for a review, see Roediger & Karpicke, 2006; see also meta-analysis by Rowland, 2014), the finding that retention on a final test is boosted more substantially by an intervening test than by an opportunity to restudy the information (e.g., Bjork & Bjork, 1992; Carpenter & DeLosh, 2006). For example, participants in Roediger and Karpicke's (2006, Exp. 2) research read a prose passage and then were assigned to one of three conditions. In the first condition (SSSS), they studied the passage four times. In the second condition

(SSST), they studied the passage three times before attempting to recall the passage (a test). In the third condition (STTT), they initially studied the passage, followed by three tests. All participants then took recall tests 5 minutes and 1 week later. Recall performance on the 5-minute test was best for the SSSS group, followed by the SSST group, and worst for STTT. However, after 1 week, the pattern was exactly the opposite. Performance was best in STTT group, followed by the SSST group, and worst for SSSS. In short, participants who initially attempted to recall the passage multiple times dramatically boosted their retention of the passage on the final test relative to those who only restudied the passage. Thus, forgetting was substantially reduced.

Research on the testing effect has revealed a number of variables that moderate the effect. For instance, a meta-analysis by Rowland (2014) found that when the initial tests involved less cue support—free or cued recall—the effect size of the impact on subsequent test performance was substantially larger (Hedge's $g = .82$ and $.72$) than if the initial test involved greater cue support—recognition ($g = .36$). In addition, the impact of the retention interval also influenced the size of the testing effect. When the retention interval between the end of the acquisition period and final testing was less than 1 day ($g = .58$; although this impact was significant), the impact was lower than when it was a day or longer ($g = .78$). Looked at in the context of eyewitness memory, these findings suggest that the impact of open-ended interview questions during an initial interview is likely to provide a stronger boost to retention than closed-ended questions. Furthermore, these effects of an initial interview are more likely to be observed when memory is assessed over longer periods. More broadly, the testing effect literature suggests that interviews not only serve as opportunities to collect information about an eyewitness event but can also be a potent learning event in their own right and help witnesses reduce forgetting of event details. As will be seen, studies conducted on the impact of interviews on subsequent memory are broadly consistent with this conclusion.

The impact of interviewing on subsequent eyewitness memory has also been examined in the literature. For instance, it has generally been found that initial interviews help reduce subsequent forgetting without substantial effects on accuracy (e.g., Goodman et al., 1992; La Rooy et al., 2005). This is particularly true if the interview questions are primarily open-ended and not leading. Unfortunately, this is not always the case with standard police interviews (see Fisher & Geisleman, 1992, for discussion). However, the Cognitive Interview (CI) is a technique developed based on research findings in the memory literature (Fisher & Geiselman, 1992). The CI includes a focus on helping witnesses to reinstate the context of the witnessed event, takes account of a witness's limited cognitive resources, involves asking questions in a manner that is compatible with a witness's mental representation of the event, and instructs the witness to try to retrieve the event in a number of varied ways (for a more complete description, see Fisher & Schreiber, 2007). The extensive literature on CI has shown it has robust memorial advantages over standard interviewing techniques (for meta-analyses, see Köhnken et al., 1999; Memon, Meissner, et al., 2010) and increases the comprehensiveness of a witness's report without decreasing the proportion of accurate information. There is also evidence that administering the CI after a witnessed event can improve subsequent retention of event details and help combat the impact of post-event suggestions (e.g., Geiselman et al., 1986; Memon, Zaragoza, et al., 2010). Participants in Memon, Zaragoza, et al. (2010) watched a video, were subsequently forced to fabricate misinformation about the event depicted in the video, and later completed source monitoring and recognition tests about the event. The manipulation concerned whether participants completed a CI or free recall for the event in the video before the forced fabrication phase or afterward. Results revealed that the CI enhanced retention of accurate details and reduced reporting of the fabricated details on the final memory tests when it was administered prior to the forced fabrication phase but not afterward. Thus, the results suggest that the administration of interview techniques like CI soon after a witnessed event can help inoculate witnesses against the potential effects of post-event misinformation.

More recently, there has been significant progress in creating easy-to-use tools that can make this benefit available to witnesses soon after an eyewitness event. A prominent example is the Self-Administered Interview (SAI; Gabbert et al., 2009), which was developed based on the general principles used to develop the Cognitive Interview (Geiselman & Fisher, 1989). The shorter SAI was developed specifically to administer to an eyewitness soon after the witnessed event. Often police officers are unable to conduct extensive interviews at a crime scene, particularly when there are multiple witnesses, and the SAI is useful for collecting information for potential follow-up interviews. Just as important, research has revealed that the SAI helps reduce subsequent forgetting (Gabbert et al., 2009, Exp. 2; Hope et al., 2014). In their initial study on the topic, Gabbert and colleagues (2009) found that, relative to a control condition, completing the SAI after viewing a mock crime improved free recall performance a week later. In a subsequent study (Hope et al., 2014), explored the generality of these findings. Participants viewed a mock crime and then either completed the SAI, completed a free-recall test, or did no initial recall (control). All participants then completed a CI a week afterward. Results revealed that participants who had initially completed the SAI remembered more and were more accurate than either free-recall or control participants. Altogether, the SAI is a promising applied tool that has the potential to enhance eyewitness memory by guiding witnesses to engage in high-quality retrieval soon after the witnessed event. Interestingly, other research suggests that witnesses who complete the SAI also appear to learn to better probe their memory when they later try to remember other events (Gawrylowicz et al., 2013).

Remembering Modifies Memory
Retrieval-Induced Forgetting

In addition to the beneficial impacts of retrieval discussed earlier, there is also the potential for negative impacts. In some situations, retrieval of information can lead to the reduced accessibility of related information on a subsequent test, a phenomenon known as RIF (Anderson et al., 1994; see Anderson, 2003, for a review). Most laboratory studies on RIF use a retrieval practice paradigm (Anderson et al., 1994). Participants study pairs of words that have a category–exemplar relationship (e.g., fruit–banana, red–blood) and then retrieve half of the pairs in each category three times using a cued-stem recall test (e.g., fruit–ba____) during the retrieval phase. After a filler period, participants complete a cued-recall test for all exemplar words. There are three major types of items on the test: (1) practiced exemplars (Rp+), (2) unpracticed exemplars from practiced categories (Rp−), and (3) unpracticed exemplars from unpracticed categories (Nrp). The consistent pattern of results for these studies is that memory for practiced exemplars is *enhanced* (a retrieval-practice effect) but that recall of unpracticed exemplars from practiced categories is *worse* than recall of unpracticed exemplars from unpracticed categories. Anderson (2003) have argued that these and a number of findings of studies in this research literature (e.g., cue independence, retrieval specificity, strength independence) are most consistent with an inhibitory cognitive control mechanism. Specifically, when a cue is presented for retrieval, a number of related items are activated. However, this activation creates competition. To retrieve a target item, the competitive items are inhibited. This inhibitory effect lingers and these items are rendered less accessible on subsequent tests. Although the inhibitory account is perhaps predominant, alternative explanations of RIF that emphasize increased competition or impacts on contextual cues remain viable (e.g., Camp et al., 2007; Spitzer & Bäuml, 2007; for a review, see Murayama et al., 2014).

Regardless of the specific mechanism underlying RIF, there is evidence that this phenomenon can be observed under conditions that mimic real-world conversations (e.g., Coman et al., 2009; Cuc et al., 2007). For example, Cuc et al. (2007, Exp. 2 & 3) had participants read stories during the encoding phase of their experiments. During the practice phase, one person selectively recalled stories while the other member of the pair listened. In Experiment 2, this recall was guided via sentence completion but was an unguided conversation in Experiment 3. After a filler period, participants completed a final cued-recall test for all the stories. Items from the stories could be classified as RP+, RP–, and Nrp, as with previous laboratory studies of RIF. Results were consistent with prior research as well, with performance best for Rp+ items and worst for RP– items, with Nrp items in between. Importantly, this pattern was obtained not only when the participant was a speaker but also for stories that were recalled when the participant was a listener. In other words, although each participant had read the story, when details were omitted by the speaker (called "silences"), the listener was also less likely to subsequently remember it. Cuc and colleagues referred to this finding as *socially shared RIF*. Subsequent research has confirmed this finding and extended it to situations where the speaker and listener have different memories about the same event (September 11; Coman et al., 2009). In short, these studies show that RIF extends to more complex memories and that discussions following a person's experience can potentially lead them to forget, or simply make it more difficult to retrieve, aspects of that experience. In the context of eyewitness interviews, this suggests the importance of using more open-ended questions over closed-ended questions that might limit the focus of retrieval when remembering the crime. However, it also highlights the potential effects of discussions between witnesses before they are interviewed. Even if post-event information is not introduced, these conversations could potentially impact whether non-discussed information is remembered during the subsequent interview.

Telling Stories—Conversations about Memories

Participants in laboratory studies of memory are often told to provide a complete and accurate account of their prior experience. But, like the protagonists in *The Things They Carried* (O'Brien, 1990), people discuss their experiences in everyday life for a variety of different reasons (e.g., Hyman & Faries, 1992; E. Marsh & Tversky, 2004; Pillemer, 1992). For instance, Hyman and Faries (1992) asked participants in their studies to describe situations where they recalled their previous experiences and found that they often did so in conversations to facilitate relationships with other people, such as talking about a memory to illustrate an aspect of themselves or discussing a memory similar to one provided by a conversational partner. Participants in Elizabeth Marsh and Tversky (2004) recorded their retelling of personal memories over a month-long period, and the results revealed that they typically talked about their memories to convey facts and emotions (e.g., to get a sympathetic reaction) and to entertain others. These participants also rated the extent to which their described memories faithfully represented the original event. Participants said that 42% of their retellings were inaccurate (although they noted that even retellings rated as accurate also include some memory distortions). Not surprisingly, participants noted they were most likely to exaggerate the details of their memories when attempting to entertain others (in contrast to factual retellings, whereby they were more likely to omit extraneous details). Thus, people talk about their memories with other people for a variety of reasons (see also McCann & Higgins, 1988) and do so in ways that may sometimes be inaccurate or highly selective.

One question that emerges from this work is whether the way that a memory is discussed has consequences for a person's later ability to recount the original episode. Research on the topic suggests that it clearly does (e.g., Dudokovic et al., 2004; Lane et al., 2001; E. Marsh et al., 2005; Tversky & Marsh, 2000). For example, in one study, participants first read a story about the characteristics of two college roommates (Tversky & Marsh, 2000). Subsequently, they either (1) attempted to recall the story, (2) wrote a letter recommending one of the roommates for a fraternity or sorority, or (3) wrote a letter complaining about one of the roommates to housing administrators. Subsequently, all participants were asked to recall the original story. Relative to the intervening recall condition, those in both letter-writing conditions accurately remembered more information about the roommate that was relevant to their perspective (e.g., they remembered more fun things about the roommate when they had recommended them for the fraternity/sorority) and falsely remembered more perspective-relevant information that was true of the non-described roommate (e.g., they falsely attributed fun characteristics from one roommate to the other that had been recommended). Importantly, their findings revealed that these errors occurred even when they had not been mentioned during rehearsal (i.e., writing the letter). Thus, the biased perspective that participants adopted following encoding influenced their subsequent recall of the original event, presumably because participants were using a schema they had developed during rehearsal to later guide their retrieval of the original event. As we discuss in the following, this and other findings in the research literature raises a serious concern about the potential impact of post-event conversations on eyewitness memory.

Other related research on this topic has used scenarios that explore specific issues relevant to eyewitness memory (e.g., Gabbert et al., 2006; Lane et al., 2001; E. Marsh et al., 2005). For instance, Lane et al. (2001, Exp. 1) had participants view a videotaped crime and subsequently answer questions about the crime that included misinformation. Some participants were then instructed to do a written review of their memory for the crime at a detailed level, some participants were instructed to do a written review of their memory for the crime at a general level (a summary), and a third group did no review. All participants subsequently completed a source monitoring test of their memory for the video and the questionnaire. Results revealed that participants who did the detailed review were more likely to misattribute misinformation items to the video than those who only did the summary. Furthermore, additional analyses revealed that not only were detail review participants more likely to have written down the misinformation items in their review than summary review participants, but they were also more likely to misattribute misinformation items to the video even when they did not write down any suggested items (i.e., they were also more likely to think about them during the review). These findings suggest that memory for a witnessed event can be affected by the specificity of a subsequent review. In this particular study, the detailed review increased eyewitness suggestibility because misinformation items were primarily peripheral to the primary actions (e.g., *the thief pulled a window shade down*). Thus, the impact of specificity of review may differ with a number of factors, including the type of misinformation suggested.

Other research has examined the influence of the way that witnesses talk about the witnessed event after its occurrence (E. Marsh et al., 2005). In this study, participants first viewed a video depicting a violent set of murders. Following the video, one group was asked to construct an accurate written account of the details of the video (factual focus group), a second group was asked to write down their emotional reaction to the video (emotional focus), and a third group only did filler tasks (control condition). The retellings were consistent with instructions as factual-focus participants produced longer, more detailed accounts and emotional-focus participants produced accounts that focused on their experienced emotions and contained more references to self. Following a 25-minute delay, all participants completed a series of memory tests for the events in the video. Although participants in both focus conditions recalled more than the control condition, participants in the emotional-focus condition were more likely to commit major errors in their recall of the events in the video than were factual-focus participants. Performance on cue-based tests such as recognition showed no significant differences. Altogether, the findings of Elizabeth Marsh et al. (2005) suggest that, particularly in open-ended recall formats more typical of eyewitness interviews, the perspective adopted while retelling a witnessed event has the potential to influence what cues are used to probe memory when later recalling the event. To the extent that this retelling perspective reduces retrieval cues that aid in remembering factual details, this could influence the accuracy or comprehensiveness of subsequent eyewitness testimony.

Conversations about crimes are also likely to occur between witnesses. In fact, in a survey of real-world eyewitnesses conducted by Skagerberg and Wright (2008), 58% of witnesses said they had talked about the event with at least one co-witness. Research on memory conformity, which typically involves participants witnessing a mock crime and then subsequently discussing the event with a fellow participant or a confederate of the experimenter, finds very high levels of conformity among research participants on subsequent memory tests (e.g., Gabbert et al., 2004, 2006; Meade & Roediger, 2002; Wright et al., 2000). Research in this area has revealed three different types of processes that lead to these errors: normative influence, informational influence, and memory distortion (see Wright et al., 2009, for discussion). Someone may report an error on the final memory test because the cost of disagreeing with someone else is high (normative influence, e.g., from a biased interviewer), because a witness believes another witness is likely to have a more accurate memory (informational influence, e.g., because they got a better view of the crime), or because a witness genuinely believes the new detail was actually seen in the original event (memory distortion or source monitoring error). Regardless of the mechanism involved in any specific situation, this research suggests that law enforcement officers should caution witnesses from post-event discussions with each other and identify circumstances where witnesses have already discussed the crime.

The research described in this section helps highlight the importance of considering what witnesses do when they are not being interviewed. Eyewitness events are quite often emotional and salient episodes in witnesses' lives, and therefore exactly the type of memories that are likely to be discussed with other people (e.g., E. Marsh & Tversky, 2004). Sometimes, these memories might be discussed with fellow witnesses and new details incorporated into their reports of what happened. Other times, a witness might just need to convey, in the form of a vivid, compelling story, just what the experience felt like to a friend or family member. The types of details that are included in this story, and the ones that are left out, have the potential to influence what is later remembered about the event. Although remembering that takes place outside the interview room is largely taken for granted by the legal system, the potential impact on the accuracy of memories of eyewitness events is considerable.

Reconsolidation

As described in the introductory chapter, once information from the experience of an event is encoded into a memory trace, this trace is vulnerable to disruption for several hours afterward but is gradually stabilized in a process called *consolidation* (e.g., McGaugh, 2000). For many years, it was thought that this stabilization process was relatively permanent once it was completed. However, more recent research in both animals and humans has suggested that consolidated memories are made temporarily unstable when they are reactivated (*reconsolidation*; e.g., Nader et al., 2000; Schiller & Phelps, 2011), leaving open the possibility that they can be modified or forgotten during a brief period before the memory is consolidated once again (although the specific mechanism underlying this effect is still debated; e.g., Elsey et al., 2018).

Researchers studying memory in the eyewitness suggestibility paradigm have argued that reconsolidation can be an important explanatory construct (e.g., Chan & LaPaglia, 2013). For instance, participants in Chan and LaPaglia (2013) first watched an episode of the television show 24 that depicted a terrorist attack. Their memory for the episode was either reactivated or not prior to receiving post-event information. On a final recognition test, participants who had their memories reactivated before being exposed to the misinformation, but not afterward, were less accurate at identifying correct event details. Altogether, Chan and LaPaglia argued that the results of six experiments were most parsimoniously explained by a reconsolidation process in which the memory of the original item was modified by the post-event information. However, other researchers (Rindal et al., 2016) have argued that alternative explanations from earlier research on the misinformation effect better explain these findings (McCloskey & Zaragoza, 1985). Specifically, McCloskey and Zaragoza (1985) noted that participants may endorse misinformation because they do not remember the original information or they place more trust in the misleading information than in their original memory. Rindal et al. (2016) had participants watch a slide show of a mock crime and subsequently reactivated their memory for the event using a brief test. Participants were then exposed to misinformation or accurate information, before completing a final memory test. Importantly, Rindal et al. found that the reactivation phase could increase choosing the misinformation item at test, as in Chan and LaPaglia. However, when participants were given a forced choice between the original test item and a new item (see modified test procedure, McCloskey & Zaragoza, 1985), the effect of reactivation was no longer observed. Instead, the results showed that participants could still remember the original item from the slides after exposure to misinformation. Altogether, these results are consistent with the idea that reactivation of a memory can influence memory reporting but not with the idea that the original memory is reconsolidated.

Conclusion

The act of remembering is not simply the nonreactive accessing of a memory representation of an experience. Instead, the retrieval process has the potential to influence whether and how that memory representation might be remembered in the future. For instance, attempting to recall an event repeatedly can allow us to access information that we otherwise would not in a single attempt (e.g., Payne, 1987). Furthermore, retrieval can increase the likelihood that we will be able to access that information at a later point in time (e.g., Roediger & Karpicke, 2006).

However, it is also the case that retrieving some information about an event has the potential to reduce accessibility to related information that was not retrieved (e.g., Anderson, 2003). The way we choose to remember events can also have consequences. Remembering in the service of other types of activities, such as telling stories to others about our experience, can alter what we later remember about the original experience (e.g., Marsh, 2007). And remembering events with other people can sometimes lead us to incorporate new information about these events into our memories (e.g., Wright et al., 2009). Altogether, research on the topics discussed in this chapter paints a clear picture of human memory as dynamic in nature.

The U.S. legal system largely ignores the impact of remembering on subsequent memory. Interviews are seen nearly exclusively as a means to obtain forensically relevant information from a witness about a crime rather than as a means to reduce subsequent forgetting. Furthermore, as illustrated in the previously discussed example of witnesses who remember additional details over multiple interviews, the benefit of these interviews can become a liability as defense attorneys argue that the added information is indicative of an unreliable memory (see Fisher et al., 2009). The potential importance of conversations or other discussions about the witnessed event outside the interview room is also largely ignored, with the possible exception of discussions with other witnesses.

What is the way forward? To date, the most promising applications to the legal context involve interview techniques. The SAI (Gabbert et al., 2009) was designed so that witnesses could have a high-quality initial recall of the witnessed event, and there is evidence that administering the SAI soon after an event increases retention of event details (e.g., Hope et al., 2014). In addition, research has also suggested that early administration of high-quality interviews (e.g., the CI) not only improves retention but appears to help ameliorate the negative impact of post-event misinformation (Memon, Zaragoza, et al., 2010). But what about the effects of storytelling or other kinds of remembering that occur outside of interviews? Despite the likely ubiquity of such retrievals, it is not clear that witnesses would be able to accurately estimate how often they occurred or characterize the circumstances under which they took place. Furthermore, even if such estimates were accurate, it is as of yet unclear how to evaluate the impact of such retrievals on memory for the event. In addition, although law enforcement personnel can physically separate witnesses from each other and admonish them to not talk with each other, it is unlikely that an admonition to refrain from telling one's friends and family about their experience of the crime is likely to be successful. Instead, the early administration of high-quality interviews such as the SAI might be the best way to reduce the impact of such retrievals, although this conjecture remains to be confirmed empirically.

In previous chapters, we have discussed topics such as how people remember and describe their encounters with other people (chapter 1), how it might be possible to discriminate between true and false memories in ourselves and others (chapter 4), and how stress and emotional arousal influence what is remembered about an event (chapter 5). In the final chapter, we take a step back and ask what research on these and other topics suggest can be done to improve the accuracy and comprehensiveness of eyewitness testimony. As will be seen, there are multiple ways that the utility of eyewitness evidence can be improved.

7

Helping Eyewitness Memory

Throughout this book, we have presented some of the ways in which the processes of memory are affected by the viewing and experiencing of a crime. From emotion and stress to recollection and familiarity to genuine compared to false memories, the ways in which these mechanisms can influence the accuracy and reliability of eyewitness memory has been highlighted. Therefore, in this chapter, we turn our attention to the ways in which this knowledge can be used to help eyewitness memory and, more specifically, those who practice in the field where eyewitness evidence may be necessary to the successful outcome of their case.

American Psychology–Law Society Scientific Review Recommendations

In 1998, the American Psychology–Law Society (hereafter AP-LS) produced a scientific review paper that covered the scientific advances made at the time regarding our understanding of how memory "works" in eyewitness environments. The original 1998 paper contained four recommendations for practitioners with regards to how to work within the confines of the capabilities of memory so as not to jeopardize a case (Wells et al., 1998). At the time of writing this chapter, AP-LS has commissioned an update to the original scientific review paper, which has added an additional five recommendations for practice based on the advances in research that have occurred since the original review (Wells et al., 2020). A draft of the updated review was released in February 2019 and was the subject of a discussion panel at the 2019 annual conference of the AP-LS. In this chapter, we cover each of the now nine recommendations for practice from the AP-LS review, linking them into the literature and topics covered thus far in this book. Please see Wells et al. (2020) for full information on each recommendation.

Recommendation 1: Evidence-Based Suspicion

Full Text Recommendation: There should be evidence-based grounds to suspect that an individual is guilty of the specific crime before conducting an identification procedure involving that individual.

Wells et al. (2020) likely placed this as their first recommendation as it may be the most important in terms of reducing mistaken eyewitness identifications. Previous research has estimated that the suspect is innocent in 65% of lineups that are shown to witnesses (data from Houston, Texas, Police Department; see Wixted et al., 2016). Data such as these suggest that lineups are being used to exclude suspects rather than to identify perpetrators. The utilization of lineups in this way is problematic due to the many memory errors that can occur that lead to the identification of the individual as the suspect in the first instance, followed up by issues surrounding the potential recoding of memories after the suspect has been encountered in the context of an identification parade. As was the subject of chapter 1, the initial description of a perpetrator given by a witness is likely to be vague and incomplete and to focus on population norms and therefore may not be the strongest evidence on which to base inclusion in a lineup. Many factors, combined or in isolation, such as stress and anxiety, intoxication, and opportunity to view have effects on the accuracy and reliability of person descriptions. Furthermore, it is important to note that these factors discussed in chapter 1 often occur in addition to the issues discussed in chapter 2 regarding familiarity and attempting to recognize an unfamiliar face.

More than one third of U.S. law enforcement agencies claim that under current procedures, they need no evidence beyond a "hunch" that a particular individual may be a suspect before placing them in a lineup (see Wise et al., 2011). That hunch could come from an incomplete and unreliable person description provided by a witness previously unfamiliar with the perpetrator whose only experience with the individual in question was in a highly emotionally charged encounter (see chapters 2 and 5). The scientific literature strongly argues that any of these factors in isolation are sufficient to reduce the reliability of the eyewitness's identification decision, and while they are yet to be studied in combination, it is not a large leap of logic to assume that they could have a cumulative effect.

As Wells et al. (2020) point out, the cumulative effect of these factors results in an increased likelihood of presenting a witness with a target-absent lineup (one in which the suspect is not the perpetrator). As it is recommended further in their report that lineups not be repeated with the same witness due to the possibility of contaminating witness memories for the perpetrator, this leads to the recommendation that other, more concrete forms of evidence be gathered to place a suspect in a lineup. While this ideal scenario may be possible in cases in which evidence outside of eyewitness memory exists, such as DNA, fingerprints, and video footage, which implicate the suspect, cases in which the only evidence is witness testimony present a more problematic scenario. In such cases, the eyewitness evidence may be the best evidence available to implicate a suspect as the perpetrator. Based on the reviews of the literature contained herein, for cases in which the only evidence is eyewitness memory, the interviewing officers may need to be extremely careful when interviewing the witnesses so as not to introduce biases or collect accounts based on stereotypes, to be aware of the limitations of person descriptions and the effects of cognitive processes such as familiarity that can be artificially created through exposure to mugshots in the context of a legal setting.

Recommendation 2: Pre-Lineup Interview

Full Text Recommendation: Before conducting an identification procedure and as soon as practicable after the commission of a crime, an officer should interview the witness to document their description of the culprit, obtain their self-report of viewing conditions and attention during the crime, document any claims of prior familiarity with the culprit, instruct witnesses to not discuss the event with co-witnesses, and warn the witness against attempting to identify the perpetrator on their own.

This recommendation links primarily to chapter 1. Recommendation 2 advises interviewing officers should collect a documented description of the culprit as soon as is practicable. However, as the scientific literature reviewed in chapter 1 demonstrates, these descriptions can be incomplete and often rely on population norms. Unfortunately, as we have learned in multiple chapters in this volume (introduction, chapters 2, 3, and 6), once encoded, memories are not set in stone; they change, they are re-created with new information, and they can become less reliable and accurate than they originally were. Forgetting can also occur. For these reasons, Wells et al. (2020) recommend that person descriptions be documented as soon as is practicably possible. However, it should be noted that this is not a safeguard that will ensure that memories of person descriptions are complete and reliable. While documenting person descriptions early on in the legal process will ensure that the memory is written down and stored before substantial opportunities for forgetting can occur, this kind of memory is still incomplete and vague and relies on subjective assessments of factors such as age, height, and weight that tend to conform to population norms. Thus, although documenting the memory/person description early in the investigation is undoubtedly a positive step forward, caution still needs to be urged in placing a reliance on person descriptions given their unreliable nature. One area where such documentation may be beneficial is in allowing fact finders, such as judges and juries, to evaluate the potential for deviation between the witness's initial memory and any subsequent memory reports, thus providing an assessment of the reliability of their memory report.

Recommendation 3: Double-Blind or Equivalent

Full Text Recommendation: Lineups should be conducted using a double-blind procedure (i.e. neither the administrator nor the witness should know who the suspect is in the lineup) or an equally effective method of preventing the administrator from inadvertently influencing the witness.

While not a topic covered in this book, the aim of this recommendation is to reduce bias during the administration of the lineup. Research has shown that when the person administering the lineup knows who the suspect is, the witness is more likely to choose that suspect compared to when the administrator is unaware of the suspect (see Wells et al., 1998; also see Kovera & Evelo, 2017). While this may not sound problematic and may sound advantageous on the face on it, this effect has been found even when the suspect is innocent (see Charman & Quiroz, 2016). Furthermore, lineup administrators who are aware of the placement of the suspect in the lineup have been found to be less likely to record an identification when the witness identifies a known filler instead of the suspect (Rodriguez & Berry, 2014). Thus, the purpose of this recommendation is to ensure that such potentials for bias are reduced if not eliminated by making sure that no one administering the lineup procedure is aware of which member of the lineup is the suspect. As noted by Wells et al. (2020), at no time is the suggestion made that those administering the lineups are aware of the influence they are exerting over the witnesses or that such influence is intentional—scientists are subject to the same biases, which is why double-blind experimental procedures are the gold standard of science.

Recommendation 4: Lineup Fillers

Full Text Recommendation: There should only be one suspect per lineup and the lineup should contain at least five appropriate fillers who do not make the suspect stand out in the lineup due to physical appearances or other factors such as clothing, or background.

As demonstrated in the case of Vincent Moto (see chapter 2), and more broadly the work of the Innocence Project writ large, mistaken eyewitness identification is often touted as the leading cause of wrongful conviction. One method of attempting to control for errors inherent in eyewitness memory is to ensure that the lineups themselves are created in a way that works *with* memory rather than against it. Placing a suspect in a lineup and ensuring that they look sufficiently similar to the fillers (the known innocents) helps ensure that any decision made by the witness is based on memory of the suspect. If a suspect stands out in the parade, such as being the only person with a distinctive scar above their eye (as was described by the witness), then the identification decision may be made because they are the only person with a scar in the lineup and not necessarily on the recognition of that individual as the perpetrator. In other words, ensuring that the suspect stands out from the fillers on the basis of similarity to the person description provided, on the basis of clothing, or any other identifiable aspect, essentially removes the ability of the witness to make a decision on the basis of their memory for the crime. Instead, the witness may be likely to pick the suspect because they have faith in the officers to have succeeded in not only finding someone who matches the description but who is also actually the perpetrator. Unfortunately, field data and laboratory-based research combined demonstrate that such a basis for an identification decision is unreliable (Dysart et al., 2006; Fitzgerald et al., 2013; N. M. Steblay et al., 2003). Of course, this is not to argue that simply making sure the fillers more closely resemble the suspect will ensure that the witness ceases to make any errors. Furthermore, questions remain as to the best way to approach this issue—should the fillers be selected on their physical match to the actual suspect, or should the fillers be selected based on the witness's description of the suspect (see Malpass et al., 2007)? Research has shown no real advantage for either strategy when it comes to improving the reliability of lineup procedures (see Darling et al., 2008; Wells et al., 2020). However, as covered in chapter 1, the initial description of the suspect may be unreliable and may simply resemble population norms (Malpass et al., 2007), thus complicating the process further. Therefore, this recommendation is an example of attempts not to remove error completely from this process, as that would be an impossible task given the issues and limitations of utilizing memory as evidence, but to create circumstances that reduce the amount and potential for error as much as possible.

Recommendation 5: Pre-Lineup Instructions

Full Text Recommendation: When inviting an eyewitness to attend a lineup procedure (photo lineup or live lineup), police should not suggest that the suspect who will be in the lineup has been arrested or that the culprit will be present in the identification procedure. The eyewitness should be instructed that (a) the lineup administrator does not know which person is the suspect and which persons are fillers; (b) the culprit might not be in the lineup at all, so the correct answer might be "not present" or "none of these"; (c) if they feel unable to make a decision they have the option of responding "don't know"; (d) after making a decision they will be asked to state how confident they are in that decision; and (e) the investigation will continue even if no identification is made.

Recent research suggests that 90% of witnesses approach a lineup task with the belief that the perpetrator is present (see Memon et al., 2004). A concern regarding this belief is that it may motivate witnesses to pick someone from the lineup, even in cases where they do not recognize anyone as the perpetrator. Therefore, to reduce this bias, it is recommended by Wells et al. (2020) that all witnesses be informed that the perpetrator may not be present in the lineup they are about to view and that they are given the option to record a "don't know" decision.

As discussed in chapter 2, faces may be recognized based on familiarity or recollection: Familiarity is the weaker of two processes and gives rise to the phenomenological experience of a face being familiar but the exact basis for the familiarity being unknown (Do I recognize you from the grocery store where you work or from the crime scene? See

Yovell & Paller, 2004). For crimes in which the perpetrator is known by the victim (such as their being a family member, close friend, etc.), recognition judgments are likely to be based on recollection. However, when the perpetrator is unknown to the victim/witness, the sheer act of describing the perpetrator and/or viewing mugshots of potential suspects have been shown to lead to the witness to be more likely to pick the person from the lineup who most closely resembles the description/the mugshot, even if that person is innocent and even when the real perpetrator is also in the lineup (see Memon et al., 2002). Such errors in recognition occur due to a source monitoring error, whereupon the witness is unable to detect why the face in the lineup is familiar, and thus, they make the assumption that the face is familiar because it is the face of the perpetrator. Research has shown that utilizing lineup instructions that do not give witnesses a don't-know option and/or do not contain the instruction that the perpetrator may or may not be present, led to a higher rate of misidentifications (e.g., Clark, 2005). On the basis of this research, Wells et al. (2020) recommend that the preceding instructions be utilized to ensure that the witness has the freedom to reject the lineup or to give a "don't know" response rather than feeling under pressure to identify a lineup member as the perpetrator.

Recommendation 6: Confidence Statement

Full Text Recommendation: A confidence statement should be taken from the witness as soon as an identification decision is made.

In chapter 4, we discussed the role of confidence in discriminating between accurate and inaccurate memories. As noted in that chapter, historically, there was some disagreement between the basic memory literature and the eyewitness identification literature about the utility of confidence in making this discrimination (for reviews, see N. Brewer & Weber, 2008; Roediger et al., 2012). More recently, researchers from both fields have coalesced around the conclusion that eyewitness confidence *at the time of identification* is useful when a witness chooses someone from the lineup (e.g., Roediger et al., 2012). Confidence estimates provided after the lineup event (e.g., at court), however, are much more malleable, and confidence expressed in the rejection of a lineup ("the perpetrator is not there") is relatively unreliable (e.g., Sauer et al., 2010).

As noted in chapter 4, an important issue concerns how triers of fact (judges and jury members) might utilize initial eyewitness confidence judgments, especially when witnesses increase their confidence at the time of trial. Initial research on the topic suggests that such a discrepancy would need to be highlighted at trial (e.g., Bradfield & McQuiston, 2004; although this is not foolproof, see Jones et al., 2008). Furthermore, other work suggests that triers of fact might be able to utilize information about the witness's calibration (e.g., Tenney et al., 2007) to appropriately adjust their assessment of witness confidence. More broadly, the fact that the research literature on people's ability to use confidence in their deliberations about eyewitness accuracy is relatively sparse suggests the importance of further research in the area. This particular recommendation will only realize its full value when empirically derived recommendations about its presentation to triers of fact are also available.

Recommendation 7: Video Recording

Full Text Recommendation: The entire identification procedure, including pre-lineup instructions and witness confidence statement, should be video recorded.

There has long been a call to video record interrogations in a bid to ensure an objective record (see Kassin et al., 2009). Beyond providing a complete and objective record, a benefit of recording interrogations is also to hold police accountable for the interrogation techniques used and to provide evidence for review by experts in cases of a suspected false confession. Wells et al. (2020) call for the video recording of identification procedures for similar reasons. First, Wells et al. argue that video recording the identification procedure, from the beginning of pre-lineup instructions to the obtaining of confidence estimates from the witness, will produce an objective and reviewable record of the procedures utilized. Such a recording, as akin to recording suspect interrogations, not only removes the potential for incomplete records of identification procedures to be kept but may entice lineup administrators to conform to best-practice guidelines, thus further reducing bias and unreliability inherent in lineup identifications (Wells et al., 2020).

Recommendation 8: Avoid Repeated Identifications

Full Text Recommendation: Repeating an identification procedure with the same suspect and same eyewitness should be avoided regardless of whether the eyewitness identified the suspect in the initial identification procedure.

Wells et al. (2020) state that the importance of this recommendation cannot be overemphasized. The reason for this emphasis is due to the potential for source monitoring errors. As discussed in chapter 3, the source monitoring framework (see M. K. Johnson & Raye, 1981), is the process by which we attribute a source to our memories. The concern with repeated identification attempts with the same suspect is that the witness may begin to experience familiarity with the suspect's image due to the repeated exposure rather than due to the suspect being the perpetrator. Thereafter, the witness may make a source monitoring error and incorrectly attribute the familiarity they experience with the suspect's image as due to exposure to the suspect during the crime (see Yovell & Paller, 2004). Such "false familiarity" has been manipulated in the laboratory and termed the "false fame effect." The false fame effect is a process by which participants can be persuaded a name or face is famous by repeatedly being exposed to the name or face in the context of a laboratory study. Jacoby et al. (1989) first reported this effect and found that 24 hours after repeated exposure to names, participants would incorrectly claim that nonfamous names were, in fact, famous—in essence, they misattributed the familiarity they developed with the non-famous names the previous day (see Jacoby et al., 1989). The false fame effect has been replicated with faces, with older adults being particularly susceptible (see Bartlett & Fulton, 1991).

A further concern with repeated identification attempts that contain the same suspect involves the commitment effect. A highly cited meta-analysis of the eyewitness literature found that if a witness makes an error and incorrectly identifies an innocent suspect in the first identification attempt, that mistake is repeated in subsequent identification attempts containing the same suspect (Deffenbacher et al., 2004). The theory underlying this effect has multiple facets; it could be that the witness remembers their earlier decision and doesn't want to appear inconsistent and thus recommits to their initial decision (Deffenbacher et al., 2006); it could be that the very act of identifying an innocent suspect the first time changed their memory for the perpetrator and led the witness to essentially rewrite their memory for the crime to now involve the innocent suspect rather than the actual perpetrator (Steblay et al., 2013; Valentine et al., 2012). It could also simply be that the witness has such faith in the police that repeatedly encountering the same suspect in the identification attempts is taken to communicate that the person who appears repeatedly is the police suspect. Knowing or being able to guess who the police suspect is has been shown in previous research to induce bias and increase the likelihood of the witness identifying that individual regardless of whether that individual matches the witness's memory for the perpetrator (see Wells & Luus, 1990). Therefore, by limiting the identification procedures to one attempt to identify, these biases can be removed from the identification procedure, thus helping improve the reliability of the identification attempt and reduce errors.

Recommendation 9: Showups

Full Text Recommendation: Showups should be avoided whenever it is possible to conduct a lineup (e.g. if probable cause exists to arrest the person then a showup should not be conducted). Cases in which it is necessary to conduct a showup should use the procedural safeguards that are recommended for lineups, including the elimination of suggestive cues, a warning that the detained person might not be the culprit, video recording the procedure, and securing a confidence statement.

Wells et al. (2020) recommend show-ups be avoided for reasons already outlined in the previous eight recommendations—they can lead to biases, misidentification, false familiarity, and source monitoring errors. A showup is an identification procedure whereby the witness is shown a single suspect and asked whether they recognize that individual as being the perpetrator of the crime. As Wells et al. (2020) point out, the major difference between a showup and a lineup is the lack of fillers: Whereas a lineup will contain fillers in an attempt to make it difficult for the witness to detect which lineup member is the suspect and thus reduce bias, a showup affords no such protections. Furthermore, Wells et al. argue that showups typically occur with the police taking the witness back to the scene of the crime, or close to the scene of the crime, to view a person who has been detained on the basis of matching the description of the perpetrator. Showups seem to be used fairly frequently by police as an identification procedure, with Flowe et al. (2001) reporting the use of showups in 55% of the 488 cases they reviewed. Showups have been shown repeatedly by the extant literature to be highly biased and to produce a higher volume of false identifications (i.e., when the suspect is not the perpetrator but the witness positively identifies them as such) than lineups (see Dysart & Lindsay, 2007, for a review).

As noted in chapter 1, person descriptions that lead to a specific individual being identified as the suspect in the first place are often incomplete, vague, and conform to population norms. Therefore, as Wells et al. (2020) argue, the target of the show-up procedure may have been detained by police due to their similarity to an item of clothing or a distinguishing physical feature such as a scar or a tattoo. Thus, the likelihood that the witness may make a positive identification on the basis of these features alone, rather than recognition of the perpetrator's face, increases the bias of a showup procedure (Wells et al., 2020). Wells et al. argue that if showups must be used, the clothing of the individual should be covered up to ensure the witness does not base their identification decision on the similarity to the perpetrator's clothes rather than similarity to the perpetrator's face. However, their overarching recommendation is not to use showups if they can be avoided and the suspect instead should be placed in a regular lineup.

CONCLUSION. The recommendations of Wells et al. (2020) are based on the results of thousands of studies examining eyewitness identification and the factors that influence its accuracy. As noted in the introduction to this chapter, many of these recommendations are updated versions of those offered in the AP-LS white paper from 1998. Despite their long-standing nature, adoption by law enforcement in the United States has been relatively slow (although it has been more substantial in countries like the United Kingdom). Although the scientific research base continues to grow, this underscores the critical importance of public policy efforts to implement these recommendations as a means of reducing the impact of eyewitness error on criminal cases.

Improving Eyewitness Memory: Key Issues and Future Directions

As demonstrated throughout this volume, memory is malleable, error-prone, and incomplete, and therefore, the only way to truly ensure that errors such as these are removed from criminal cases would be to remove the reliance on memory evidence entirely. Given such a recommendation is impracticable if not impossible, we are motivated to find methods to decrease the unreliability of this form of evidence while keeping in mind that such methods do not automatically make this form of evidence error-free. In this section, we discuss issues surrounding other ways to improve eyewitness memory, beyond eyewitness identification, focusing on promising new directions for research.

Searching for a Magic Bullet? Deterministic Versus Probabilistic Cues to Accuracy

Will it ever be possible to point to a particular marker (e.g., brain activity or a subjective judgment) that definitively discriminates between true and false memories across different people and situations? Perhaps. It seems unwise to bet against the ingenuity of future scientists and engineers, but the constructive nature of the memory system also suggests this could be a staggeringly difficult goal to accomplish (e.g., see Hassabis & Maguire, 2007; Newman & Lindsay, 2009, for relevant discussion). However, there are many cues we have discussed in this volume that are diagnostic of memory accuracy (e.g., areas of brain activity, confidence, and other aspects of phenomenal experience; see chapter 4). It seems unreasonable to suggest that this type of information would not be of use in deciding the outcome of a legal case (N. Brewer & Weber, 2008). Yet, some researchers within the eyewitness domain have downplayed the usefulness of cues, such as confidence, that are only probabilistically associated with accuracy, presumably because they are perceived to be inconsistent with the notion of a definitive judgment of guilt or innocence. However, this attitude seems problematic in ways that are suggested by the proverb "Perfect is the enemy of (the) good." Diagnostic cues could be useful in the legal context in a number of circumstances. One potential use of such cues is in the investigative portion of criminal investigations. For example, knowing the confidence of a witness and the latency of his or her identification response might inform whether an identified suspect is judged worthy of additional investigation (N. Brewer et al., 2012; Roediger et al., 2012). Furthermore, diagnostic cues could also be useful at later points in the case. Providing the confidence a witness expressed at the time of identification to triers-of-facts (judges and jurors) might be useful for judging his or her accuracy, as long as it is not the only evidence against a defendant. More broadly, it is important to keep in mind that *all* forensic evidence is probabilistic in nature (e.g., National Research Council, 2009; Roediger et al., 2012). However, much more work in this area is needed. For example, one goal would be to more precisely characterize the diagnosticity of different cues to witness accuracy (similar to efforts to gauge the effects of different estimator variable factors on eyewitness memory; see, e.g., Deffenbacher et al., 2008; G. Loftus & Harley, 2005). In addition, research is needed to establish how different cues might be integrated together to provide stronger diagnostic evidence to accuracy.

Supporting the Discrimination of True and False Memories

Ultimately, one hoped-for outcome of research on false memory is that it leads to new and better strategies for improving the utility of eyewitness memory. In an investigation, there are two main ways to do this: (1) help the witness better distinguish between veridical and false memories in his or her report and (2) help the decision-maker (investigators, jurors or judges) more accurately evaluate the veridicality of a witness account. Although we have discussed some of these issues in chapter 4, we briefly describe a few promising directions.

HELPING THE WITNESS. One of the key ways to improve discrimination between true and false memories is to ensure that people's expectations about a memory task (metamnemonic knowledge) are consistent with its actual features (e.g., knowing which characteristics of phenomenal experience are diagnostic of different sources; Gallo, 2013; Lane et al., 2007). To the extent a person is well calibrated, he or she should be better able to form more discriminative retrieval cues to probe memory (e.g., Jacoby et al., 2005) or use more effective criteria when evaluating retrieved information (e.g., M. K. Johnson et al., 1993). As discussed in a previous section, false memories can be reduced in a number of ways, including using test formats that focus people on diagnostic features (e.g., criterial recollection task; Gallo et al., 2010), by providing warnings before the test (e.g., Starns et al., 2007), or by giving feedback about the accuracy of initial test judgments (e.g., Lane et al., 2007). There are some barriers to directly applying any of these options to real-world witnesses. For example, to use techniques that call attention to specific features of a memory, an investigator would have to know which features to encourage a witness to use. Because it is unlikely that even a small set of features would be diagnostic across all the different situations encountered by witnesses, it would require that researchers identify such features through research (Lane et al., 2007). Even if this information was available to professionals, it would still be necessary for the investigator to diagnose which standard situation was the closest match to that of a particular witness. Furthermore, even general warnings are not always effective in reducing memory errors (see the review in Chambers & Zaragoza, 2001), and feedback can actually hurt memory accuracy if it is inaccurate (Lane et al., 2007). This is not to say that any of these particular approaches might eventually be useful for real-world witnesses but rather that considerable work would be necessary to address the constraints of the environment.

Other techniques may also be usefully applied to the investigative context. For instance, because witnesses might not consider the nature of the memory task they are being asked to perform before beginning an interview (e.g., which sources they must distinguish and which features distinguish between them), it is possible that they could be trained how to identify and incorporate the constraints of the task into their memory decisions (Lane et al., 2007). Other alternatives include training witnesses to better assess their own memories. For instance, source monitoring training has been shown to enhance the accuracy of young children's memory performance (e.g., Poole & Lindsay, 2002; Thierry & Spence, 2002). Although this specific type of training is unlikely to be helpful for adolescents and adults (who already understand how to make such judgments), a more effective training method might involve teaching these older witnesses to consider features in memory that may be available but that are not routinely utilized in memory judgments. This training could be paired with measures from the literature that have been designed to elicit careful consideration of phenomenal experience, such as graded recollection (e.g., Gallo et al., 2010; Palmer et al.,

2010) or the Memory Characteristics Questionnaire (M. K. Johnson et al., 1988). A more speculative addition would be mindfulness training; a technique that has recently been shown to improve metacognitive accuracy on a memory task, presumably by increasing people's sensitivity to their internal states (Baird et al., 2014). Although all of these potential directions appear promising based on previous research, it is clear that further development is needed to adapt the techniques for the investigative context, along with tests of their efficacy for reducing memory errors.

HELPING THE DECISION-MAKER. To date, there have been few attempts to develop training aids to improve people's ability to judge the accuracy of witness memory. One recent approach, called the I-I-Eye aid, involves teaching people to evaluate witnesses by considering the procedures used by investigators to elicit that person's eyewitness account, as well as factors during the witnessed event that might influence the accuracy of their account such as view of the perpetrator or lighting (Pawlenko et al., 2013; Wise et al., 2009). The results of one experiment revealed that I-I-Eye mock juror participants were better able to discriminate between a "strong" and a "weak witness" depicted in a trial transcript than were participants in a control condition (Pawlenko et al., 2013). Note that this approach focuses primarily on identifying external factors that may have affected a particular witness and is more likely to be useful for jurors or judges than investigators (although the latter might benefit from considering factors present during the event). In contrast, we previously reviewed a number of techniques used to focus participants on particular features present in true versus false memory reports (e.g., judgment of memory characteristics questionnaire [JMCQ]; Clark-Foos et al., 2014; Short & Bodner, 2010; see chapter 4). Much like the research on people's sensitivity to features in their own memories (e.g., Lane et al., 2007), these studies suggest that people can improve their ability to discriminate between accurate and false memory accounts if their attention to particular features of reports is guided (e.g., Short & Bodner, 2010) and reinforced (Clark-Foos et al., 2014).

One promising approach is to pair the use of the JMCQ with computational techniques that could be used to more optimally weight characteristics to maximize discrimination (Short & Bodner, 2010). In other words, decision-making could be improved with the use of both human and algorithmic inputs. Despite the potential of these techniques, the current gap between the laboratory and the field is wide. At this point, the JMCQ has not been directly adapted for use in legal settings, and this is an important future research direction.

Integrating Information to Better Predict Accuracy

Many cues to memory accuracy (e.g., confidence) are diagnostic rather than deterministic. As argued earlier, such cues can still be useful in the context of an investigation or trial (N. Brewer & Weber, 2008). However, it may be possible to further improve discrimination by integrating multiple cues into decision-making (see also Bernstein & Loftus, 2009). A recent meta-analysis suggests that such an approach appears useful in deception detection, as clusters of cues appear to better predict the veracity of a statement than individual cues (Hartwig & Bond, 2014). A key issue for approaching this task involves selecting appropriate cues and weighting them in ways that maximize the discrimination between accurate and false memories or between more or less accurate witnesses. Candidates for measures include verifiable information about the conditions present during the witnessed crime (e.g., lighting), characteristics of retrieval decisions (e.g., confidence and response time for eyewitness identification; e.g., N. Brewer et al., 2012), the verbal content of the witness's account (e.g., Short & Bodner, 2010), or neuroscientific data such as event-related potentials or functional magnetic resonance imaging (Abe et al., 2008; Gonsalves et al., 2004; Slotnick & Schacter, 2004). It may also be possible to administer a set of standardized measures to witnesses during the investigative phase of a case to evaluate characteristics such as visual acuity, working memory capacity, or episodic memory (see D. Davis & Loftus, 2007, for other candidate measures). Of course, any measure used in such situations must be shown to demonstrate cross-situation stability, such as has recently been found for recognition response criterion (Kantner & Lindsay, 2012), as a step toward establishing predictive validity. Finally, the task of determining the optimal weighting of cues is likely to be aided by the use of advanced computational techniques (Bernstein & Loftus, 2009).

Ultimately, investigators want to figure out what happened (*the ground truth*) during a crime or other event. One noteworthy strategy for accomplishing this goal involves using a mathematical model to use information obtained from eyewitnesses and other sources of information (e.g., physical evidence) as a means to reconstruct the event. The literature provides two recent examples of such an approach (Dunn & Kirsner, 2011; Waubert de Puiseau et al., 2012), both of which involve integrating information provided by multiple witnesses. Dunn and Kirsner (2011) evaluated historical accounts from eyewitnesses to the 1941 sinking of the HMAS *Sydney II* off the coast of Australia. These accounts varied widely, but Dunn and Kirsner's approach was to classify these accounts into different categories and then utilize the information from all the accounts (integrated with other physical information) to calculate a candidate location for the sunken ship. This estimate subsequently turned out to be fairly accurate when the ship was later discovered. Waubert de Puiseau and colleagues (2012) evaluated the use of a model to reconstruct a video event that was witnessed by multiple participants who each subsequently gave yes or no answers to a series of factual questions. For any given question, their model weights the answers of witnesses who had greater overall competence (as measured by a higher proportion of shared responses with other witnesses) higher than witnesses with lower competence. Results revealed that this technique provided a more accurate reconstruction of the event than a majority rule strategy, particularly when there were larger groups of witnesses. Both studies thus highlight the potential utility of formal modeling to aid investigators in their use of eyewitness testimony, although much research is needed to establish the generalizability of these techniques.

Conclusion

As we have discussed in this section, future improvements in the collection and use of eyewitness evidence are likely to come from asking new questions, or in taking advantage of new conceptual or technological developments. Broadly, these involve ways of getting high-quality information from witnesses, better predicting the accuracy of a given witness (or aspects of a single witness's account), and helping others (e.g., investigators, judges, jurors) make better decisions from this information. We note that most of the ideas in this section were primarily inspired by theoretical or computational approaches from outside the field. This is not to say that eyewitness memory research cannot generate new and exciting applications but, rather, that the field can benefit from new and fresh perspectives on the eyewitness memory "problem." However, as we also noted, many of these ideas have not been truly tested in situations that better approximate the conditions experienced by real-life witnesses. Thus again, we see the potential for fruitful interaction between researchers of different types.

Final Thoughts

The fragile, constructive, and malleable nature of memory makes reliance on it particularly fraught in high-stakes situations such as eyewitness memory. Yet, as we have argued throughout this volume, we do not have the luxury of being able to abandon its use in a court of law. Rather, we need to understand when we can best trust eyewitness memory as a source of evidence, and when we should have less confidence. To do so, we need to use our understanding of human cognitive processes in the context of complex, real-world events to find ways of using it to its fullest potential. We must also continue to expand research that focuses on the cognitive processes of those who must interpret and make decisions based on eyewitness evidence. Furthermore, these goals are most likely to be achieved through the collaboration of scientists who work in and outside the field of eyewitness memory.

Although much has been learned about eyewitness memory, we both feel strongly that our scientific understanding has not increased as rapidly as perhaps it should have but that there are clear paths for achieving that goal. We hope that the research and ideas presented in this volume have generated ideas of your own. This is an exciting time to grapple with the complexity of eyewitness memory and to try to find solutions that will reduce the human cost of erroneous testimony. If this book has motivated even a single person to take up the challenge, we have been successful.

ACKNOWLEDGMENTS

We owe a debt of gratitude to the many people who made this project a reality.

We first thank Jennifer Hammer, Veronica Knutson, and other staff at the NYU Press. We deeply appreciate your commitment to this project and your help overcoming the challenges along the way.

Both of us acknowledge our colleagues and institutions for their support during this project. I (S. L.) appreciate my supportive colleagues in the Department of Psychology at Louisiana State University (LSU) and, subsequently, at the University of Alabama in Huntsville. Initial work on this project was funded by an ATLAS grant from the Louisiana Board of Regents. I want to acknowledge Ann Whitmer, College of Humanities and Social Sciences at LSU, who provided critical support of my grant proposal. Thank you as well to the graduate and undergraduate students who worked in my laboratory over the years and never failed to inspire me with their curiosity and commitment. In addition, I am deeply grateful to Barbara Basden, Maria Zaragoza, and Marcia Johnson, all of whom played important roles in my development as a scientist. Thank you to my colleagues Scott Gronlund and Roy Malpass for your friendship and illuminating conversations about the nature of eyewitness memory. Finally, a special thanks to Chris Meissner. Our work together inspired me to pursue this project.

I (K. H.) have had some wonderful mentors during my career. To Amina Memon, Brian Clifford, and Louise Phillips, the three people who first ignited my interest in the scientific study of eyewitness memory, thank you. I will always be indebted to you for your supervision and mentorship; you taught me the importance of a rigorous scientific process. I also wish to thank Christian Meissner, my postdoctoral supervisor, who taught me the importance of ensuring that our research is applicable to the field environment. Chris taught me that science can be a true vehicle for change, especially if we as researchers take the step to engage with the system and those who work within it. To Roy Malpass, who was a mentor to me during my time at the University of Texas at El Paso, thank you for your guidance and willingness to share your experiences with me; you taught me how to be an educator and how to remain eternally curious. To the people I work with every day at Texas A&M International University—students, faculty, and staff—you inspire me, and I feel extremely fortunate to be counted among your ranks. Finally, to the law enforcement practitioners I have worked with throughout the years who strive to learn how the science of eyewitness memory impacts their role in the criminal justice system—I feel honored to be on those journeys with you.

We also wish to thank family and friends who were there for us before and during the long process of completing this book. I (S. L.) thank my parents, Philip and Mary Jo Lane, for cultivating a deep desire to understand the world and the intellectual humility to avoid easy answers. I (K. H.) would like to thank my family for their support, not only during this project but also in everything that I turn my hand to, and especially my husband, Keaton, and our son, Iain, who give me the drive to continue to work in this area and advocate for science-based practice.

—Sean M. Lane and Kate A. Houston

NOTES

INTRODUCTION

1 Details about this case were obtained from Innocenceproject.org, and articles that appeared in the *Baton Rouge Advocate* (Roberts, 2005) and the *Chicago Tribune* (Possley, 2005).
2 Although the concept of basic and applied research is useful, it is important to think about research as falling along a continuum. At the most extreme, basic research is undertaken to gain knowledge for its own sake, with little thought given to real-world application of the results (Whitley & Kite, 2013). Its motivation is theoretical (i.e., building or testing theories), and it is conducted under controlled conditions, usually in the laboratory. At the other extreme, applied research is undertaken to solve a real-world problem, and its results should be readily useful for that purpose. It may or may not be theoretically motivated and is conducted in field settings where researchers will often have less control over all the variables of interest. Most studies will not fall so neatly in one category or the other. For instance, many applied studies of eyewitness memory are conducted in the laboratory, although the materials may be designed to closely approximate important elements encountered by real-world witnesses.
3 Although most contemporary research on eyewitness memory has been conducted since the 1970s (e.g., E. Loftus et al., 1979), research on the topic began over a century ago (e.g., Munsterberg, 1899; Stern, 1904; Whipple, 1911).
4 Researchers also have evidence that memory plays a role in imagining the future (e.g., for reviews, see Schacter & Addis, 2007; Szpunar, 2010).

CHAPTER 3. GENUINE AND FALSE MEMORIES

1 The term *source monitoring* describes the general process of discriminating the origin of a memory. When a witness picks someone out of lineup, they are attributing their memory for that person to the context of the crime. The terms *source confusion* or *source misattribution error* describes a specific type of error in which someone mistakenly claims that an item (e.g., a person or an object) that originated from one source actually originated from another source. Lineup identifications involve source monitoring processes, but memory errors that occur in such judgments are not necessarily source misattribution errors (see, e.g., Perfect & Harris, 2003).

2 Other major theories used to motivate research on false memory include fuzzy trace theory (Reyna & Brainerd, 1995) and activation-monitoring theory (Roediger et al., 2001).

CHAPTER 4. DISTINGUISHING BETWEEN GENUINE AND FALSE MEMORIES

1 When we evaluate the accuracy of memories of people we know well, we often have other useful knowledge, such as whether the person has been known to have an accurate memory in other situations.
2 Some of the measures discussed in this paragraph were originally developed to distinguish between truthful statements and lies (e.g., CBCA; Undeustch, 1989), and others were adapted from memory research to apply to lie detection (JMCQ; Sporer & Sharman, 2006). It is only more recently that researchers have attempted to distinguish between true memories, false memories, and lies in the same study (e.g., Blandón-Gitlin et al., 2009; Short & Bodner, 2010).

REFERENCES

Abe, N., Okuda, J., Suzuki, M., Sasaki, H., Matsuda, T., Mori, E., Tsukada, M., & Fujii, T. (2008). Neural correlates of true memory, false memory, and deception. *Neuron*, *18*(12), 2811–2819.

Alonzo, J., & Lane, S. M. (2010). Saying versus judging: Assessing juror knowledge of eyewitness memory. *Applied Cognitive Psychology*, *24*(9), 1245–1264.

Altman, C. M., Schreiber Compo, N., McQuiston, D., Hagsand, A. V., & Cervera, J. (2018). Witnesses' memory for events and faces under elevated levels of intoxication. *Memory*, *26*(7), 946–959. doi:10.1080/09658211.2018.1445758

American Society for the Positive Care of Children. (2019). *Child maltreatment statistics in the U.S.* https://americanspcc.org/child-abuse-statistics/

Anderson, M. C. (2003). Rethinking interference theory: Executive control and the mechanisms of forgetting. *Journal of Memory and Language*, *49*(4), 415–445.

Anderson, M. C., Bjork, R. A., & Bjork, E. L. (1994). Remembering can cause forgetting: retrieval dynamics in long-term memory. *Journal of Experimental Psychology: Learning, Memory, and Cognition*, *20*(5), 1063–1087.

Anderson, N. D., & Craik, F. I. M. (2005). Memory in the aging brain. In E. Tulving, & Craik, F. I. M (Eds.), The Oxford handbook of memory (pp. 411–425). Oxford University Press

Angie, A. D., Connelly, S., Waples, E. P., & Kligyte, V. (2011). The influence of discrete emotions on judgment and decision-making: A meta-analytic review. *Cognition & Emotion*, *25*(8), 1393–1422. doi:10.1080/02699931.2010.550751

Arnold, M., & Lindsay, D. S. (2005). Remembrance of remembrance past. *Memory*, *13*(5), 533–549.

Atkinson, R. C., & Shiffrin, R. M. (1968). Human memory: A proposed system and its control processes. *The Psychology of Learning and Motivation*, *2*(4), 89–195.

Baddeley, A. (2000). The episodic buffer: A new component of working memory?. *Trends in Cognitive Sciences*, *4*(11), 417–423.

Baddeley, A., & Hitch, G. J. (1974). Working memory. In G. Bower (Ed.), *Recent advances in learning and motivation* (Vol. 8, pp. 47–89). Academic Press.

Bahrami, B., Olsen, K., Latham, P. E., Roepstorff, A., Rees, G., & Frith, C. D. (2010). Optimally interacting minds. *Science*, *329*(5995), 1081–1085.

Baird, B., Mrazek, M. D., Phillips, D. T., & Schooler, J. W. (2014). Domain-specific enhancement of metacognitive ability following meditation training. *Journal of Experimental Psychology: General*, *143*(5), 1972–1979.

Banaji, M. R., & Crowder, R. G. (1989). The bankruptcy of everyday memory. *American Psychologist, 44*(9), 1185–1193.

Banaji, M. R., & Crowder, R. G. (1994). Experimentation and its discontents. In P. E. Morris & M. Gruneberg (Eds.), *Aspects of memory* (2nd ed., pp. 296–308). Routledge.

Bar, M. (2007). The proactive brain: Using analogies and associations to generate predictions. *Trends in Cognitive Sciences, 11*(7), 280–289.

Barnier, A. J., Sharman, S. J., McKay, L., & Sporer, S. L. (2005). Discriminating adults' genuine, imagined, and deceptive accounts of positive and negative childhood events. *Applied Cognitive Psychology, 19*(8), 985–1001.

Bartlett, F. C. (1932). *Remembering: An experimental and social study*. Cambridge University Press.

Bartlett, J. C., & Fulton, A. (1991). Familiarity and recognition of faces: The factor of age. *Memory & Cognition, 19*, 229–238.

Bartlett, J. C., & Memon, A. (2007). Eyewitness memory in young and older eyewitnesses. In R. C. L. Lindsay, D. F. Ross, J. D. Read, & M. P. Toglia (Eds.), *The Handbook of Eyewitness Psychology: Vol. 2. Memory for people* (pp. 309–338). Erlbaum.

Bayen, U. J., Murnane, K., & Erdfelder, E. (1996). Souce discrimination, item detection, and multinomial models of source monitoring. *Journal of Experimental Psychology: Learning, Memory, and Cognition, 22*(1), 197–215.

BBC News. (2008). *Coltrane used on NZ wanted poster*. http://news.bbc.co.uk/2/hi/entertainment/7548090.stm

Bell, B. E., & Loftus, E. F. (1988). Degree of detail of eyewitness testimony and mock juror judgments. *Journal of Applied Social Psychology, 18*(14), 1171–1192.

Bell, B. E., & Loftus, E. F. (1989). Trivial persuasion in the courtroom: the power of (a few) minor details. *Journal of Personality and Social Psychology, 56*(5), 669–679.

Benton, T. R., Ross, D. F., Bradshaw, E., Thomas, W. N., & Bradshaw, G. S. (2006). Eyewitness memory is still not common sense: Comparing jurors, judges and law enforcement to eyewitness experts. *Applied Cognitive Psychology, 20*(1), 115–129.

Bernstein, D. M., & Loftus, E. F. (2009). How to tell if a particular memory is true or false. *Perspectives on Psychological Science, 4*(4), 370–374.

Bjork, R. A., & Bjork, E. L. (1992). A new theory of disuse and an old theory of stimulus fluctuation. In A. Healy, S. Kosslyn, & R. Shiffrin (Eds.), *From learning processes to cognitive processes: Essays in honor of William K. Estes* (Vol. 2, pp. 35–67). Erlbaum.

Blandón-Gitlin, I., Pezdek, K., Lindsay, D. S., & Hagen, L. (2009). Criteria-based content analysis of true and suggested accounts of events. *Applied Cognitive Psychology, 23*(7), 901–917.

Bonner, L., Burton, A. M., & Bruce, V. (2003). Getting to know you: How we learn new faces. *Visual Cognition, 10*(5), 527–536. doi:10.1080/13506280244000168

Bornstein, B. H., & LeCompte, D. C. (1995). A comparison of item and source forgetting. *Psychonomic Bulletin & Review, 2*(2), 254–259.

Bornstein, B. H., Liebel, L. M., & Scarberry, N. C. (1998). Repeated testing in eyewitness memory: a means to improve recall of a negative emotional event. *Applied Cognitive Psychology, 12*(2), 119–131.

Bower, G. H., Black, J. B., & Turner, T. J. (1979). Scripts in memory for text. *Cognitive Psychology, 11*(2), 177–220.

Bradfield, A., & McQuiston, D. E. (2004). When does evidence of eyewitness confidence inflation affect judgments in a criminal trial? *Law and Human Behavior, 28*(4), 369–387.

Brainerd, C. J., Reyna, V. F., Wright, R., & Mojardin, A. H. (2003). Recollection rejection: false-memory editing in children and adults. *Psychological Review, 110*(4), 762–784.

Brewer, N., & Weber, N. (2008). Eyewitness confidence and latency: Indices of memory processes not just markers of accuracy. *Applied Cognitive Psychology, 22*(6), 827–840.

Brewer, N., Weber, N., & Guerin, N. (2020). Police lineups of the future? *American Psychologist, 75*(1), 76–91.

Brewer, N., & Wells, G. L. (2006). The confidence-accuracy relationship in eyewitness identification: Effect of lineup instructions, foil similarity, and target-absent base rates. *Journal of Experimental Psychology: Applied, 12*(1), 11–30.

Brewer, N., Weber, N., Wootton, D., & Lindsay, D. S. (2012). Identifying the bad guy in a lineup using confidence judgments under deadline pressure. *Psychological Science, 23*(10), 1208–1214.

Brewer, W. F. (1996). What is recollective memory? In D. C. Rubin (Ed.), *Remembering our past: Studies in autobiographical memory* (pp. 19–66). Cambridge University Press.

Brigham, J. C., Bennett, L. B., Meissner, C. A., & Mitchell, T. L. (2007). The influence of race on eyewitness memory. In R. C. L. Lindsay, D. F. Ross, J. D. Read, & M. P. Toglia (Eds.), *The Handbook of Eyewitness Psychology, Vol. 2. Memory for people* (pp. 257–282). Erlbaum.

Brigham, J. C., & Malpass, R. S. (1985). The role of experience and contact in the recognition of faces of own and other-race persons. *Journal of Social Issues, 41*(3), 139–155.

Brimacombe, C. A. E., Quinton, N., Nance, N., & Garrioch, L. (1997). Is age irrelevant? Perception of young and old eyewitnesses. *Law and Human Behavior, 21*(6), 619–634.

Brown, C., & Lloyd-Jones, T. J. (2005). Verbal facilitation of face recognition. *Memory & Cognition, 33*(8), 1442–1456.

Brown, S. C., & Craik, F. I. M. (2005). Encoding and retrieval of information. In E. Tulving & Craik, F. I. M. (Eds.), *The Oxford handbook of memory* (pp. 93–107). Oxford University Press.

Bruce, V. Henderson, Z., Greenwood, K., Hancock, P. J. B., Burton, A. M. & Miller, P. (1999). Verification of face identities from images captured on video. *Journal of Experimental Psychology: Applied, 5*(4), 339–360. doi:10.1037/1076-898X.5.4.339.

Bruce, V., Henderson, Z., Newman, C., & Burton, A. M. (2001). Matching identities of familiar and unfamiliar faces caught on CCTV images. *Journal of Experimental Psychology: Applied*, 7(3), 207–218.

Bruce, V., & Young, A. (1986). Understanding face recognition. *British Journal of Psychology*, 77(3), 305–327.

Burke, A., Heuer, F., & Reisberg, D. (1992). Remembering emotional events. *Memory and Cognition*, 20(3), 277–290.

Burton, A. M., Wilson, S., Cowan, S., & Bruce, V. (1999). Face recognition in poor quality video: Evidence from security surveillance. *Psychological Science*, 10(3), 243–248.

Cabeza, R., Rao, S. M., Wagner, A. D., Mayer, A. R., & Schacter, D. L. (2001). Can medial temporal lobe regions distinguish true from false? An event-related functional MRI study of veridical and illusory recognition memory. *Proceedings of the National Academy of Sciences*, 98(8), 4805–4810.

Cacioppo, J. T. (2007). Presidential column: Psychology is a hub science. *APS Observer*, 20(8). https://www.psychologicalscience.org

Camp, G., Pecher, D., & Schmidt, H. G. (2007). No retrieval-induced forgetting using item-specific independent cues: Evidence against a general inhibitory account. *Journal of Experimental Psychology: Learning, Memory, and Cognition*, 33(5), 950–958.

Campbell, D. T., & Fiske, D. W. (1959). Convergent and discriminant validation by the multitrait-multimethod matrix. *Psychological Bulletin*, 56(2), 81–105.

Candel, I., Merckelbach, H., & Zandbergen, M. (2003). Boundary distortions for neutral and emotional pictures. *Psychonomic Bulletin and Review*, 10(3), 691–695.

Carmichael, L., Hogan, H. P., & Walter, A. A. (1932). An experimental study of the effect of language on the reproduction of visually perceived form. *Journal of Experimental Psychology*, 15(1), 73–86.

Carlson, C. A., Pleasant, W. E. Weatherford, D. R., Carlson, M. A., & Bednarz J. E. (2016). The weapon focus effect: Testing an extension of the unusualness hypothesis. *Applied Psychology in Criminal Justice*, 12(2), 87–100.

Carpenter, S. K., & DeLosh, E. L. (2006). Impoverished cue support enhances subsequent retention: Support for the elaborative retrieval explanation of the testing effect. *Memory & Cognition*, 34(2), 268–276.

Carstensen, L. L., Issacowitz, D. M., & Charles, S. T. (1999). Taking time seriously: A theory of socioemotional selectivity. *American Psychologist*, 54(3), 165–181.

Carstensen, L. L., & Mikels, J. A. (2005). At the intersection of cognition and emotion: Aging and the positivity effect. *Current Directions in Psychological Science*, 14(3), 117–121.

Carstensen, L. L., Mikels, J. A., & Mather, M. (2006). Aging and the intersection of cognition, motivation and emotion. In J. Birren & K. W. Schaie (Eds.), *Handbook of the psychology of aging* (6th ed., pp. 343–362). Academic Press.

Chambers, K. L., & Zaragoza, M. S. (2001). Intended and unintended effects of explicit warnings on eyewitness suggestibility: Evidence from source identification tests. *Memory & Cognition, 29*(8), 1120–1129.

Chan, J. C., & LaPaglia, J. A. (2013). Impairing existing declarative memory in humans by disrupting reconsolidation. *Proceedings of the National Academy of Sciences, 110*(23), 9309–9313.

Charles, S. T., Mather, M., & Carstensen, L. L. (2003). Aging and emotional memory: The forgettable nature of negative images for older adults. *Journal of Experimental Psychology: General, 132*(2), 310–324.

Charman, S. D., & Quiroz, V. (2016). Blind sequential lineup administration reduces both false identifications and confidence in those identifications. *Law and Human Behavior, 40*(5), 477–487. doi:10.1037/lhb0000197

Chase, W. G., & Simon, H. A. (1973). Perception in chess. *Cognitive Psychology, 4*(1), 55–81.

Christiansen, R. E., & Ochalek, K. (1983). Editing misleading information from memory: Evidence for the coexistence of original and postevent information. *Memory & Cognition, 11*(5), 467–475.

Christianson, S. (1992). Emotional stress and eyewitness memory: A critical review. *Psychological Bulletin, 112*(2), 284–389.

Christianson, S., & Loftus, E. F. (1991). Remembering emotional events: The fate of detailed information. *Cognition and Emotion, 5*, 81–108.

Clark, S. E. (2003). A memory and decision model for eyewitness identification. *Applied Cognitive Psychology, 17*(6), 629–654.

Clark, S. E. (2005). A re-examination of the effects of biased lineup instructions in eyewitness identification. *Law and Human Behavior, 29*(4), 395–424. doi:10.1007/s10979-005-5690-7

Clark, S. E. (2008). The importance (necessity) of computational modelling for eyewitness identification research. *Applied Cognitive Psychology, 22*(6), 803–813.

Clark, S. E., & Gronlund, S. D. (1996). Global matching models of recognition memory: How the models match the data. *Psychonomic Bulletin & Review, 3*(1), 37–60.

Clark-Foos, A., Brewer, G., & Marsh, R. L. (2015). Judging the reality of others' memories. *Memory, 23*(3), 427–436.

Clifford, B. R., & Hollin, C. R. (1981). Effects of the type of incident and the number of perpetrators on eyewitness memory. *Journal of Applied Psychology, 66*(3), 634–370.

Clifford, B. R., & Scott, J. (1978). Individual and situational factors in eyewitness testimony. *Journal of Applied Psychology, 63*(3), 352–359.

Clutterbuck, R., & Johnston, R. A. (2005). Demonstrating how unfamiliar faces become familiar using a face matching task. *European Journal of Cognitive Psychology, 17*(1), 97–116.

Cohen, N. J., & Squire, L. R. (1980). Preserved learning and retention of pattern-analyzing skill in amnesia: dissociation of knowing how and knowing that. *Science, 210*(4466), 207–210.

Cohen, R. L. (1989). Memory for action events: The power of enactment. *Educational Psychology Review, 1*(1), 57–80.

Coman, A., Manier, D., & Hirst, W. (2009). Forgetting the unforgettable through conversation: Socially shared retrieval-induced forgetting of September 11 memories. *Psychological Science, 20*(5), 627–633.

Cook, T. D., Campbell, D. T., & Day, A. (1979). *Quasi-experimentation: Design & analysis issues for field settings* (Vol. 351). Houghton Mifflin.

Cowan, N. (1999). An embedded-processes model of working memory. In A. Miyake & P. Shah (Eds.), *Models of working memory: Mechanisms of active maintenance and executive control* (pp. 62–101). Cambridge University Press.

Cowan, N., Elliott, E. M., Saults, J. S., Morey, C. C., Mattox, S., Hismjatullina, A., & Conway, A. R. (2005). On the capacity of attention: Its estimation and its role in working memory and cognitive aptitudes. *Cognitive Psychology, 51*(1), 42–100.

Craik, F. I. M. (1983). On the transfer of information from temporary to permanent memory. *Philosophical Transactions of the Royal Society of London, B, 302*(1110), 341–359.

Cuc, A., Koppel, J., & Hirst, W. (2007). Silence is not golden: A case for socially shared retrieval-induced forgetting. *Psychological Science, 18*(8), 727–733.

Cutler, B. L. (2013). *Reform of eyewitness identification procedures*. American Psychological Association Press.

Cutler, B. L., Penrod, S. D., & Dexter, H. R. (1990). Juror sensitivity to eyewitness identification evidence. *Law and Human Behavior, 14*(2), 185–191.

Cutler, B. L., Penrod, S. D., & Stuve, T. E. (1988). Juror decision making in eyewitness identification cases. *Law and Human Behavior, 12*(1), 41–55.

Darling, S., Valentine, T., & Memon, A. (2008). Selection of lineup foils in operational contexts. *Applied Cognitive Psychology, 22*(2), 159–168. https://doi.org/10.1002/acp.1366

Davies, G., Shepherd, J., & Ellis, H. (1979). Effects of interpolated mugshot exposure on accuracy of eyewitness identification. *Journal of Applied Psychology, 64*(2), 232–237.

Davis, D., & Loftus, E. F. (2007) Internal and external sources of misinformation in adult witness memory. In M. P. Toglia, J. D. Read, D. F. Ross, & R. C. L. Lindsay (Eds.), *Handbook of Eyewitness Psychology, Vol. 1. Memory for events* (pp. 195–237). Erlbaum.

Davis, G., Tarrant, A., & Flin, R. (1989). Close encounters of the witness kind. Children's memory for a simulated health inspection. *British Journal of Psychology, 80*(4), 415–429.

DeCarlo, L. T. (2003). An application of signal detection theory with finite mixture distributions to source discrimination. *Journal of Experimental Psychology: Learning, Memory, and Cognition, 29*(5), 767–778.

Deese, J. (1959). Influence of inter-item associative strength upon immediate free recall. *Psychological Reports, 5*(3), 305–312.

Deffenbacher, K. A., Bornstein, B. H., McGorty, E. K., & Penrod, S. D. (2008). Forgetting the once-seen face: Estimating the strength of an eyewitness's memory representation. *Journal of Experimental Psychology: Applied, 14*(2), 139–150.

Deffenbacher, K. A., Bornstein, B. H., & Penrod, S. D. (2006). Mugshot exposure effects: Retroactive interference, mugshot commitment, source confusion, and unconscious transference. *Law and Human Behavior, 30*(3), 287.

Deffenbacher, K. A., Bornstein, B. H., Penrod. S. D., & McGorty, E. K. (2004). A meta-analytic review of the effects of high stress on eyewitness memory. *Law & Human Behavior, 28*(6), 687–706.

Deffenbacher, K. A., & Loftus, E. F. (1982). Do jurors share a common understanding concerning eyewitness behavior? *Law and Human Behavior, 6*(1), 15–30.

Dent, H., & Stephenson, G. (1979). An experimental study of the effectiveness of different techniques of questioning child witnesses. *British Journal of Social and Clinical Psychology, 18*(1), 41–51.

Desmarais, S. L., & Read, J. D. (2011). After 30 years, what do we know about what jurors know? A meta-analytic review of lay knowledge regarding eyewitness factors. *Law and Human Behavior, 35*(3), 200–210.

Diana, R. A., Reder, L. M., Arndt, J., & Park, H. (2006). Models of recognition: A review of arguments in favour of a dual process account. *Psychological Bulletin and Review, 13*(1), 1–21.

Dobbins, I. G., Rice, H. J., Wagner, A. D., & Schacter, D. L. (2003). Memory orientation and success: Separable neurocognitive components underlying episodic recognition. *Neuropsychologia, 41*(3), 318–333.

Dodson, C. S., & Schacter, D. L. (2002). When false recognition meets metacognition: The distinctiveness heuristic. *Journal of Memory and Language, 46*(4), 782–803.

Donaldson, W. (1996). The role of decision processes in remembering and knowing. *Memory & Cognition, 24*(4), 523–533.

Dougal, S., & Rotello, C. M. (2007). "Remembering" emotional words is based on response bias, not recollection. *Psychonomic Bulletin & Review, 14*(3), 423–429.

D'Souza, D. C., Perry, E., MacDougall, L., Ammerman, Y., Cooper, T., Wu, Y-T, Braley, G., Gueorguieva, R., & Krustal, J. H. (2004). The psychotomimetic effects of intravenous delta-9-tetrahydrocannabinol in healthy individuals: implications for psychosis. *Neuropsychopharmacology, 29*(8), 1558–1572.

Dubois, S., Rossion, B., Schiltz, C., Bodart, D, M., Michel, C., Bruyer, R., & Crommelinck, M. (1999). Effects of familiarity on the processing of human faces. *NeuroImage, 9*(3), 278–289.

Dudukovic, N. M., Marsh, E. J., & Tversky, B. (2004). Telling a story or telling it straight: The effects of entertaining versus accurate retellings on memory. *Applied Cognitive Psychology, 18*(2), 125–143.

Dunlosky, J., & Hertzog, C. (2000). Updating knowledge about encoding strategies: A componential analysis of learning about strategy effectiveness from task experience. *Psychology and Aging, 15*(3), 462–474.

Dunn, J. C. (2004). Remember-know: A matter of confidence. *Psychological Review, 111*(2), 524–542.

Dunn, J. C., & Kirsner, K. (2011). The search or HMAS Sydney II: Analysis and integration of survivor reports. *Applied Cognitive Psychology, 25*(3), 513–527.

Dysart, J. E., & Lindsay, R. C. L. (2007). Show-up identifications: Suggestive technique or reliable method? In R. C. L. Lindsay, D. F. Ross, J. D. Read, & M. P. Toglia (Eds.), *The Handbook of Eyewitness Psychology, Vol. 2. Memory for people* (pp. 137–153). Erlbaum.

Dysart, J. E, Lindsay, R. C. L., & Dupuis, P. R. (2006). Show-ups: The critical issue of clothing bias. *Applied Cognitive Psychology, 20*(8), 1009–1023.

Easterbrook, J. A. (1959). The effect of emotion on cue utilisation and the organisation of behavior. *Psychological Review, 66*(3), 183–201.

Ebaid, D., & Crewther, S. G. (2018). Temporal aspects of memory: A comparison of memory performance, processing speed and time estimation between young and older adults. *Frontiers in Aging Neuroscience, 10*, Article 352. doi:10.3389/fnagi.2018.00352

Ebbesen, E. B., & Konecni, V. J. (1996). Eyewitness memory research: Probative v. prejudicial value. *Expert Evidence, 5*(3), 2–28.

Edelstein, R. S., Alexander, K. W., Goodman, G. S., & Newton, J. W. (2004). Emotion and eyewitness memory. In D. Reisberg & P. Hertel (Eds.), *Memory and emotion* (pp. 272–307). Oxford University Press.

Eldridge, L. L., Sarfatti, S., & Knowlton, B. J. (2002). The effect of testing procedure on remember-know judgments. *Psychonomic Bulletin & Review, 9*(1), 139–145.

Ellis, H. D., Deregowski, J. B., & Shepherd, J. W. (1975). Descriptions of White and Black faces by White and Black subjects. *International Journal of Psychology, 10*(2), 119–123.

Ellis, H. D., Shepherd, J. W., & Davies, G. M. (1979). Identification of familiar and unfamiliar faces from internal and external features: Some implications for theories of face recognition. *Perception, 8*(4), 431–439. doi:10.1068/p080431

Ellis, H. D., Shepherd, J. W., & Davies, G. M. (1980). The deterioration of verbal descriptions of faces over different delay intervals. *Journal of Political Science and Administration, 8*(1), 101–106.

Elsey, J. W., Van Ast, V. A., & Kindt, M. (2018). Human memory reconsolidation: A guiding framework and critical review of the evidence. *Psychological Bulletin, 144*(8), 797–848.

Engle, R. W. (2001). What is working memory capacity? In H. L. Roediger, J. S. Nairne, I. Neath, & A. M. Suprenant (Eds.), *The nature of remembering: Essays in honor of Robert G. Crowder* (pp. 297–314). American Psychological Association.

Evans, J. R., Meissner, C. A., Brandon, S. E., Russano, M. R., & Kleinman, S. M. (2010). Criminal versus HUMINT interrogations: The importance of psychological science to improving interrogative practice. *Journal of Psychiatry & Law, 38*(1–2), 215–249.

Evans, J. R., Schreiber Compo, N., & Russano, M. B. (2009). Intoxicated witnesses and suspects: Procedures and prevalence according to law enforcement. *Psychology, Public Policy, and Law, 15*(3), 194–221. doi:10.1037/a0016837

Fabiani, M., Stadler, M. A., & Wessels, P. M. (2000). True but not false memories produce a sensory signature in human lateralized brain potentials. *Journal of Cognitive Neuroscience, 12*(6), 941–949.

Falshore, M., & Schooler, J. W. (1995). The verbal vulnerability of perceptual expertise. *Journal of Experimental Psychology: Learning, Memory and Cognition, 21*(6), 1608–1623.

Fawcett, J. M., Peace, K. A., & Greve, A. (2016). Looking down the barrel of a gun: What do we know about the weapon focus effect? *Journal of Applied Research in Memory and Cognition, 5*, 257–263.

Ferguson, S. A., Hashtroudi, S., & Johnson, M. K. (1992). Age differences in using source-relevant cues. *Psychology and Aging, 7*(3), 443–452.

Festinger, L. (1962). Cognitive dissonance. *Scientific American, 207*, 93–106.

Finegold, G. A. (1914). The influence of environment on the identification of persons and things. *Journal of Criminal Law and Political Science, 5*, 39–51.

Fisher, R., & Schreiber, N. (2007). Interviewing protocols to imporove eyewitness memory. In M. Toglia, R. Lindsay, D. Ross, & J. D. Read (Eds.), *The Handbook for Eyewitness Psychology: Vol. 1. Memory for events* (pp. 53–80). Erlbaum.

Fisher, R. P., Brewer, N. and Mitchell, G. (2009). The relation between consistency and accuracy of eyewitness testimony: Legal versus cognitive explanations. In R. Bull, T. Valentine, & T. Williamson (Eds.), *Handbook of psychology of investigative interviewing: Current developments and future directions* (pp. 121–136). Wiley-Blackwell.

Fisher, R. P., & Geiselman, R. E. (1992). *Memory enhancing techniques for investigative interviewing: The Cognitive Interview*. Charles C Thomas.

Fitzgerald, R. J., Price, H. L., Oriet, C., & Charman, S. D. (2013). The effect of suspect-filler similarity on eyewitness identification decisions: A meta-analysis. *Psychology, Public Policy, and Law, 19*(2), 151–164. doi:10.1037/a0030618

Flowe, H., Ebbesen, E. B., Burke, C., & Chivabunditt, P. (2001, July). *At the scene of the crime: An examination of the external validity of published studies on line-up identification accuracy* [Paper presentation]. American Psychology Society Annual Convention, Toronto, Ontario, Canada.

Freyd, J. J., & Gleaves, D. H. (1996). "Remembering" words not presented in lists: Relevance to the current recovered/false memory controversy. *Journal of Experimental Psychology: Learning, Memory, and Cognition, 22*(3), 811–813.

Frith, C. D. (2012). The role of metacognition in human social interactions. *Philosophical Transactions of the Royal Society B: Biological Sciences, 367*(1599), 2213–2223.

Fung, H. H., & Carstensen, L. L. (2003). Sending memorable messages to the old: Age differences in preferences and memory for advertisements. *Journal of Personality and Social Psychology, 85*(1), 163–178.

Gabbert, F., Hope, L., & Fisher, R. P. (2009). Protecting eyewitness evidence: Examining the efficacy of a self-administered interview tool. *Law and Human Behavior, 33*(4), 298–307.

Gabbert, F., Memon, A., Allan, K., & Wright, D. B. (2004). Say it to my face: Examining the effects of socially encountered misinformation. *Legal and Criminological Psychology, 9*(2), 215–227.

Gabbert, F., Memon, A., & Wright, D. B. (2006). Memory conformity: Disentangling the steps toward influence during a discussion. *Psychonomic Bulletin & Review, 13*(3), 480–485.

Gallo, D. A. (2004). Using recall to reduce false recognition: Diagnostic and disqualifying monitoring. *Journal of Experimental Psychology: Learning, Memory, and Cognition, 30*(1), 120–128.

Gallo, D. A. (2010). False memories and fantastic beliefs: 15 years of the DRM illusion. *Memory & Cognition, 38*(7), 833–848.

Gallo, D. (2013). *Associative illusions of memory: False memory research in DRM and related tasks.* Psychology Press.

Gallo, D. A., McDonough, I. M., & Scimeca, J. (2010). Dissociating source memory decisions in the prefrontal cortex: fMRI of diagnostic and disqualifying monitoring. *Journal of Cognitive Neuroscience, 22*(5), 955–969.

Gallo, D. A., Roberts, M. J., & Seamon, J. G. (1997) Remembering words not presented in lists: Can we avoid creating false memories? *Psychonomic Bulletin & Review, 4*(2), 271–276.

Gallo, D. A., Weiss, J. A., & Schacter, D. L. (2004). Reducing false recognition with criterial recollection tests: Distinctiveness heuristic versus criterion shifts. *Journal of Memory and Language, 51*(3), 473–493.

Gardiner, J. M., & Java, R. I. (1990). Recollective experience in word and nonword judgments. *Memory & Cognition, 18*(1), 23–30.

Gardiner, J. M., & Java, R. I. (1993). Recognizing and remembering. In A. Collins, S. Gathercole, & P. Morris (Eds.), *Theories of memory* (pp. 163–188). Erlbaum.

Gardiner, J. M., & Parkin, A. J. (1990). Attention and recollective experience in recognition memory. *Memory & Cognition, 18*(6), 579–583.

Gardiner, J. M., Ramponi, C., & Richardson-Klavehn, A. (2002). Recognition memory and decision processes: A meta-analysis of remember, know, and guess responses. *Memory, 10*(2), 83–98.

Garner, W. R., Hake, H. W., & Eriksen, C. W. (1956). Operationism and the concept of perception. *Psychological Review, 63*(3), 149–159.

Garry, M., Manning, C. G., Loftus, E. F., & Sherman, S. J. (1996). Imagination inflation: Imagining a childhood event inflates confidence that it occurred. *Psychonomic Bulletin & Review, 3*(2), 208–214.

Gates, A. I. (1917). *Recitation as a factor in memorizing* (Archives of Psychology, No. 40). The Science Press.

Gawrylowicz, J., Memon, A., & Scoboria, A. (2014). Equipping witnesses with transferable skills: The Self-Administered Interview©. *Psychology, Crime & Law, 20*(4), 315–325.

Geiselman, R. E., & Fisher, R. P. (1989). The cognitive interview technique for victims and witnesses of crime. In D. C. Raskin (Ed.), *Psychological methods in criminal investigation and evidence* (p. 191–215). Springer.

Geiselman, R. E., Fisher, R. P., Cohen, G., Holland, H., & Surtes, L. (1986). Eyewitness responses to leading and misleading questions under the cognitive interview. *Journal of Police Science & Administration, 14*(1), 31–39.

Geraerts, E., Lindsay, D. S., Merckelbach, H., Jelicic, M., Raymaekers, L., Arnold, M. M., & Schooler, J. W. (2009). Cognitive mechanisms underlying recovered-memory experiences of childhood sexual abuse. *Psychological Science, 20*(1), 92–98.

Geraerts, E., McNally, R. J., Jelicic, M., Merckelbach, H., & Raymaekers, L. (2008). Linking thought suppression and recovered memories of childhood sexual abuse. *Memory, 16*(1), 22–28.

Ghetti, S., & Castelli, P. (2006). Developmental differences in false-event rejection: Effects of memorability-based warnings. *Memory, 14*(6), 762–776.

Gillund, G., & Shiffrin, R. M. (1984). A retrieval model for both recognition and recall. *Psychological Review, 91*(1), 1–67.

Goff, L. M., & Roediger, H. L. (1998). Imagination inflation for action events: Repeated imaginings lead to illusory recollections. *Memory & Cognition, 26*(1), 20–33.

Goldstein, A. G., & Chance, J. E. (1980). Memory for faces and schema theory. *Journal of Psychology, 105*(1), 47–59.

Goodman, G. S., Taub, E. P., Jones, D. P. H., England, P., Port, L. K., Rudy, L., Prado, L., Myers, J. E. B., & Melton, G. B. (1992). Testifying in criminal court: Emotional effects on child sexual assault victims. *Monographs of the Society for Research in Child Development, 57*(5), 1–155.

Gonsalves, B., Reber, P. J., Gitelman, D. R., Parrish, T. B., Mesulam, M. M., & Paller, K. A. (2004). Neural evidence that vivid imagining can lead to false remembering. *Psychological Science, 15*(10), 655–660.

Graf, P., & Schacter, D. L. (1985). Implicit and explicit memory for new associations in normal and amnesic subjects. *Journal of Experimental Psychology: Learning, Memory, and Cognition, 11*(3), 501–518.

Gronlund, S. D., Wixted, J. T., & Mickes, L. (2014). Evaluating eyewitness identification procedures using receiver operating characteristic analysis. *Current Directions in Psychological Science, 23*(1), 3–10.

Han, S., & Dobbins, I. G. (2009). Regulating recognition decisions through incremental reinforcement learning. *Psychonomic Bulletin & Review, 16*(3), 469–474.

Hartwig, M., & Bond, C. F. (2014). Lie detection from multiple cues: A meta-analysis. *Applied Cognitive Psychology, 28*(5), 661–676.

Hassabis, D., & Maguire, E. A. (2007). Deconstructing episodic memory with construction. *Trends in Cognitive Sciences, 11*(7), 299–306.

Haw, R. M., Dickinson, J. J., & Meissner, C. A. (2007). The phenomenology of carryover effects between showup and lineup identification. *Memory, 15*(1), 117–127.

Heaps, C. M., & Nash, M. (2001). Comparing recollective experience in true and false autobiographical memories. *Journal of Experimental Psychology: Learning, Memory, and Cognition, 27*(4), 920–930.

Helmholtz, H. V. (1867). LXIII. On Integrals of the hydrodynamical equations, which express vortex-motion. *The London, Edinburgh, and Dublin Philosophical Magazine and Journal of Science, 33*(226), 485–512.

Herrmann, D., & Gruneberg, M. (1993). The need to expand the horizons of the practical aspects of memory movement. *Applied Cognitive Psychology, 7*(7), 553–565.

Heuer, F., & Reisberg, D. (1990). Vivid memories of emotional events: The accuracy of remembered minutiae. *Memory, 18*(5), 496–506.

Hicks, J. L., & Marsh, R. L. (2001). False recognition occurs more frequently during source identification than during old–new recognition. *Journal of Experimental Psychology: Learning, Memory, and Cognition, 27*(2), 375–383.

Hintzman, D. L. (1988). Judgments of frequency and recognition memory in a multiple-trace memory model. *Psychological Review, 95*(4), 528–551.

Hintzman, D. L., & Curran, T. (1994). Retrieval dynamics of recognition and frequency judgments: Evidence for separate processes of familiarity and recall. *Journal of Memory and Language, 33*(1), 1–18.

Hirst, W., & Echterhoff, G. (2012). Remembering in conversations: The social sharing and reshaping of memories. *Annual Review of Psychology, 63*(1), 55–79.

Hornberger, M., Morcom, A. M., & Rugg, M. D. (2004). Neural correlates of retrieval orientation: Effects of study-test similarity. *Journal of Cognitive Neuroscience, 16*(7), 1196–1210.

Hope, L., Gabbert, F., Fisher, R. P., & Jamieson, K. (2014). Protecting and enhancing eyewitness memory: The impact of an initial recall attempt on performance in an investigative interview. *Applied Cognitive Psychology, 28*(3), 304–313.

Hosch, H. M., Jolly, K. W., Schmersal, L. A., & Smith, B. A. (2009). Expert psychology testimony on eyewitness identification: Consensus among experts? In B. L. Cutler (Ed.), *Expert testimony on the psychology of eyewitness identification* (pp. 143–168). Oxford University Press.

Houston, K. A., Clifford, B. R., Phillips, L. H., & Memon, A. (2013). The emotional eyewitness: The effects of emotion on specific aspects of eyewitness recall and recognition performance. *Emotion, 13*(1), 118–128.

Hyman, I. E., & Faries, J. M. (1992). The functions of autobiographical memory. In M. A. Conway, D. C. Rubin, H. S. Pinnler, & W. A. Wagenaar (Eds.), *Theoretical perspectives on autobiographical memory* (pp. 207–221). Springer.

Hyman Jr, I. E., & Pentland, J. (1996). The role of mental imagery in the creation of false childhood memories. *Journal of Memory and Language, 35*(2), 101–117.

The Innocence Project. (2019a). *Troy Webb*. https://www.innocenceproject.org/

The Innocence Project. (2019b). *Vincent Moto*. https://www.innocenceproject.org

The Innocence Project. (2019c). *Eyewitness identification reform*. https://www.innocenceproject.org/

The Innocence Project. (2019d). *Ronald Cotton*. https://www.innocenceproject.org/

The Innocence Project. (2020). *DNA Exonerations in the United States*. https://www.innocenceproject.org/

Israel, L., & Schacter, D. L. (1997). Pictorial encoding reduces false recognition of semantic associates. *Psychonomic Bulletin & Review, 4*(4), 577–581.

Ito, T. A., Cacioppo, T. A., & Lang, P. J. (1998). Eliciting affect using the international affective picture system: Trajectories through evaluative space. *Personality and Social Psychology Bulletin, 24*(8), 855–879.

Itoh, Y. (2005). The facilitating effect of verbalization on the recognition memory of incidentally learned faces. *Applied Cognitive Psychology, 19*(4), 421–433. doi:10.1002/acp.1069

Jacoby, L. L. (1991). A process dissociation framework: Separating automatic from intentional uses of memory. *Journal of Memory and Language, 30*(5), 513–541.

Jacoby, L. L., Kelley, C., Brown, J., & Jashecko, J. (1989). Becoming famous overnight: Limits on the availability to avoid unconscious influences of the past. *Journal of Personality and Social Psychology, 56*(3), 326–338.

Jacoby, L. L., Kelley, C. M., & Dywan, J. (1989). Memory attributions. In H. L. Roediger III & F. I. M. Craik (Eds.), *Varieties of memory and consciousness: Essays in honour of Endel Tulving* (pp. 391–422). Erlbaum.

Jacoby, L. L., Kelley, C. M., & McElree, B. D. (1999). The role of cognitive control: Early selection vs. late correction. In S. Chaiken & Y. Trope (Eds.), *Dual-process theories in social psychology* (pp. 383–400). Guilford Press.

Jacoby, L. L., Shimizu, Y., Daniels, K. A., & Rhodes, M. G. (2005). Modes of cognitive control in recognition and source memory: Depth of retrieval. *Psychonomic Bulletin & Review, 12*(5), 852–857.

Jacoby, L. L., Woloshyn, V., & Kelley, C. (1989). Becoming famous without being recognized: Unconscious influences of memory produced by dividing attention. *Journal of Experimental Psychology: General, 118*(2), 115–125.

Jaeger, A., Cox, J. C., & Dobbins, I. G. (2012). Recognition confidence under violated and confirmed memory expectations. *Journal of Experimental Psychology: General, 141*(2), 282–301.

James, W. (1890), *The Principles of Psychology*. Dover.

Johnson, M. K. (1992). MEM: Mechanisms of recollection. *Journal of Cognitive Neuroscience, 4*(3), 268–280.

Johnson, M. K., Bush, J. G., & Mitchell, K. J. (1998). Interpersonal reality monitoring: Judging the sources of other people's memories. *Social Cognition, 16*(2), 199–224.

Johnson, M. K., & Chalfonte, B. L. (1994). Binding complex memories: The role of reactivation and the hippocampus. In D. L. Schacter & E. Tulving (Eds.), *Memory systems 1994* (pp. 311–350). MIT Press.

Johnson, M. K., Foley, M. A., Suengas, A. G., & Raye, C. L. (1988). Phenomenal characteristics of memories for perceived and imagined autobiographical events. *Journal of Experimental Psychology: General*, 117(4), 371–376.

Johnson, M. K., Hashtroudi, S., & Lindsay, D. S. (1993). Source monitoring. *Psychological Bulletin*, 114(1), 3–28.

Johnson, M. K., & Raye, C. L. (1981). Reality monitoring. *Psychological Review*, 88(1), 67–85.

Johnson, M. K., & Raye, C. L. (2000). Cognitive and brain mechanisms of false memories and beliefs. In D. L. Schacter & E. Scarry (Eds.), *Memory and belief* (pp. 35–86). Harvard University Press.

Johnson, M. K., Raye, C. L., Mitchell, K. J., & Ankudowich, E. (2011). The cognitive neuroscience of true and false memories. In R. F. Belli (Ed.), *True and false recovered memories: Toward a reconciliation of the debate* (Vol. 58, Nebraska Symposium on Motivation, pp. 15–52). Springer.

Johnson, M. K., Raye, C. L., Mitchell, K. J., Greene, E. J., Cunningham, W. A., & Sanislow, C. A. (2005). Using fMRI to investigate a component process of reflection: Prefrontal correlates of refreshing a just-activated representation. *Cognitive, Affective, & Behavioral Neuroscience*, 5(3), 339–361.

Johnson, M. K., Raye, C. L., Wang, A. Y., & Taylor, T. H. (1979). Fact and fantasy: The roles of accuracy and variability in confusing imaginations with perceptual experiences. *Journal of Experimental Psychology: Human Learning and Memory*, 5(3), 229–240.

Johnson, M. K., & Sherman, S. J. (1990). Constructing and reconstructing the past and the future in the present. In E. T. Higgins & R. M. Sorrentino (Eds.), *Handbook of motivation and social cognition: Foundations of social behavior* (pp. 482–526). Guilford Press.

Johnson, M. K., & Suengas, A. G. (1989). Reality monitoring judgments of other people's memories. *Bulletin of the Psychonomic Society*, 27(2), 107–110.

Johnson, M. R., Mitchell, K. J., Raye, C. L., D'Esposito, M., & Johnson, M. K. (2007). A brief thought can modulate activity in extrastriate visual areas: Top-down effects of refreshing just-seen visual stimuli. *NeuroImage*, 37(1), 290–299.

Jones, E. E., Williams, K. D., & Brewer, N. (2008). "I had a confidence epiphany!": Obstacles to combating post-identification confidence inflation. *Law and Human Behavior*, 32(2), 164–176.

Juslin, P., Olsson, N., & Winman, A. (1996). Calibration and diagnosticity of confidence in eyewitness identification: Comments on what can be inferred from the low confidence–accuracy correlation. *Journal of Experimental Psychology: Learning, Memory, and Cognition*, 22(5), 1304–1316.

Kane, M. J., Conway, A. R. A., Hambrick, D. Z., & Engle, R. W. (2007). Variation in working-memory capacity as variation in executive attention and control. In A. R. A. Conway, C. Jarrold, M. J. Kane, A. Miyake, & J. Towse (Eds.), *Variation in working memory* (pp. 21–48). Oxford University Press.

Kane, M. J., Bleckley, M. K., Conway, A. R., & Engle, R. W. (2001). A controlled-attention view of working-memory capacity. *Journal of Experimental Psychology: General, 130*(2), 169–183.

Kantner, J., & Lindsay, D. S. (2010). Can corrective feedback improve recognition memory? *Memory and Cognition, 38*(4), 389–406.

Kantner, J., & Lindsay, D. S. (2012). Response bias in recognition memory as a cognitive trait. *Memory and Cognition, 40*(8), 1163–1177.

Karpel, M. E., Hoyer, W. J., & Toglia, M. P. (2001). Accuracy and qualities of real and suggested memories nonspecific age differences. *The Journals of Gerontology Series B: Psychological Sciences and Social Sciences, 56*(2), 103–110.

Kassin, S. M., & Barndollar, K. A. (1992). The psychology of eyewitness testimony: A comparison of experts and prospective jurors. *Journal of Applied Social Psychology, 22*(16), 1241–1241.

Kassin, S. M., Drizin, S. A., Grisso, T., Gudjonsson, G. H., Leo, R. A., & Redlich, A. D. (2009). Police-induced confessions: risk factors and recommendations. *Law and Human Behavior, 34*(1), 3–38. doi:10.1007/s10979-009-9188-6

Kassin, S. M., Leo, R. A., Meissner, C. A., Richman, K. D., Colwell, L. H., Leach, A.-M., & Fon, D. (2007). Police interviewing and interrogation: A self-report survey of police practices and beliefs. *Law and Human Behavior, 31*(4), 381–400.

Kassin, S. M., Tubb, V. A., Hosch, H. M., & Memon, A. (2001). On the "general acceptance" of eyewitness testimony research: A new survey of the experts. *American Psychologist, 56*(5), 405–416.

Kensinger, E. A. (2009a). Remembering the details: Effects of emotion. *Emotion Review, 1*(2), 99–113.

Kensinger, E. A. (2009b). How emotion affects older adults' memories for event details. *Memory, 17*(2), 208–219.

Keogh, L., & Markham, R. (1998). Judgements of other people's memory reports: Differences in reports as a function of imagery vividness. *Applied Cognitive Psychology, 12*(2), 159–171.

Kersten, D., Mamassian, P., & Yuille, A. (2004). Object perception as Bayesian inference. *Annual Review of Psychology, 55*, 271–304.

Knott, L. M., Howe, M. L., Toffalini, E., Shah, D., & Humphreys, L. (2018). The role of attention in immediate emotional false memory enhancement. *Emotion, 18*(8), 1063–1077. doi:10.1037/emo0000407

Knutsson, J., Allwood, C. M., & Johansson, M. (2011). Child and adult witnesses: The effect of repetition and invitation-probes on free recall and metamemory realism. *Metacognition and Learning, 6*(3), 213–228.

Köhnken, G., Milne, R., Memon, A., & Bull, R. (1999). The cognitive interview: A meta-analysis. *Psychology, Crime and Law, 5*(1–2), 3–27.

Kolers, P. A., & Roediger, H. L. (1984). Procedures of mind. *Journal of Verbal Learning and Verbal Behavior, 23*(4), 425–449.

Koriat, A., Bjork, R. A., Sheffer, L., & Bar, S. K. (2004). Predicting one's own forgetting: The role of experience-based and theory-based processes. *Journal of Experimental Psychology: General, 133*(4), 643–656.

Koriat, A., & Goldsmith, M. (1996). Monitoring and control processes in the strategic regulation of memory accuracy. *Psychological Review, 103*(3), 490–517.

Kosslyn, S. M., & Thompson, W. L. (2000). Shared mechanisms in visual imagery and visual perception: Insights from cognitive neuroscience. In M. S. Gazzaniga (Ed.), *The new cognitive neurosciences* (2nd ed., pp. 975–986). MIT Press.

Kovera, M. B., & Evelo, A. J. (2017). The case for double-blind lineup administration. *Psychology, Public Policy, and Law, 23*(4), 421–437. doi:10.1037/law0000139

Kramer, R. S. S., Young, A. W., & Burton, A. M. (2018). Understanding face familiarity. *Cognition, 172*(1), 46–58. doi:10.1016/j.cognition.2017.12.005

Kramer, T. H., Buckhout, R., & Eugenio, P. (1990). Weapon focus, arousal and eyewitness memory: Attention must be paid. *Law and Human Behavior, 14*(2), 167–184.

Kramer, T. H., Manesi, Z., Towler, A., Reynolds, M. G., & Burton, A. M. (2018). Familiarity and within-person facial variability: The importance of internal and external features. *Perception, 47*(1), 3–15. doi:10.1177/0301006617725242

Kuehn, L. L. (1974). Looking down a gun barrel: Person descriptions and violent crime. *Perceptual and Motor Skills, 39*(3), 1159–1164.

Lampinen, J. M., Meier, C. R., Arnal, J. D., & Leding, J. K. (2005). Compelling untruths: content borrowing and vivid false memories. *Journal of Experimental Psychology: Learning, Memory, and Cognition, 31*(5), 954–963.

Lampinen, J. M., Neuschatz, J. S., & Cling, A. D. (2012). *Psychology of eyewitness memory*. Psychological Press.

Lampinen, J. M., Neuschatz, J. S., & Payne, D. G. (1998). Memory illusions and consciousness: Examining the phenomenology of true and false memories. *Current Psychology, 16*(3–4), 181–224.

Lampinen, J. M., Odegard, T., & Neuschatz, J. S. (2004). Robust recollection rejection in the memory conjunction paradigm. *Journal of Experimental Psychology: Learning, Memory, and Cognition, 30*(2), 332–342.

Lampinen, J, M., Ryals, B. D., & Smith, K. (2008). Compelling untruths: The effect of retention interval on content borrowing and vivid false memories. *Memory, 16*(2), 149–156.

Lane, S. M. (2006). Dividing attention during a witnessed event increases eyewitness suggestibility. *Applied Cognitive Psychology, 20*(2), 199–212.

Lane, S. M., & Karam-Zanders, T. (2014). What do people know about memory? In T. J. Perfect & D. S. Lindsay (Eds.), *The SAGE handbook of applied memory* (pp. 348–365). Sage Publications.

Lane, S. M., Mather, M., Villa, D., & Morita, S. (2001). How events are reviewed matters: Effects of varied focus on eyewitness suggestibility. *Memory & Cognition, 29*(7), 940–947.

Lane, S. M., & Meissner, C. A. (2008). A 'middle road' approach to bridging the basic-applied divide in eyewitness identification research. *Applied Cognitive Psychology*, 22(6), 779–787.

Lane, S. M., Roussel, C. C., Villa, D., & Morita, S. (2007). Features and feedback: Enhancing metamnemonic knowledge at retrieval reduces source monitoring errors. *Journal of Experimental Psychology: Learning, Memory & Cognition*, 33(6), 1131–1142.

Lane, S. M., Roussel, C. C., Villa, D., Starns, J. J., & Alonzo, J. D. (2008). Providing information about diagnostic features at retrieval reduces false recognition. *Memory*, 16(6), 836–851.

Lane, S. M., & Zaragoza, M. S. (1995). The recollective experience of cross-modality source confusions. *Memory and Cognition*, 23(5), 607–610.

Lane, S. M., & Zaragoza, M. S. (2007). A little elaboration goes a long way: The role of generation in eyewitness suggestibility. *Memory and Cognition*, 35(6), 1255–1266.

Laney, C., Campbell, H. V., Heuer, F., & Reisberg, D. (2004). Memory for thematically arousing events. *Memory and Cognition*, 32(7), 1149–1159.

Laney, C., Heuer, F., & Reisberg, D. (2003). Thematically-induced arousal in naturally-occurring emotional memories. *Applied Cognitive Psychology*, 17(8), 995–1004.

La Rooy, D., Pipe, M. E., & Murray, J. E. (2005). Reminiscence and hypermnesia in children's eyewitness memory. *Journal of Experimental Child Psychology*, 90(3), 235–254.

Laughery, K. R., Alexander, J. F., & Lane, A. B. (1971). Recognition of human faces: Effects of target exposure time, target position, pose position and type of photograph. *Journal of Applied Psychology*, 55(5), 477–483.

LePort, A. K., Mattfeld, A. T., Dickinson-Anson, H., Fallon, J. H., Stark, C. E., Kruggel, F., & McGaugh, J. L. (2012). Behavioral and neuroanatomical investigation of highly superior autobiographical memory (HSAM). *Neurobiology of Learning and Memory*, 98(1), 78–92.

Levine, L. J., & Edelstein, R. S. (2009). Emotion and memory narrowing: A review and goal-relevance approach. *Cognition and Emotion*, 23(5), 833–875.

Levine, L. J., & Pizarro, D. A. (2004). Emotion and memory research: A grumpy review. *Social Cognition*, 22(5), 530–554.

Levy, B. J., & Wagner, A. D. (2013). Measuring memory reactivation with functional MRI implications for psychological theory. *Perspectives on Psychological Science*, 8(1), 72–78.

Lindsay, D. S. (1990). Misleading suggestions can impair eyewitnesses' ability to remember event details. *Journal of Experimental Psychology: Learning, Memory, and Cognition*, 16(6), 1077–1083.

Lindsay, D. S. (2008). Source monitoring. In J. Byrne (Series Ed.) & H. L. Roediger, III (Vol. Ed.), *Learning and Memory: A Comprehensive Reference, Vol. 2. Cognitive psychology of memory* (pp. 325–348). Elsevier.

Lindsay, D. S., (2014). Memory source monitoring applied. In T. Perfect & D. S. Lindsay (Eds.), *SAGE handbook of applied memory* (pp 59–75). SAGE Publications.

Lindsay, D. S., & Briere, J. (1997). The controversy regarding recovered memories of childhood sexual abuse pitfalls, bridges, and future directions. *Journal of Interpersonal Violence*, 12(5), 631–647.

Lindsay, D. S., & Johnson, M. K. (1989). The eyewitness suggestibility effect and memory for source. *Memory & Cognition*, 17(3), 349–358.

Lindsay, D. S., & Johnson, M. K. (2000). False memories and the source monitoring framework: A reply to Reyna and Lloyd (1997). *Learning and Individual Differences*, 12(2), 145–161.

Lindsay, D. S., Johnson, M. K., & Kwon, P. (1991). Developmental changes in memory source monitoring. *Journal of Experimental Child Psychology*, 52(3), 297–318.

Lindsay, D. S., & Kantner, J. (2011). A search for influences of feedback on recognition of music, poetry, and art. In P. Higham & J. Leboe (Eds.), *Constructions of remembering and metacognition: Essays in honour of Bruce Whittlesea* (pp. 137–154). Palgrave Macmillan.

Lindsay, D. S., & Read, J. D. (1994). Psychotherapy and memories of childhood sexual abuse: A cognitive perspective. *Applied Cognitive Psychology*, 8(4), 281–338.

Lindsay, D. S., Read, J. D., & Sharma, K. (1998). Accuracy and confidence in person identification: The relationship is strong when witnessing conditions vary widely. *Psychological Science*, 9(3), 215–218.

Lindsay, R. C., Wells, G. L., & O'Connor, F. J. (1989). Mock-juror belief of accurate and inaccurate eyewitnesses. *Law and Human Behavior*, 13(3), 333–339.

Lindsay, R. C. L., Martin, R., & Webber, L. (1994). Default values in eyewitness descriptions. A problem for the match-to-description lineup foil selection strategy. *Law and Human Behavior*, 18(5), 527–541.

Loftus, E. F. (1993). The reality of repressed memories. *American psychologist*, 48(5), 518–537.

Loftus, E. F., Loftus, G. R., & Messo, J. (1987). Some facts about "weapon focus." *Law and Human Behavior*, 11(1), 55–62.

Loftus, E. F., Miller, D. G., & Burns, H. J. (1978). Semantic integration of verbal information into visual memory. *Journal of Experimental Psychology: Human Learning and Memory*, 4(1), 19–31.

Loftus, E. F., & Palmer, J. C. (1974). Reconstruction of automobile destruction: An example of the interaction between language and memory. *Journal of Verbal Learning and Verbal Behavior*, 13(5), 585–589.

Loftus, E. F., & Pickrell, J. E. (1995). The formation of false memories. *Psychiatric Annals*, 25(12), 720–725.

Loftus, G. R., & Harley, E. M. (2005). Why is it easier to identify someone close than far away? *Psychonomic Bulletin & Review*, 12(1), 43–65.

Lyle, K., & Johnson, M. (2006). Importing perceived features into false memories. *Memory*, 14(2), 197–213.

Lyle, K. B., & Johnson, M. K. (2007). Source misattributions may increase the accuracy of source judgments. *Memory & Cognition*, 35(5), 1024–1033.

MacLin, O. H., Maclin, M. K., & Malpass, R. S. (2001). Race, arousal, attention, exposure and delay: An examination of factors moderating face recognition. *Psychology, Public Policy, and Law, 7*(1), 134–152. doi:10.1037/1076-8971.7.1.134

MacLin, O. H., & Malpass, R. S. (2001). Racial categorization of faces: The ambiguous race face effect. *Psychology, Public Policy and Law, 7*, 98–118.

Macmillan, N. A., & Creelman, C. D. (2005). *Detection theory: A user's guide.* Erlbaum.

Malmberg, K. J. (2008). Recognition memory: A review of the critical findings and an integrated theory for relating them. *Cognitive Psychology, 57*(4), 335–384.

Malpass, R. S., & Kravitz, J. (1969). Recognition for faces of own and other race. *Journal of Personality and Social Psychology, 13*(4), 330–334.

Malpass, R. S., Tredoux, C. G., & McQuiston-Surrett, D. E. (2007). Lineup construction and lineup fairness. In R. C. L. Lindsay, D. F. Ross, J. D. Read, & M. P. Toglia (Eds.), *The Handbook of Eyewitness Psychology, Vol. 2: Memory for people* (pp. 155–178. Erlbaum.

Mandler, G. (1980). Recognizing: The judgment of previous occurrence. *Psychological Review, 87*(3), 252–271.

Marsh, E. J. (2007). Retelling is not the same as recalling: Implications for memory. *Current Directions in Psychological Science, 16*(1), 16–20.

Marsh, E. J., & Tversky, B. (2004). Spinning the stories of our lives. *Applied Cognitive Psychology, 18*(5), 491–503.

Marsh, E. J., Tversky, B., & Hutson, M. (2005). How eyewitnesses talk about events: Implications for memory. *Applied Cognitive Psychology, 19*(5), 531–544.

Marsh, R. L., Cook, G. I., & Hicks, J. L. (2006). An analysis of prospective memory. In *Psychology of Learning and Motivation* (Vol. 46, pp. 115–153). Elsevier.

Marsh, R. L., & Hicks, J. L. (1998). Event-based prospective memory and executive control of working memory. *Journal of Experimental Psychology: Learning, Memory, and Cognition, 24*(2), 336–349.

Marsh, R. L., Meeks, J. T., Cook, G. I., Clark-Foos, A., Hicks, J. L., & Brewer, G. A. (2009). Retrieval constraints on the front end create differences in recollection on a subsequent test. *Journal of Memory and Language, 61*(3), 470–479.

Mather, M. (2004). Aging and emotional memory. In D. Reisberg & P. Hertel (Eds.), *Memory and emotion* (pp. 272–307). Oxford University Press.

Mather, M. (2007). Emotional arousal and memory binding: An object-based framework. *Perspectives on Psychological Science, 2*(1), 33–52.

Mather, M., Henkel, L., & Johnson, M. K. (1997). Evaluating characteristics of false memories: Remember/know judgments and memory characteristics questionnaire compared. *Memory & Cognition, 25*(5), 826–837.

Mazzoni, G., Scoboria, A., & Harvey, L. (2010). Nonbelieved memories. *Psychological Science, 21*(9), 1334–1340.

McCann, C. D., & Higgins, E. T. (1988). Motivation and affect in interpersonal relations: The role of personal orientations and discrepancies. In L. Donohew, H. E.

Sypher, & E. T. Higgins (Eds.), *Communication, social cognition, and affect* (pp. 53–79). Erlbaum.

McCloskey, M., & Zaragoza, M. (1985). Misleading postevent information and memory for events: arguments and evidence against memory impairment hypotheses. *Journal of Experimental Psychology: General*, 114(1), 1–16.

McDermott, K. B. (1996). The persistence of false memories in list recall. *Journal of Memory and Language*, 35(2), 212–230.

McDermott, K. B., Szpunar, K. K., & Christ, S. E. (2009). Laboratory-based and autobiographical retrieval tasks differ substantially in their neural substrates. *Neuropsychologia*, 47(11), 2290–2298.

McDuff, S. G., Frankel, H. C., & Norman, K. A. (2009). Multivoxel pattern analysis reveals increased memory targeting and reduced use of retrieved details during single-agenda source monitoring. *The Journal of Neuroscience*, 29(2), 508–516.

McGaugh, J. L. (2000). Memory—a century of consolidation. *Science*, 287(5451), 248–251.

Meade, M. L., & Roediger, H. L. (2002). Explorations in the social contagion of memory. *Memory & Cognition*, 30(7), 995–1009.

Megreya, A. M., & Burton, A. M. (2006). Unfamiliar faces are not faces: Evidence from a matching task. *Memory and Cognition*, 34(4), 865–876.

Meissner, C. A., & Brigham, J. C. (2001). Thirty years of investigating the other-race effect in memory for faces: A meta-analytic review. *Psychology, Public Policy and Law*, 7(1), 3–35.

Meissner, C. A., Brigham, J. C., & Butz, D. A. (2005). Memory for own- and other-race faces: A dual-process approach. *Applied Cognitive Psychology*, 19(5), 545–567.

Meissner, C. A., Sporer, S. L., & Schooler, J. W. (2007). Person descriptions as eyewitness evidence. In R. C. L. Lindsay, D. F. Ross, J. D. Read, & M. P. Toglia (Eds.), *The Handbook of Eyewitness Psychology, Vol. 2. Memory for people* (pp. 3–34). Erlbaum.

Melton, A. W., & Irwin, J. M. (1940). The influence of degree of interpolated learning on retroactive inhibition and the transfer of specific responses. *American Journal of Psychology*, 53, 173–203.

Memon, A., & Bartlett, J. (2002). The effects of verbalisation on face recognition in young and older adults. *Applied Cognitive Psychology*, 16(6), 635–650.

Memon, A., Gabbert, F., & Hope, L. (2004). The ageing eyewitness. In J.Adler (Ed.), *Forensic psychology: Debates, concepts and practice* (pp. 96–112). Willan.

Memon, A., Hope, L., Bartlett, J., & Bull, R. (2002). Eyewitness recognition errors: The effects of mugshot viewing and choosing in young and old adults. *Memory and Cognition*, 30(8), 1219–1227.

Memon, A., Meissner, C. A., & Fraser, J. (2010). The cognitive interview: A meta-analytic review and study space analysis of the past 25 years. *Psychology, Public Policy, and Law*, 16(4), 340–372.

Memon, A., Zaragoza, M., Clifford, B. R., & Kidd, L. (2010). Inoculation or antidote? The effects of cognitive interview timing on false memory for forcibly fabricated events. *Law and Human Behavior, 34*(2), 105–117.

Meyer, M. M., Bell, R., & Buchner, A. (2015). Remembering the snake in the grass: Threat enhances recognition but not source memory. *Emotion, 15*(6), 721–730. doi:10.1037/emo0000065

Meyersburg, C. A., Bogdan, R., Gallo, D. A., & McNally, R. J. (2009). False memory propensity in people reporting recovered memories of past lives. *Journal of Abnormal Psychology, 118*(2), 399–404.

Mishkin, M., Malamut, B., & Bachevalier, J. (1984). Memories and habits: Two neural systems. In G. Lynch, J. L. McGaugh, & N. M. Weinberger (Eds.), *Neurobiology of learning and memory* (pp. 65–77). Guilford Press.

Mitchell, K. J., & Johnson, M. K. (2000). Source monitoring: Attributing mental experiences. In E. Tulving & F. I. M. Craik (Eds.), *The Oxford handbook of memory* (pp. 179–195). Oxford University Press.

Mitchell, K. J., & Johnson, M. K. (2009). Source monitoring 15 years later: What have we learned from fMRI about the neural mechanisms of source memory? *Psychological Bulletin, 135*(4), 638–677.

Mohler-Kuo, M., Dowdall, G. W., Koss, M. P., & Wechsler, H. (2004). Correlates of rape while intoxicated in a national sample of college women. *Journal of Studies on Alcohol, 65*(4), 37–55. doi:10.1037/a0027840

Morgan, C. A., III, Hazlet, G., Baranoski, M., Doran, A., Southwick, S., & Loftus, E. F. (2007). Accuracy of eyewitness identification is significantly associated with performance on a standardized test of face recognition. *International Journal of Law and Psychiatry, 30*(3), 213–223.

Morgan, C. A., III, Hazlet, G., Doran, A., Garrett, S., Hoyt, G., Thomas, P., Baranoski, M., & Southwick, S. M. (2004). Accuracy of eyewitness memory for persons encountered during exposure to highly intense stress. *International Journal of Law and Psychiatry, 27*(3), 265–279.

Morgan, C. A. III., Hazlett, G., Wang, S., Richardson, E. G. Jr., Schnurr, P., & Southwick, S. M. (2001). Symptoms of dissociation in humans experiencing acute, uncontrollable stress: a prospective investigation. *American Journal of Psychiatry, 158*(8), 1239–1247. doi:10.1176/appi.ajp.158.8.1239

Morgan, C. A. III., Wang, S., Mason, J., Southwick, S. M., Fox, P., Hazlett, G., Charney, D. S., & Greenfield, G. (2000). Hormone profiles in humans experiencing military survival training. *Biological Psychiatry, 47*(10), 891–901. doi:10.1016/s0006-3223(99)00307-8

Morgan, C. A. III., Wang, S., Southwick, S. M., Rasmusson, A., Hazlett, G., Hauger, R. L., & Charney, D. S. (2000). Plasma neuropeptide-Y concentrations in humans exposed to military survival training. *Biological Psychiatry, 47*(10), 902–909. doi:10.1016/s0006-3223(99)00239-5

Morris, C. D., Bransford, J. D., & Franks, J. J. (1977). Levels of processing versus transfer appropriate processing. *Journal of Verbal Learning and Verbal Behavior, 16*(5), 519–533.

Moulin, C. J. A., Thompson, R. G., Wright, D. B., & Conway, M. A. (2007). Eyewitness memory in older adults. In M. P. Toglia, J. D. Read, D. F. Ross & R. C. L. Lindsay (Eds.), *The Handbook of Eyewitness Psychology: Vol. 1. Memory for events* (pp. 627–646). Erlbaum.

Munsterberg, H. (1899). Psychology and history. *Psychological Review, 6*(1), 1–31.

Murayama, K., Miyatsu, T., Buchli, D., & Storm, B. C. (2014). Forgetting as a consequence of retrieval: A meta-analytic review of retrieval-induced forgetting. *Psychological Bulletin, 140*(5), 1383–1409.

Murphy, N. A., & Issacowitz, D. M. (2008). Preferences for emotional information in older and younger adults: A meta-analysis of memory and attention tasks. *Psychology and Aging, 23*(2), 263–286.

Nader, K., Schafe, G. E., & Le Doux, J. E. (2000). Fear memories require protein synthesis in the amygdala for reconsolidation after retrieval. *Nature, 406*(6797), 722–726.

National Institute of Justice. (2008). *Most victims know their attacker.* https://nij.ojp.gov/topics/articles/most-victims-know-their-attacker

National Institute of Justice Technical Group for Eyewitness Evidence. (1999). *Eyewitness evidence: A guide for law enforcement.* U.S. Department of Justice, Office of Justice Programs, National Institute of Justice.

National Research Council. (2009). *Strengthening forensic science in the United States: A path forward.* National Academies Press.

Neil v. Biggers, 409 U.S. 188 (1972).

Neisser. U. (1967). *Cognitive psychology.* Appleton Century Crofts.

Neisser, U. (1978). Anticipations, images, and introspection. *Cognition, 6*(2), 169–174.

Neisser, U. (1982). Memory: What are the important questions? In U. Neisser (Ed.), *Memory observed: Remembering in natural contexts* (pp. 3–19). W. H. Freeman.

Nelson, T. O. (1996). Consciousness and cognition. *American Psychologist, 51*(2), 102–116.

Neuschatz, J. S., Lampinen, J. M., Preston, E. L., Hawkins, E. R., & Toglia, M. P. (2002). The effect of memory schemata on memory and the phenomenological experience of naturalistic situations. *Applied Cognitive Psychology, 16*(6), 687–708.

Neuschatz, J. S., Payne, D. G., Lampinen, J. M., & Toglia, M. P. (2001). Assessing the effectiveness of warnings and the phenomenological characteristics of false memories. *Memory, 9*(1), 53–71.

Newman, E. J., & Lindsay, D. S. (2009). False memories: What the hell are they for? *Applied Cognitive Psychology, 23*(8), 1105–1121.

Norman, K. A., & Schacter, D. L. (1997). False recognition in younger and older adults: Exploring the characteristics of illusory memories. *Memory & Cognition, 25*(6), 838–848.

Nyberg, L., McIntosh, A. R., Houle, S., Nilsson, L. G., & Tulving, E. (1996). Activation of medial temporal structures during episodic memory retrieval. *Nature, 380*(6576), 715–717.

O'Brien, T. (1990). *The things they carried.* Houghton Mifflin.

O'Craven, K. M., & Kanwisher, N. (2000). Mental imagery of faces and places activates corresponding stimulus-specific brain regions. *Journal of Cognitive Neuroscience, 12*(6), 1013–1023.

Ochsner, K. N., Schacter, D. L., & Edwards, K. (1997). Illusory recall of vocal affect. *Memory, 5*(4), 433–455.

O'Donnell, C., & Bruce, V. (2001). Familiarisation with faces selectively enhances sensitivity to changes made to the eyes. *Perception, 30*(6), 755–764.

Odegard, T., & Lampinen, J. (2004). Memory conjunction errors for autobiographical events: More than just familiarity. *Memory, 12*(3), 288–300.

Office of Juvenile Justice and Delinquency Prevention. (2016). *Statistical briefing book.* https://www.ojjdp.gov/

Okado, Y., & Stark, C. E. (2005). Neural activity during encoding predicts false memories created by misinformation. *Learning & Memory, 12*(1), 3–11.

Palmer, F. T., Flowe, H. D., Takarangi, M. K. T., & Humphries, J. E. (2013). Intoxicated witnesses and suspects: An archival analysis of their involvement in criminal case processing. *Law and Human Behavior, 37*(1), 54–59. doi:10.1037/lhb0000010

Palmer, M. A., Brewer, N., McKinnon, A. C., & Weber, N. (2010). Phenomenological reports diagnose accuracy of eyewitness identification decisions. *Acta Psychologica, 133*(2), 137–145.

Patihis, L., Frenda, S. J., LePort, A. K., Petersen, N., Nichols, R. M., Stark, C. E., McGaugh, J. L., & Loftus, E. F. (2013). False memories in highly superior autobiographical memory individuals. *Proceedings of the National Academy of Sciences, 110*(52), 20947–20952.

Pawlenko, N. B., Safer, M. A., Wise, R. A., & Holfeld, B. (2013). A teaching aid for improving jurors' assessments of eyewitness accuracy. *Applied Cognitive Psychology, 27*(2), 190–197.

Payne, D. G. (1987). Hypermnesia and reminiscence in recall: a historical and empirical review. *Psychological Bulletin, 101*(1), 5–27.

Payne, D. G., Elie, C. J., Blackwell, J. M., & Neuschatz, J. S. (1996). Memory illusions: Recalling, recognizing, and recollecting events that never occurred. *Journal of Memory and Language, 35*(2), 261–285.

Perfect, T. J., & Harris, L. J. (2003). Adult age differences in unconscious transference: Source confusion or identity blending? *Memory & Cognition, 31*(4), 570–580.

Pickel, K. L. (1998). Unusualness and threat as possible causes of "weapon focus." *Memory, 6*(3), 277–295.

Pickel, K. L. (1999). The influence of context on the "weapon focus" effect. *Law and Human Behavior, 23*(3), 299–311.

Pickel, K. L. (2007). Remembering and identifying menacing perpetrators: Exposure to violence and the weapon focus effect. In R. C. L. Lindsay, D. F. Ross, J. D. Read & M. P. Toglia (Eds.), *Handbook of Eyewitness Psychology: Vol. 2. Memory for people* (pp. 339–360). Erlbaum.

Pickel, K. L., Ross, S. J., & Truelove, R. S. (2006). Do weapons automatically capture attention? *Applied Cognitive Psychology, 20*(7), 871–893.

Pigott, M., & Brigham, J. C. (1985). Relationship between accuracy of prior description and facial recognition. *Journal of Applied Psychology, 88*(3), 315–323.

Pillemer, D. B. (1992). Remembering personal circumstances: A functional analysis. In E. Winograd & U. Neisser (Eds.), *Emory Symposia in Cognition, 4. Affect and accuracy in recall: Studies of "flashbulb" memories* (pp. 236–264). Cambridge University Press. https://doi.org/10.1017/CBO9780511664069.013

Platz, S. J., & Hosch, H. M. (1988). Cross-racial/ethnic eyewitness identification: A field study. *Journal of Applied Social Psychology, 18*(11), 972–984.

Poole, D. A., & Lindsay, D. S. (2002). Reducing child witnesses' false reports of misinformation from parents. *Journal of Experimental Child Psychology, 81*(2), 117–140.

Possley, M. (2005, March 7). Jailed 23 years, freed by DNA. *Chicago Tribune*.

Pozzulo, J. (2007). Person descriptions and identification by child witnesses. In R. C. L. Lindsay, D. F. Ross, J. D. Read, & M. P. Toglia (Eds.), *The Handbook of Eyewitness Psychology, Vol. 2. Memory for people* (pp. 283–308). Erlbaum.

Pozzulo, J. D., & Warren, K. L. (2003). Descriptions and identifications of strangers by child and adult witnesses. *Journal of Applied Psychology, 88*(2), 315–323.

Prull, M. W., Gabrieli, J. D. E., & Bunge, S. A. (2000). Age-related changes in memory: A cognitive neuroscience perspective. In F. I. M. Craik & T. A. Salthouse (Eds.), *The handbook of aging and cognition* (2nd ed., pp. 91–155). Erlbaum.

Rajaram, S. (1993). Remembering and knowing: Two means of access to the personal past. *Memory & Cognition, 21*(1), 89–102.

Rajaram, S. (1998). The effects of conceptual salience and perceptual distinctiveness on conscious recollection. *Psychonomic Bulletin & Review, 5*(1), 71–78.

Rajaram, S., & Geraci, L. (2000). Conceptual fluency selectively influences knowing. *Journal of Experimental Psychology: Learning, Memory, and Cognition, 26*(4), 1070–1074.

Rapcsak, S. Z., Reminger, S. L., Glisky, E. L., Kaszniak, A. W., & Comer, J. F. (1999). Neuropsychological mechanisms of false facial recognition following frontal lobe damage. *Cognitive Neuropsychology, 16*(3–5), 267–292.

Ratcliff, R., & Starns, J. J. (2009). Modeling confidence and response time in recognition memory. *Psychological Review, 116*(1), 59–83.

Raz, N. (2000). Aging of the brain and its impact of cognitive performance: Integration of structural and functional findings. In F. I. M. Craik & T. A. Salthouse (Eds.), *The handbook of aging and cognition* (2nd ed., pp. 1–91). Erlbaum.

Read, J. D. (1995). The availability heuristic in person identification: The sometimes misleading consequences of enhanced contextual information. *Applied Cognitive Psychology, 9*(2), 91–121.

Read, J. D., & Desmarais, S. L. (2009). Lay knowledge of eyewitness issues: A Canadian evaluation. *Applied Cognitive Psychology, 23*(3), 301–326.

Reder, L.M., & Schunn, C. D. (1999). Bringing together the psychometric and strategy worlds: Predicting adaptivity in a dynamic task. In D. Gopher & A. Koriat (Eds), *Attention and Performance XVII. Cognitive regulation of performance: Interaction of theory and application* (pp. 315–342). MIT Press.

Reder, L. M., Nhouyvanisvong, A., Schunn, C. D., Ayers, M. S., Angstadt, P., & Hiraki, K. (2000). A mechanistic account of the mirror effect for word frequency: A computational model of remember–know judgments in a continuous recognition paradigm. *Journal of Experimental Psychology: Learning, Memory, and Cognition, 26*(2), 294–320.

Reisberg, D., & Heuer, F. (2004). Memory for emotional events. In D. Reisberg & P. Hertel (Eds.), *Memory and emotion* (pp. 3–41). Oxford University Press.

Reisberg, D., & Heuer, F. (2007). The influence of emotion on memory in forensic settings. In M. P. Toglia, J. D. Read, D. F. Ross, & R. C. L. Lindsay (Eds.), *Handbook of Eyewitness Psychology, Vol. 1. Memory for events* (pp. 81–116). Erlbaum.

Reyna, V. F., & Brainerd, C. J. (1995). Fuzzy trace theory: An interim synthesis. *Learning and Individual Differences, 7*(1), 1–75.

Rindal, E. J., DeFranco, R. M., Rich, P. R., & Zaragoza, M. S. (2016). Does reactivating a witnessed memory increase its susceptibility to impairment by subsequent misinformation? *Journal of Experimental Psychology: Learning, Memory, and Cognition, 42*(10), 1544–1558.

Rissman, J., Greely, H. T., & Wagner, A. D. (2010). Detecting individual memories through the neural decoding of memory states and past experience. *Proceedings of the National Academy of Sciences, 107*(21), 9849–9854.

Roberts, P. B. (2005, March 12). LA frees inmate, 40, believed innocent. *Baton Rouge Advocate*.

Rodin, M. J. (1987). Who is memorable to whom? A study of cognitive disregard. *Social Cognition, 5*(2), 144–165.

Rodriguez, D. N., & Berry, M. A. (2014). The effect of line-up administrator blindness on the recording of eyewitness identification decisions. *Legal and Criminal Psychology, 19*(1), 69–79. doi:10.1111/j.2044-8333.2012.02058.x

Roediger, H. L. & Karpicke, J. D. (2006). The power of testing memory: Basic research and implications for educational practice. *Perspectives on Psychological Science, 1*(2), 181–210.

Roediger, H. L., & McDermott, K. B. (1995). Creating false memories: Remembering words not presented in lists. *Journal of experimental psychology: Learning, Memory, and Cognition, 21*(4), 803–814.

Roediger, H. L., & McDermott, K. B. (1996). False perceptions of false memories. *Journal of Experimental Psychology: Learning, Memory, and Cognition, 22*(3), 814–816.

Roediger, H. L., & McDermott, K. B. (2013). Two types of event memory. *Proceedings of the National Academy of Sciences of the United States of America, 110*(52), 20856–20857.

Roediger, H. L., Watson, J. M., McDermott, K. B., & Gallo, D. A. (2001). Factors that determine false recall: A multiple regression analysis. *Psychonomic Bulletin & Review, 8*(3), 385–407.

Roediger, H. L., Wixted, J. H., & DeSoto, K. A. (2012). The curious complexity between confidence and accuracy in reports from memory. In L. Nadel & W. Sinnott-Armstrong (Eds.), *Memory and law* (pp. 84–118). Oxford University Press.

Rolls, E. T. (2007). *Emotion explained*. Oxford University Press.

Rose, R. A., Bull, R., & Vrij, A. (2005). Non-biased lineup instructions do matter—a problem for older witnesses. *Psychology, Crime and Law, 11*(2), 147–159.

Ross, D. R., Ceci, S. J., Dunning, D., & Toglia, M. P. (1994). Unconscious transference and mistaken identity: When a witness misidentifies a familiar with innocent person. *Journal of Applied Psychology, 79*(6), 918–930.

Rotello, C. M., & Macmillan, N. A. (2006). Remember-know models as decision strategies in two experimental paradigms. *Journal of Memory and Language, 55*(4), 479–494.

Rotello, C. M., Macmillan, N. A., & Van Tassel, G. (2000). Recall-to-reject in recognition: Evidence from ROC curves. *Journal of Memory and Language, 43*(1), 67–88.

Rowland, C. A. (2014). The effect of testing versus restudy on retention: a meta-analytic review of the testing effect. *Psychological Bulletin, 140*(6), 1432–1463.

Sacks, O. (2013, February 21). Speak, memory. *New York Review of Books*. https://www.nybooks.com

Safer, M. A., Christianson, S., Autry, M. A., & Österlund, K. (1998). Tunnel memory for traumatic events. *Applied Cognitive Psychology, 12*(2), 99–117.

Salthouse, T. A. (1996). The processing-speed theory of adult age differences in cognition. *Psychological Review, 103*(3), 403–428.

Sauer, J., Brewer, N. & Weber, N. (2008). Multiple confidence estimates as indices of eyewitness memory. *Journal of Experimental Psychology: General, 137*(3), 528–547.

Sauer, J., Brewer, N., Zweck, T., & Weber, N. (2010). The effect of retention interval on the confidence-accuracy relationship for eyewitness identification. *Law and Human Behavior, 34*(4), 337–347.

Sauer, J. D., Brewer, N., & Weber, N. (2012). Using confidence ratings to identify a target among foils. *Journal of Applied Research in Memory and Cognition, 1*(2), 80–88.

Schacter, D. L., & Addis, D. R. (2007). The cognitive neuroscience of constructive memory: remembering the past and imagining the future. *Philosophical Transactions of the Royal Society B: Biological Sciences, 362*(1481), 773–786.

Schacter, D. L., Israel, L., & Racine, C. (1999). Suppressing false recognition in younger and older adults: The distinctiveness heuristic. *Journal of Memory and Language, 40*(1), 1–24.

Schacter, D. L., & Loftus, E. F. (2013). Memory and law: What can cognitive neuroscience contribute? *Nature Neuroscience*, *16*(2), 119–123.

Schacter, D. L., Norman, K. A., & Koutstaal, W. (1998). The cognitive neuroscience of constructive memory. *Annual Review of Psychology*, *49*(1), 289–318.

Schacter, D. L., & Slotnick, S. D. (2004). The cognitive neuroscience of memory distortion. *Neuron*, *44*(1), 149–160.

Scherer, K. S. (1999). Appraisal theory. In T. Dalgleish, & M. Power (Eds.), *Handbook of cognition and emotion* (pp. 637–663). John Wiley and Sons.

Schiller, D., & Phelps, E. A. (2011). Does reconsolidation occur in humans? *Frontiers in Behavioral Neuroscience*, *5*, Article 24. https://www.frontiersin.org

Schonfield, D., & Robertson, B. (1966). Memory storage and aging. *Canadian Journal of Psychology*, *20*(2), 228–236.

Schooler, J. W., & Eich, E. (2005). Memory for emotional events. In E. Tulving & F. I. M. Craik (Eds.), *The Oxford handbook of memory* (pp. 379–392). Oxford University Press.

Schooler, J. W., & Engstler-Schooler, T. Y. (1990). Verbal overshadowing of visual memories: Some things are better left unsaid. *Cognitive Psychology*, *22*(1), 36–71.

Schooler, J. W., Gerhard, D., & Loftus, E. F. (1986). Qualities of the unreal. *Journal of Experimental Psychology: Learning, Memory, and Cognition*, *12*(2), 171–181.

Schooler, J. W., Ryan, R. S., & Reder, L. M. (1996). The costs and benefits of verbalization. In D. Herrmann, M. Johnson, C. McEvoy, C. Hertzog, & P. Hertel (Eds.), *Basic and applied psychology: New findings* (pp 51–65). Erlbaum.

Scimeca, J. M., McDonough, I. M., & Gallo, D. A. (2011). Quality trumps quantity at reducing memory errors: Implications for retrieval monitoring and mirror effects. *Journal of Memory and Language*, *65*(4), 363–377.

Schreiber Compo, N., Evans, J. R., Carol, R. N., Kemp, D., Villalba, D., Ham, L. S., & Rose, S. (2011). Alcohol intoxication and memory for events: A snapshot of alcohol myopia in a real-world drinking scenario. *Memory*, *19*(2), 202–210. doi:10.1080/09658211.2010.546802

Scoboria, A., Boucher, C., & Mazzoni, G. (2015). Reasons for withdrawing belief in vivid autobiographical memories. *Memory*, *23*(4), 545–562.

Scoboria, A., Jackson, D., Talarico, J., Hanczakowski, M., Wysman, L., & Mazzoni, G. (2014). The role of belief in occurrence within autobiographical memory. *Journal of Experimental Psychology: General*, *143*(3), 1242–1258.

Searcy, J. H., Bartlett, J. C., & Memon, A. (1999). Age differences in accuracy and choosing in eyewitness identification and face recognition. *Memory and Cognition*, *27*(3), 538–552.

Seitz, S. J., Lord, C. G., & Taylor, C. A. (2007). Beyond pleasure: Emotion activity affects the relationship between attitudes and behavior. *Personality and Social Psychology Bulletin*, *33*(7), 933–947.

Selmeczy, D., & Dobbins, I. G. (2014). Relating the content and confidence of recognition judgments. *Journal of Experimental Psychology: Learning, Memory, and Cognition*, *40*(1), 66–85.

Semmler, C., Brewer, N., & Wells, G. L. (2004). Effects of postidentification feedback on eyewitness identification on confidence. *Journal of Applied Psychology, 89*(2), 334–346.

Shapiro, P. N., & Penrod, S. (1986). Meta-analysis of facial identification studies. *Psychological Bulletin, 100*(2), 139–156.

Shaw III, J. S., & McClure, K. A. (1996). Repeated postevent questioning can lead to elevated levels of eyewitness confidence. *Law and Human Behavior, 20*(6), 629–653.

Shepherd, J. W., & Deregowski, J. B. (1981). Races and faces—A comparison of the responses of Africans and Europeans to faces of the same and different races. *British Journal of Psychology, 20*, 125–133.

Short, J. L., & Bodner, G. E. (2011). Differentiating accounts of actual, suggested and fabricated childhood events using the judgment of memory characteristics questionnaire. *Applied Cognitive Psychology, 25*(5), 775–781.

Simons, D. J., & Chabris, C. F. (2011). What people believe about how memory works: A representative survey of the US population. *PLOS One, 6*(8), e22757.

Simons, D. J., & Rensink, R. A. (2005). Change blindness: Past, present, and future. *Trends in Cognitive Sciences, 9*(1), 16–20.

Skagerberg, E. M., & Wright, D. B. (2008). The prevalence of co-witnesses and co-witness discussions in real eyewitnesses. *Psychology, Crime & Law, 14*(6), 513–521.

Slotnick, S. D., & Schacter, D. L. (2004). A sensory signature that distinguishes true from false memories. *Nature Neuroscience, 7*(6), 664–672.

Smith, S. M. (1979). Remembering in and out of context. *Journal of Experimental Psychology: Human Learning and Memory, 5*(5), 460–471.

Snodgrass, J. G., & Corwin, J. (1988). Pragmatics of measuring recognition memory: Applications to dementia and amnesia. *Journal of Experimental Psychology: General, 117*(1), 34–50.

Spaniol, J., & Bayen, U. J. (2002). When is schematic knowledge used in source monitoring? *Journal of Experimental Psychology: Learning, Memory, and Cognition, 28*(4), 631–651.

Spitzer, B., & Bäuml, K. H. (2007). Retrieval-induced forgetting in item recognition: Evidence for a reduction in general memory strength. *Journal of Experimental Psychology: Learning, Memory, and Cognition, 33*(5), 863–875.

Spitzer, H. F. (1939). Studies in retention. *Journal of Educational Psychology, 30*(9), 641–656.

Sporer, S. L. (1996). Psychological aspects of person descriptions. In S. Sporer, R. Malpass, & G. Koehnken (Eds.), *Psychological issues in eyewitness identification* (pp. 53–86). Erlbaum.

Sporer, S. L. (2007). Person descriptions as retrieval cues: Do they really help? *Psychology, Crime & Law, 13*(6), 591–609. doi:10.1080/10683160701253986

Sporer, S. L., Kaminski, K. S., Davids, M. C., & McQuiston, D. S. (2016). The verbal facilitation effect: re-reading person descriptions as a system variable to improve identification performance. *Memory, 24*(10), 1329–1344. doi:10.1080/09658211.2015.1106561

Sporer, S. L., Penrod, S., Read, D., & Cutler, B. (1995). Choosing, confidence, and accuracy: A meta-analysis of the confidence-accuracy relation in eyewitness identification studies. *Psychological Bulletin, 118*(3), 315–327.

Sporer, S. L., & Sharman, S. J. (2006). Should I believe this? Reality monitoring of accounts of self-experienced and invented recent and distant autobiographical events. *Applied Cognitive Psychology, 20*(6), 837–854.

Squire, L. R. (2004). Memory systems of the brain: a brief history and current perspective. *Neurobiology of Learning and Memory, 82*(3), 171–177.

Starns, J. J., Lane, S. M., Alonzo, J. D., & Roussel, C. C. (2007). Metamnemonic control over the discriminability of memory evidence: A signal-detection analysis of warning effects in the associative list paradigm. *Journal of Memory & Language, 56*(4), 592–607.

Steblay, N. M. (1992). A meta-analytic review of the weapon focus effect. *Law and Human Behavior, 16*(4), 413–424.

Steblay, N. M., Dysart, J., Fulero, S., & Lindsay, R. C. L. (2003). Eyewitness accuracy rates in police showup and lineup presentations: A meta-analytic comparison. *Law and Human Behavior, 27*(5), 523–540. doi:10.1023/A:1025438223608

Steblay, N. K., Tix, R. W., & Benson, S. L. (2013). Double exposure: The effects of repeated identification lineups on eyewitness accuracy. *Applied Cognitive Psychology, 27*(5), 644–654. doi:10.1002/acp.2944

Stern, L. W. (1904). Die Aussage als geistige Leistung und als Verhorsprodukt [The statement as a mental achievement and product of interrogation]. *Beitrage zur Psychologie der Aussage, 3*, 269–415.

Strack, F., & Bless, H. (1994). Memory for nonoccurrences: Metacognitive and presuppositional strategies. *Journal of Memory and Language, 33*(2), 203–217.

Straube, B. (2012). An overview of the neuro-cognitive processes involved in the encoding, consolidation, and retrieval of true and false memories. *Behavioral and Brain Functions, 8*(1), Article 35. https://behavioralandbrainfunctions.biomedcentral.com

Suengas, A. G., & Johnson, M. K. (1988). Qualitative effects of rehearsal on memories for perceived and imagined complex events. *Journal of Experimental Psychology: General, 117*(4), 377–389.

Szpunar, K. K. (2010). Episodic future thought an emerging concept. *Perspectives on Psychological Science, 5*(2), 142–162.

Tauber, S. K., & Rhodes, M. G. (2010). Metacognitive errors contribute to the difficulty in remembering proper names. *Memory, 18*(5), 522–532.

Technical Working Group for Eyewitness Evidence. (1999). *Eyewitness evidence: A guide for law enforcement.* U.S. Department of Justice, Office of Justice Programs.

Tenney, E. R., MacCoun, R. J., Spellman, B. A., & Hastie, R. (2007). Calibration trumps confidence as a basis for witness credibility. *Psychological Science, 18*(1), 46–50.

Tenney, E. R., Spellman, B. A., & MacCoun, R. J. (2008). The benefits of knowing what you know (and what you don't): How calibration affects credibility. *Journal of Experimental Social Psychology, 44*(5), 1368–1375.

Thierry, K. L., & Spence, M. J. (2002). Source-monitoring training facilitates preschoolers' eyewitness memory performance. *Developmental Psychology, 38*(3), 428–437.

Tulving, E. (1972). Episodic and semantic memory. In E. Tulving & W. Donaldson (Eds)., *Organization of memory* (pp. 382–402). Academic Press.

Tulving, E. (1981). Similarity relations in recognition. *Journal of Verbal Learning and Verbal Behavior, 20*(5), 479–496.

Tulving, E. (1983). *Elements of episodic memory*. Oxford University Press.

Tulving, E. (1985). Memory and consciousness. *Canadian Psychology, 26*(1), 1–12.

Tulving, E., & Thomson, D. M. (1971). Retrieval processes in recognition memory: Effects of associative context. *Journal of Experimental Psychology, 87*(1), 116–124.

Tulving, E., & Thomson, D. M. (1973). Encoding specificity and retrieval processes in episodic memory. *Psychological review, 80*(5), 352–373.

Turtle, J., Read, J. D., Lindsay, D. S., & Brimacombe, C. A. (2008). Toward a more informative psychological science of eyewitness evidence. *Applied Cognitive Psychology, 22*(6), 769–778.

Tversky, B., & Marsh, E. J. (2000). Biased retellings of events yield biased memories. *Cognitive Psychology, 40*(1), 1–38.

Undeutsch, U. (1989). The development of statement reality analysis. In J.C. Yuille (Ed.), *Credibility assessment* (pp. 101–119). Kluwer.

Unsworth, N., & Engle, R.W. (2007a). The nature of individual differences in working memory capacity: Active maintenance in primary memory and controlled search from secondary memory. *Psychological Review, 114*(1), 104–132.

U.S. Census Bureau. (2016). *An aging world: 2015 international population reports.* https://census.gov/content/dam/Census/library/publications/2016/demo/p95-16-1.pdf

Valentine, T., Davis, J. P., Memon, A., & Roberts, A. (2012). Live show-ups and their influence on a subsequent video lineup. *Applied Cognitive Psychology, 26*(1), 1–23. doi:10.1002/acp.1796

Valentine, T., & Mesout, J. (2009). Eyewitness identification under stress in the London dungeon. *Applied Cognitive Psychology, 23*(2), 151–161.

Van Koppen, P. J., & Lochun, S. K. (1997). Portraying perpetrators: The validity of offender descriptions by witnesses. *Law and Human Behavior, 21*(6), 661–685.

van Zandt, T. (2000). How to fit a response time distribution. *Psychonomic Bulletin & Review, 7*(3), 424–465.

Vieira, K., & Lane, S. M. (2013). How you lie affects what you remember. *Journal of Applied Research in Memory and Cognition, 2*(3), 173–178. doi:10.1016/j.jarmac.2013.05.005

Vokey, J. R., & Read, J. D. (1992). Familiarity, memorability and the effect of typicality on the recognition of faces. *Memory and Cognition, 20*(3), 291–302.

Vredeveldt, A., Charman, S. D., Blanken, A.& Hooydank, M. (2018). Effects of cannabis on eyewitness memory: A field study. *Applied Cognitive Psychology, 32*(4), 420–428. doi:10.1002/acp.3414

Vrij, A. (2005). Criteria-based content analysis: A qualitative review of the first 37 studies. *Psychology, Public Policy, and Law, 11*(1), 3–41.

Vrij, A. (2008). Nonverbal dominance versus verbal accuracy in lie detection a plea to change police practice. *Criminal Justice and Behavior, 35*(10), 1323–1336.

Waubert de Puiseau, B., Aßfalg, A., Erdfelder, E., & Bernstein, D. M. (2012). Extracting the truth from conflicting eyewitness reports: A formal modeling approach. *Journal of Experimental Psychology: Applied, 18*(4), 390–403.

Weber, N., & Brewer, N. (2003). The effect of judgment type and confidence scale on confidence-accuracy calibration in face recognition. *Journal of Applied Psychology, 88*(3), 490–499.

Wells, G. L. (1993). What do we know about eyewitness identification? *American Psychologist, 48*(5), 553–571.

Wells, G. L., & Bradfield, A. L. (1998). "Good, you identified the suspect": Feedback to eyewitnesses distorts their reports of the witnessing experience. *Journal of Applied Psychology, 83*(3), 360–376.

Wells, G. L., & Bradfield, A. L. (1999). Distortions in eyewitnesses' recollections: Can the postidentification-feedback effect be moderated? *Psychological Science, 10*(2), 138–144.

Wells, G. L., Ferguson, T. J., & Lindsay, R. C. (1981). The tractability of eyewitness confidence and its implications for triers of fact. *Journal of Applied Psychology, 66*(6), 688–696.

Wells, G. L., Kovera, M. B., Douglass, A. B., Brewer, N., Meissner, C. A., & Wixted, J. T. (2020). Policy and procedure recommendations for the collection and preservation of eyewitness identification evidence. *Law and Human Behavior, 44*(1), 3–36.

Wells, G. L., & Leippe, M. R. (1981). How do triers of fact infer the accuracy of eyewitness identifications? Using memory for peripheral detail can be misleading. *Journal of Applied Psychology, 66*(6), 682–687.

Wells, G. L., & Luus, E. (1990). Police lineups as experiments: Social methodology as a framework for properly-conducted lineups. *Personality and Social Psychology Bulletin, 16*(1), 106–117. doi:10.1177/0146167290161008

Wells, G. L., Memon, A., & Penrod, S. D. (2006). Eyewitness evidence: Improving its probative value. *Psychological Science in the Public Interest, 7*(2), 45–75.

Wells, G. L., & Murray, D. M. (1984). Eyewitness confidence. In G. L. Wells & D. M. Murray (Eds.), *Eyewitness testimony: Psychological perspectives* (pp. 155–170). Cambridge University Press.

Wells, G. L., & Olson, E. A. (2003). Eyewitness testimony. *Annual Review of Psychology, 54*(1), 277–295.

Wells, G. L., Small, M., Penrod, S., Malpass, R. S., Fulero, S. M., & Brimacombe, C. A. E. (1998). Eyewitness identification procedures: Recommendations for lineups and photospreads. *Law and Human Behavior, 22*(6), 603–647. doi:10.1023/A:1025750605807

Wessel, I., & Merckelbach, H. (1996). The impact of anxiety on memory for details in spider phobics. *Applied Cognitive Psychology, 11*(3), 444.1–444.9.

Whipple, G. M. (1911). The psychology of testimony. *Psychological Bulletin, 8*(9), 307–309.

Whitley, B. E., Kite, M. E., & Adams, H. L. (2012). *Principles of research in behavioral science*. Routledge.

Wickelgren, W. A., & Norman, D. A. (1966). Strength models and serial position in short-term recognition memory. *Journal of Mathematical Psychology, 3*(2), 316–347.

Wickens, C. D. (2002). Multiple resources and performance prediction. *Theoretical Issues in Ergonomics Science, 3*(2), 159–177.

Wilcock, R., Bull, R., & Milne, R. (2008). Assisting vulnerable witnesses. In *Witness identification in criminal cases* (pp. 141–162). Oxford University Press.

Wise, R. A., Fishman, C. S., & Safer, M. A. (2009). How to analyze the accuracy of eyewitness testimony in a criminal case. *Connecticut Law Review, 42*(2), 435–513.

Wise, R. A., Safer, M. A., & Maro, C. M. (2011). What U.S. law enforcement officers know and believe about eyewitness factors, eyewitness interviews and identification procedures. *Applied Cognitive Psychology, 25*(3), 488–500. doi:10.1002/acp.1717

Wixted, J. T. (2004). The psychology and neuroscience of forgetting. *Annual Review of Psychology, 55*(1), 235–269.

Wixted, J. T. (2007). Dual-process theory and signal-detection theory of recognition memory. *Psychological Review, 114*(1), 152–176.

Wixted, J. T., & Mickes, L. (2010). A continuous dual-process model of remember/know judgments. *Psychological Review, 117*(4), 1025–1054.

Wixted, J. T., & Mickes, L. (2014). A signal-detection-based diagnostic-feature-detection model of eyewitness identification. *Psychological Review, 121*(2), 262–276.

Wixted, J. T., Mickes, L., Dunn, J. C., Clark, S. E., & Wells, W. (2016). Estimating the reliability of eyewitness identifications from police lineups. *Proceedings of the National Academy of Sciences of the United States of America, 113*(2), 304–309. doi:10.1073/pnas.1516814112

Wixted, J. T., & Stretch, V. (2004). In defense of the signal detection interpretation of remember/know judgments. *Psychonomic Bulletin & Review, 11*(4), 616–641.

Wolf, O. T. (2009). Stress and memory in humans: Twelve years of progress? *Brain Research, 1293*(1), 142–154.

Wright, D. B., Memon, A., Skagerberg, E. M., & Gabbert, F. (2009). When eyewitnesses talk. *Current Directions in Psychological Science, 18*(3), 174–178.

Wright, D. B., Self, G., & Justice, C. (2000). Memory conformity: Exploring misinformation effects when presented by another person. *British Journal of Psychology, 91*(Pt. 2), 189–202.

Yarmey, A. D. (1982). Eyewitness identification and stereotypes of criminals. In A. Trankell (Ed.), *Reconstructing the past: The role of psychologists in criminal trials* (pp. 205–225). Norstedt and Soners.

Yarmey, A. D. (1986). Verbal, visual, and voice identification of a rape suspect under different levels of illumination. *Journal of Applied Psychology, 71*(3), 363–370.

Yarmey, A. D. (2000). The older eyewitness. In M. B. Rothman, B. D. Dunlop & P. Entzel (Eds.), *Elders, crime and the criminal justice system: Myths, perceptions and reality in the 21st century* (pp. 127–148). Springer.

Yarmey, A. D., Jones, H. T., & Rashid, S. (1984). Eyewitness memory of elderly and young adults. In D. J. Muller, D. E. Blackman, & A. J. Chapman (Eds.), *Psychology and law* (pp. 218–228). John Wiley and Sons.

Yarmey, A. D., & Kent, J. (1980). Eyewitness identification by elderly and young adults. *Law and Human Behavior, 4*(4), 359–371.

Yonelinas, A. P. (1994). Receiver-operating characteristics in recognition memory: Evidence for a dual-process account. *Journal of Experimental Psychology: Learning, Memory and Cognition, 20*(6), 1314–1354.

Yonelinas, A. P. (1997). Recognition memory ROCs for item and associative information: The contribution of recollection and familiarity. *Memory & Cognition, 25*(6), 747–763.

Yonelinas, A. P. (2001). Components of episodic memory: The contribution of recollection and familiarity. *Philosophical Translations of the Royal Society of London, B, 356*(1413), 1363–1374.

Yonelinas, A. P. (2002). The nature of recollection and familiarity: A review of 30 years of research. *Journal of Memory and Language, 46*(3), 441–517.

Yonelinas, A. P., & Jacoby, L. L. (1994). Dissociations of processes in recognition memory: Effects of interference and of response speed. *Canadian Journal of Experimental Psychology, 48*(4), 516–534.

Yonelinas, A. P., & Jacoby, L. L. (1996). Noncriterial recollection: Familiarity as automatic, irrelevant recollection. *Consciousness and Cognition, 5*(1), 131–141.

Yovell, G., & Paller, K. (2004). The neural basis of the butcher-on-the-bus phenomenon: When a face seems familiar but if not remembered. *NeuroImage, 21*(2), 789–800.

Zacks, R. T., Hasher, L., & Li, K. Z. H. (2000). Human memory. In F. I. M. Craik & T. A. Salthouse (Eds.), *The handbook of aging and cognition* (pp. 293–357). Erlbaum.

Zaragoza, M. S., & Koshmider, J. W. (1989). Misled subjects may know more than their performance implies. *Journal of experimental psychology: Learning, Memory, and Cognition, 15*(2), 246–255.

Zaragoza, M. S., & Lane, S. M. (1994). Source misattributions and the suggestibility of eyewitness memory. *Journal of Experimental Psychology: Learning, Memory and Cognition, 20*(4), 934–945.

Zaragoza, M. S., & Lane, S. M. (1998). Processing resources and eyewitness suggestibility. *Legal and Criminological Psychology, 3*(2), 305–320.

Zaragoza, M. S., & Mitchell, K. J. (1996). Repeated exposure to suggestion and the creation of false memories. *Psychological Science, 7*(5), 294–300.

INDEX

Page numbers in *italics* indicate tables.

accessibility, 16
accuracy: autobiographical memory, 71–73; confidence related to, 87–90, 91, 97–99; feedback on, 13
activation-monitoring theory, 168n2 (chap. 3)
active-duty military personnel, 101–3
age, 118–21, 122–24
alcohol, 32–35
Altman, C. M., 34
American Psychology-Law Society (AP-LS), 143–44, 155
Amsterdam, 34–35
Anderson, M. C., 120–21, 133
anger, 117
Angie, A. D., 117–18
anxiety, 32
AP-LS. *See* American Psychology-Law Society
applied research, 5, 167n2. *See also* basic-applied divide
archival studies, 28, 29
arousal, as emotion, 116
attentional narrowing theory: central details in, 106–7; negative emotion in, 106–10, 113; peripheral details in, 106–8; thematic emotional events and, 113; weapon focus effect and, 110
autobiographical beliefs, 70
autobiographical memory accuracy, 71–73
availability, 16

Bartlett, Frederic, 48
basic-applied divide, 7–11
basic research, 4–5, 167n2
best practice recommendation, 42–43
beta, 23
bias: in college roommates study, 136; computer/statistical model of, 55; double-blind procedure and, 147; old/new recognition related to, 23; own age, 37; own-race, 38, 40; positive information, 122; pre-lineup instructions and, 149; repeated identifications and, 153
Blandón-Gitlin, I., 95–96
blood alcohol level, 33–34
Bonner, L., 46, 53
Brewer, Neil, 90–91
Brimacombe, C. A. E., 120
Bruce, V., 45–47, 52–53, 54
Burton, A. M., 47, 52–53
butcher-on-the-bus: context of, 49–50; definition of, 24; SMF and, 54–55

Cabeza, R., 91–92
calibration perspective, 98–99, 151, 157
cannabis, 34–35
Carlson, C. A., 111
Carstensen, L. L., 122, 123
CBCA. *See* criteria-based content analysis
central details, 106–8

central/peripheral effect, 105–6, 124; anger and, 117; definitions of, 114; Houston on, 115; thematic arousal and, 113–14
Chan, J. C., 139–40
chance level, 45
change blindness, 17
Charles, S. T., 122–23
childhood sexual abuse, 37–38
Children and Young Persons Act (1989), 28
choosers, 88, 89
Christianson, R. E., 107
CI. *See* Cognitive Interview
Clifford, B. R., 103–4
clothing, 154–55
Clutterbuck, R., 55
Cognitive Interview (CI), 14, 131–32, 141
cognitive psychology, 6–7
college roommates study, 135–36
Coltrane, Robbie, 28
computer/statistical model, 55
confidence, 77, 156; accuracy related to, 87–90, 91, 97–99
confidence statement, 150–51
conservative, 23
consolidation, 15–16, 139
constraints, 10
contact hypothesis, 38–39
content borrowing, 66
control condition, 137
converging operations, 9
correct rejection, 22, 26
correlation, 88–89
Cotton, Ronald, 100
counterfactual reasoning, 60–61
Craik, F. I. M., 120–21
Creelman, C. D., 23
criteria-based content analysis (CBCA), 95–96
criterial recollection, 79–80, 84
cross-race effect, 38–39

"Crovitz" technique, 73–74
Cuc, A., 134
cue-dependent remembering, 63
cued recall, 19, 20
cued-recall tests, 120–21, 133
cues, deterministic versus probabilistic, 156–57

Davis, G., 36
deadline pressure, 90–91
declarative memory, 21
Deese-Roediger-McDermott paradigm (DRM), 93, 114; false memory and, 72–73; fMRI and, 91; phenomenal experience and, 78–79, 80–81; study-recall trials with, 84–85; warning in, 82–83
Deffenbacher, K. A., 104–5
details, 95, 106–8
deterministic versus probabilistic cues, 156–57
diagnostic monitoring, 67
discrete emotions, 117–18
disqualifying monitoring, 67
distinctiveness heuristic, 68
distractors, 19
DNA testing, 2, 3, 27, 44, 100
"don't know" decision, 149–50
double-blind or equivalent lineup, 147
d-prime, 23
DRM. *See* Deese-Roediger-McDermott paradigm
dual process models of memory, 24–25, 50–51
Dubois, S., 55
Dunn, J. C., 161

early selection, 67
Easterbrook, J. A., 106, 107, 110
ecological criterion, 9
ecphoric confidence rating judgments, 90
ecphoric similarity, 90

Edelstein, R. S., 116
Ellis, H. D., 28–29, 45, 51–52
emotion, 5, 32, 100, 116, 121–22. *See also* negative emotion; stress
emotional memory, 122–23
emotional narratives, 112–13
emotional reactivity, 9
encoding, 15
encoding specificity principle, 16
Engstler-Schooler, T. Y., 41
environmental-support hypothesis, 120
environment influence, 25
episodic memory, 21–22, 55
episodic memory errors, 49–50
evaluators, 94, 168n1
Evans, J. R., 32, 34
evidence-based suspicion, 144–45
expectations, 66, 82
experiencing and remembering, 19–25
eyewitness events, 15; criminal cases and, 11–13; fear and, 12; judging of, 14; photo lineup in, 12; post-event (mis)information in, 13; testimony in, 12; time and, 12; weapon focus effect in, 13
eyewitness evidence, 3–4, 13–15
eyewitness identification reform, 2–3
eyewitness misidentification, 3
eyewitness researchers, 4–5

face recognition unit, 52
face-specific processing system, 47
false alarm, 22, 23, 26
false fame effect, 152–53
false memories, 5, 61, 168n2; definition of, 59–60; DRM and, 72–73; in lab and real-world, 70–74; metamnemonic knowledge and, 82; unconscious transference in, 76. *See also* genuine and false memories
Falshore, M., 39–40
familiarity, 24, 45, 53; in rape, 1–2, 56

familiarity and recollection, 149–50; dual-process model of memory in, 50–51; eyewitness implications in, 55; face recognition unit in, 52; familiarity process in, 51–54; identity-specific semantic codes in, 52; moderate familiarity in, 54–55; mugshot exposure effect in, 54; name code in, 52; of police officers, 53; poor-quality viewing scenarios in, 52–53; source monitoring errors in, 48–49, 51; structural code in, 51–52
Faries, J. M., 135
feedback, 13, 85–86, 157–58
field-versus-laboratory debate, 33–34
filler task, 41
flash-bulb memory, 112
Flowe, H., 154
fMRI. *See* functional magnetic resonance imaging
food and sleep deprivation, 101–3
food deprivation, 107
forgetting, 128, 133–34, 146
free recall, 19, 20
free-recall tests, 120
functional magnetic resonance imaging (fMRI), 91
Fung, H. H., 122
fuzzy trace theory, 168n2 (chap. 3)

Gabbert, F., 132
generalizability, 9–10, 103, 106
genuine and false memories, 58–74; counterfactual reasoning in, 60–61; different monitoring processes in, 67–68; different types of control at retrieval in, 67; false memories in lab and real-world, 72–74; nonmemorial information in, 69–71; remembering and knowing in, 68–69; SMF in, 62–66, 167n2 (chap. 3); theoretical view and mechanisms in, 67–71; veridical (true) memory in, 59–60

genuine and false memories, distinguishing between, 75–99; internal cues in, 75; judging other people's memories in, 94–99; neural activity and, 91–94; phenomenal experience in, 77–91; physiological measures in, 75–76; reliability in, 75; research on, 75; SMF in, 76; source monitoring error in, 61–62
Gonsalves, B., 92

Heuer, F., 103, 106–7
heuristic decisions, 64–65
highly superior autobiographical memory (HSAM), 73
high road research, 6–8
high-stress interrogations, 101–2
hits, 22, 26
Hollin, C. R., 103–4
Houston, K. A., 114–15
HSAM. *See* highly superior autobiographical memory
hunch, 144–45
Hyman, I. E., 135
hypermnesia, 129

IAPS. *See* International Affective Picture System
identity-specific semantic codes, 52
I-I-Eye aid, 159
image recognition, 46–47
imagination, 78, 92, 126
implicit memory, 22
informational influence, 138
initial interview, 130–31
Innocence Project, 3, 44, 148
innocent bystander effect, 49
interference, 17
internal validity, 10
International Affective Picture System (IAPS), 122–23
interpersonal reality monitoring, 94

intoxication, 32–35
Issacowitz, D. M., 123

Jacoby, L. L., 50–51, 152–53
JMCQ. *See* judgment of memory characteristics questionnaire
Johnson, M. K., 48, 55, 62, 94
journals, 11
judging other people's memories: calibration perspective in, 98–99; CBCA in, 95–96, 168n2 (chap. 4); evaluators in, 94, 168n1; interpersonal reality monitoring in, 94; mere inflation in, 98; qualitative characteristics of reports on, 94–97
judgment of memory characteristics questionnaire (JMCQ), 96, 159–60, 168n2 (chap. 4)

key issues, 155–61
Kirsner, K., 161
Kramer, Robin, 55
Kuehn, L. L., 28–29

laboratory-based experiments, 28–29
Lane, S. M., 7–8, 83, 84, 85–86
Laney, C., 112–14, 115
LaPaglia, J. A., 139–40
late correction, 67
Laugherty, K. R., 31
Law and Order, 12
law enforcement officers, 53, 56, 57
Levine, L. J., 116, 117
liberal, 23
lies, 168n2 (chap. 4)
Lindsay, Roderick, 29, 60–61
lineup fillers, 147–49, 154
lineups, 40–42, 62, 76, 88; evidence-based suspicion and, 144–45, 147, 149–50
list word recall, 84–85
Lochun, G. R., 29

Loftus, Elizabeth, 109–10
long-term memory, 20–21
low road research, 6–8
low-stress interrogations, 101–2
lures, 19

Maclin, O. H., 31
Macmillan, N. A., 23
Mandler, G., 24
Marsh, Elizabeth, 135–38
Mather, M., 80–81, 122
McCloskey, M., 140
MCQ. *See* Memory Characteristics Questionnaire
Megreya, A. M., 47
Meissner, C. A., 7–8, 30
Memon, A., 131–32
memory, 15–18, 168n1; conversations about, 135–39; for persons, 27–35
Memory Characteristics Questionnaire (MCQ), 14–15, 69, 77, 84, 158; JMCQ as, 96, 159–60, 168n2 (chap. 4)
memory distortion, 138
memory measurement, 19–20
memory test, 82
memory traces, 66
memory types, 20–22
Mesout, J., 104–5
meta-analysis, 42, 117–18, 123, 130, 131, 153, 160
metacognitive information, 99, 159
metamnemonic knowledge, 81–87, 157
methodological fixation, 9
middle road research: in basic-applied divide, 8–11; converging operations in, 9; ecological criterion in, 9; generalizability in, 9–10; methodological fixation and, 9; prediction from, 8; theory and method in, 8
miss, 22, 26
Morgan, C. A., 107

Morgan, Charles, III, 101–3
Moto, Vincent, 44, 56, 148
mugshot exposure effect, 54
multiple interviews, 141
multiple measures, 9
Murphy, N. A., 123

name code, 52
National Institute of Justice, 44–45, 56
negative emotion, 116–17; attentional narrowing theory and, 106–10, 113; presentation medium and, 111–15; recall memory and, 105–8, 122–25; recognition memory and, 108–11; weapon focus effect and, 109–11
Neil v. Biggers (1972), 97
Neisser, Ulrich, 6–7, 18
neural activity: behavioral studies and, 93; fMRI in, 91; imagination and, 92; limitations related to, 93–94; retrieval and, 93; sensory reactivation hypothesis in, 91; time related to, 93; visual processing areas in, 92
neutral conditions, 113–15
"new," 22–23, 26
Newman, E. J., 60–61
New Zealand, 28
nonbelieved memory, 70
nonchoosers, 88, 89
noncriterial recollection, 79
nondeclarative memory, 21, 22
nonmemorial information, 69–71
Norman, K. A., 80–81
normative influence, 138
Notre Dame Cathedral fire, 48–49

Obama, Barack, 60
object appearance, 80
object location in the scene, 80
O'Brien, T., 126, 135
O'Donnell, C., 45–46

older adult witnesses, 118–24, 158; cued-recall tests of, 120–21; emotion of, 121–22; environmental-support hypothesis and, 120; old/new recognition of, 123; positive emotions of, 123; recall memory of, 120; recognition tests of, 121; Searcy on, 119–20; socioemotional selectivity theory and, 123
old/new recognition, 26, 86; of older adult witnesses, 123; SDT and, 22–23
open-ended questions, 134, 137–38
opportunity to view, 30–32
own-age bias, 37
own-race bias, 38, 40

Palmer, F., 32–33
past lives memory, 72
Patihis, L., 73
perceiver's own descriptors, 30
peripheral details, 106–8
perpetrator's memory, 125
person descriptions, 27–35; descriptors in, 28–29; intoxication in, 32–35; opportunity to view in, 30–32; race and, 38–40; stress and anxiety in, 32
person descriptions by child witnesses, 37–38
person descriptors and face recognition relationship: cognitive processing in, 40–41; filler task in, 41; lineup decision and, 40–42; meta-analysis on, 42; mock-crime video in, 41; verbal-facilitation effect in, 40–42; verbal-overshadowing in, 41–42
phenomenal experience, 77–91; associations in, 81; avoiding false memories and, 81–87; confidence related to, 77, 87–91; criterial recollection in, 79–80; diagnostic features of, 83–84; expectations in, 82; feedback in, 85–86; imagination of, 78; list word recall in, 84–85; metamnemonic knowledge in, 81–82; noncriterial recollection in, 79; object appearance in, 80; object location in the scene in, 80; qualitative characteristics of, 77–81; reactions or feelings of, 80–81; reexperience of, 77–78; remember/know judgment in, 78–79; sensory reactivation hypothesis in, 81; sound of word's presentation in, 81; theme words and, 78–79, 80–81; vividness of, 77, 78; word's position in list in, 81
physical evidence collection and maintenance, 14
physiological measures, 75–76
Pickel, K. L., 110–11
Pizarro, D. A., 116, 117
Poole, Booby, 100
poor-quality viewing scenarios, 52–53
population norms, 28, 42, 148–49, 154
positive emotions, 116, 123, 125
positive feedback, 3
post-event information, 3, 134
post-event misinformation, 13, 61–62
post-experiment questionnaire, 83–84
post-identification feedback, 89
postretrieval decision processes, 82
Pozzulo, J., 36–37
Practical Aspects of Memory movement, 7
prediction, 8
pre-lineup instructions, 149–50
pre-lineup interview, 145–46
presentation medium, 111–15
primary memory, 20
priming memory, 22
prior retrievals, 127–28
proactive interference, 17–18
probabilism, 156
procedural memory, 22

race, 3, 38–40
race/ethnicity, 29–30

rape: familiarity in, 1–2, 45, 56; intoxication related to, 32–33; wrongful convictions of, 1–2, 27, 100
Raye, C. L., 48
Raz, N., 119
Read, J. D., 31
Reality Monitoring Framework, 48
reality monitoring model, 48
real-world eyewitness situation, 10
recall memory, 105–8, 120, 122–25
recall tests, 19
receiving operating characteristics (ROC), 23
recognition memory, 108–11
recognition tests, 19, 20, 121
recognizing familiar and unfamiliar faces, 44–50
recollection, 24
recollection rejection, 68
recommendations: confidence statement in, 150–51; evidence-based suspicion in, 144–45; lineup fillers in, 147–49; pre-lineup instructions in, 149–50; pre-lineup interview, 145–46; repeated identifications avoidance in, 152–53; showups in, 153–55; video recording in, 151–52
reconsolidation, 16, 139–40
recovered (repressed) memory debate, 70
Reisberg, D., 103, 106–7
relational information, 83
remembering, 5, 25. *See also* experiencing and remembering
remembering changes memory, 141–42; conversations about memories in, 135–39; enhancement in, 128–32; forgetting in, 133–34, 146; mechanical recording systems and, 127; prior retrievals in, 127–28; reconsolidation in, 139–40; storytelling in, 126; testing effect in, 129–30
remember/know judgment, 78–79

reminiscence, 129
repeated exposure, 55, 57
repeated identifications avoidance, 152–53
reproduction, 16–17
research, 3–5, 11, 167nn2–3; collaboration in, 162–63. *See also* high road research; middle road research
retention interval, 130
retrieval, 15–16, 18, 121
retrieval fluency, 64
retrieval-induced forgetting (RIF), 128, 133–34
retrieval mode, 21–22
retrieval orientation, 67
retroactive interference, 17
RIF. *See* retrieval-induced forgetting
Rindal, E. J., 140
ROC. *See* receiving operating characteristics
Rotello, C. M., 51
Rowland, C. A., 130

Safer, M. A., 108–9
SAI. *See* Self-Administered Interview
Salthouse, T. A., 119
same-race descriptors, 39–40
Sauer, J., 90
Schacter, D. L., 80–81, 92
Schooler, J. W., 39–40, 41, 80, 94–95
Schreiber Compo, N., 33–34
SDT. *See* Signal Detection Theory
Searcy, J. H., 119–20
selective processing, 25
Self-Administered Interview (SAI), 132, 141, 142
semantic memory, 21–22
sensory reactivation hypothesis, 81, 91
sexual abuse, children, 37–38. *See also* rape
short-term memory, 20
showups, 153–56

Signal Detection Theory (SDT): beta in, 23; confidence and, 87; dual process models of memory and, 24–25; ecphoric similarity and, 90; ROC and, 23; single process model as, 24–25
single process model, 24–25
Skagerberg, E. M., 138
Slotnick, S. D., 92
SMF. *See* Source Monitoring Framework
socially shared RIF, 134
socioemotional selectivity theory, 123
source confusion, 167n1 (chap. 3)
source constrained retrieval, 67
source memory test, 19–20, 85
source misattribution error, 152, 167n1 (chap. 3)
source monitoring, 136, 150, 167n1 (chap. 3)
source monitoring errors: in familiarity and recollection, 48–49, 51; in genuine and false memories, distinguishing between, 61–62
Source Monitoring Framework (SMF), 158; agenda in, 64; butcher-on-the-bus and, 54–55; construction in, 62–63; cue-dependent remembering in, 63; distinctiveness heuristic in, 68; distraction in, 65–66; expectations in, 66; in genuine and false memories, 62–66, 167n2 (chap. 3); in genuine and false memories, distinguishing between, 76; heuristic decisions in, 64–65; memory traces in, 66; nonmemorial information in, 70; Notre Dame fire related to, 48–49; reality-monitoring model related to, 48; recollection rejection in, 68; retrieval fluency in, 64; sex and age in, 65; source errors in, 65
Spellman, B. A., 98
Sporer, S. L., 88
staged crimes and real crimes, 29
Starns, J. J., 83
storage, 15

storytelling, 126
stress, 5, 25, 25, 32; ethics related to, 102; food and sleep deprivation and, 101–3; nonviolent crime event and, 103–4; recall and memory related to, 104–5; violent crime event and, 103–4. *See also* negative emotion
structural code, 51–52
survival school training, 101–3
suspicion, 96

target-absent lineup, 145
targets, 19, 53
testing effect, 129–30
thematic arousal, 112–14
theme words, 80–81
theories, 4, 5, 8, 123, 167n2. *See also specific theories*
The Things They Carried (O'Brien), 126, 135
third parties verification, 112
Thompson, Jennifer, 100
trace, 15–16, 18, 168n2 (chap. 3)
true and false discrimination: decision-maker help in, 159–60; information integration in, 160–61; witness help in, 157–59
true memories, 168n2 (chap. 4)
Tulving, E., 21
Tversky, B., 135

unconscious transference, 76
unfamiliar faces: external features of, 45, 56–57; eyes in, 46; face-matching study on, 46–47; generic object recognition system for, 47; internal features of, 45–46, 56–57; processing shift with, 45–46

Valentine, T., 104–5
Van Koppen, P. J., 29
verbal-facilitation effect, 40–42

verbal-overshadowing, 41–42
veridical (true) memory, 59–60
video camera versus human memory, 17–18, 25
video recording identification procedure, 151–52
videotaped crime, 41, 46–47, 103–4, 136–38
violent videotaped crime, 137–38
visually induced reactions, 112
Vredeveldt, A., 34–35

Warren, K. L., 36–37
Waubert de Puiseau, B., 161
weapon focus effect: attentional narrowing theory and, 110; in eyewitness events, 13; negative emotion and, 109–11
Webb, Troy, 27
Wells, G. I., 144–47, 149–52; on show-ups, 154–55

"where, what, and when," 21
Wickens, C. D., 23
Wilcock, R., 120
Williams, Michael Anthony, 1–3
Wixted, J. T., 23
WMC. *See* working memory capacity
working memory, 20–21
working memory capacity (WMC), 21
Wright, D. B., 138
written reviews, 136
wrongful conviction cases, 3, 44, 56, 148
wrongful convictions: of rape, 1–2, 27, 100

Yarmey, A. D., 30–31, 120
yes/no recognition, 22, 84, 123
Yonelinas, A. P., 50–51
Young, A., 52–53

Zaragoza, M. S., 131–32, 140

ABOUT THE AUTHORS

Sean M. Lane, PhD, is Professor of Psychology and Dean of the College of Arts, Humanities, and Social Sciences at the University of Alabama in Huntsville. Formerly, he was Professor of Cognitive and Brain Sciences in the Department of Psychology at Louisiana State University. Dr. Lane's research examines the mechanisms underlying learning and memory and how these mechanisms influence behavior in complex, real-world settings such as eyewitness situations. He has worked to further the productive interaction between basic and applied research, including serving on the governing board of the Society for Applied Research in Memory and Cognition and as associate editor of *Applied Cognitive Psychology*. He received his PhD from Kent State University.

Kate A. Houston, PhD, is Associate Professor of Criminal Justice at Texas A&M International University. She is an experimental psychologist specializing in legal psychology, particularly in the areas of emotion and memory, interpersonal communication, social influence, and rapport. Kate's research has received funding from the Economic and Social Research Council in the United Kingdom and, more recently, the Federal Bureau of Investigation/High-Value Detainee Interrogation Group in the United States. She received her PhD from the University of Aberdeen in Scotland.